SATAN Would Be A Democrat!

Examining the Democrat Party Platform in Light of God's Word – the Holy Bible

JEFFERSON DANIEL SEAL

SATAN WOULD BE A DEMOCRAT!
Examining the Democrat Party Platform
In Light of God's Word – The Holy Bible

Copyright © 2019 by Jefferson Daniel Seal
All rights reserved. No part of this book shall be reproduced, stored in a retrieval system, or transmitted by any means without written permission from the author.

ISBN
International Standard Book Number:
978-1-61422-703-8

ORDER OTHER BOOKS ON PROPHECY:

The End is Near!
The Time is Near! – Volume I
The Time is Near! – Volume II
Antichrist Revealed!
Holy Week – The Bible Detective
How to Study the Bible
Unmasking the Antichrist – The Bible Detective

First Edition 2019
Printed in the United States of America

PUBLISHED through DWJD MINISTRIES

DWJD MINISTRIES = Doing What Jesus Did
Info@DWJDMinistries.com
Content copyright 2019.
DWJDMINISTRIES.COM.
All rights reserved.

Watch for these other informative titles:

The Time is Near! – Volume III
Un-Holy Week
The Lord's Prayer
Creation Week

DWJD MINISTRIES mission is to spread the truth about the Word of God throughout the world

- Our goal is to live by: "doing what Jesus did"
- We are a "non-profit" corporation
- All profits are directed back into the ministry
- We exist for the sole purpose of fulfilling our mission statement

DWJD's Mission Statement:

"This gospel of the kingdom shall be preached in the whole world as a testimony to all the nations, and then the end will come.

Matthew 24:14

The adjacent verse is the spoken words of Jesus Christ, as recorded in the pages of the Holy Bible. His message is quite clear. The Good News about God's kingdom *will* be delivered to the people of the entire world. We at DWJD Ministries are dedicated to following Jesus Christ. Our every effort is to remain obedient to God's Word while faithfully completing the tasks He has given to us. Our work is guided by the principle: "Doing what Jesus did."

We invite you to join us! All that's required is for you to feel the Holy Spirit motivating you to act. You can assist us in "<u>d</u>oing <u>w</u>hat <u>J</u>esus <u>d</u>id" by spreading God's Word. Start by telling others about Jesus. DWJD ministries is here to help. Go to our website and purchase our books and materials—and then get them into the hands of those most needful of the Gospel. Contribute from your surplus. Any gift you bring is always greatly treasured. May God richly bless you for anything done in His Name.

-Amen

Prologue

For the whole of human history, there's been a war raging of epic proportion. It's the ongoing struggle between good and evil. Paul, in his letter to the Ephesians said; "For we do not wrestle against flesh and blood, but against authorities, against the cosmic powers over this present darkness, against the spiritual forces of evil in the heavenly places." Generally speaking, "good" can be defined as anything relating to God, His Son Jesus Christ, His Holy Spirit, and His Word—the Holy Bible. And "evil" can be defined as being everything else. So, this book discusses the particulars as to how this battle is being waged through political parties.

First off, you might think I believe all Democrats are evil or bad. No, that's not true at all. In fact, I will *never* say Democrats are evil. But, as will be definitively shown within these pages, the goals of the Democrat Party work in complete opposition to God's Word—the holy Bible. Not just some of them, but each and every one. This means the Democrat Party is being led by Satan. He's the only entity capable of achieving such a victory. And, he's doing it by swindling, conning and defrauding people into following his lead. Just like with a conman working a scam out on the street, Satan is working the Democrat side of the fence; and he's been at it since man was kicked out of the Garden of Eden.

And in the same vein, I am not saying therefore; Republicans are good, and thus are the party of God. Nope. I would never sing the praises of the

Republicans either. But, for the time being, they are the individuals who, for whatever reason, are the ones able to resist the wiles of Satan and his demons. Some are able to withstand the satanic work due to their being followers of Jesus. They have put on the armor of God and are thus well protected. Others have learned to obey the law of sowing and reaping. They work very hard at sowing good seed within their lives, such that good crops are the resulting harvest.

You will learn the policies of the United States' largest political party did not come about by accident. Planks in the platform of the 2016 Democrat convention will be used to prove the Democrat Party is operating under the hand of Satan himself. I will reveal before your intellectual eyes all the proof you should require. I'm going to use the pages of the Bible to prove it to you. Each plank, when closely examined, can be shown to utilize guidance which goes directly opposite of God's Word. Every single plank is part of this vast conspiracy.

There can only be one explanation: Satan's behind it. He's using powerful demonic influence to drive his evil plan for the enslavement of humanity. And, what better place to start than inside the largest political party of the world's most powerful country. After reading this book, you'll never view the Democrat Party in the light of being just an opposing philosophical ideology to the conservatives. Your eyes will be opened to the evil scheme being played out right before you. The good news is: You'll never see the Bible in the same way again either.

Table of

I. Recent History 1

Truth Be Told	1
Mandatory Reading	11
It's All About Money	17
Seeing Is Believing	25
A Crooked Candidate	34
From Out of Nowhere	43
Who's in Your Heart?	51

II. Democrat Defined 61

Followers of Satan	61
Silencing the Demons Inside	70
Who's Your Daddy?	78
God is Never Ridiculed	87
Corruption Leading to Destruction	95

III. Demonic Preamble 103

The Party of Conflict	103
There is Virtue in Success	110
Use a Carrot Vice a Stick	117
Big Promises Make for Big Lies	124

IV. A Brawl Over Power 135

Unionize then Demonize	135
God's Power is Always Good	143
A Most Wicked and Odious Sin	151
Granting Wrong Rights	161

Contents

V.	**Stealing the Vote**	**171**
	The Guise of Protection	171
	Campaign Mis-Finance	180
	Outright Lying Hypocrisy	187
VI.	**Global Warming Hoax**	**197**
	Ice Age Evidence	197
	Crisis Fabrication 101	204
	You Cain't Fix Stoopid!	213
	An Impotent Lying Lion	221
VII.	**Health & Safety Ruse**	**229**
	Death, Domination & Dejection	229
	Satan's Security Number	237
	Clinging Tightly to Faith	244
	Demons of the Airwaves	253
	Sons of Disobedience	262
VIII.	**Brainwashing 101**	**271**
	Testing All Voices	271
	Israel's Right to Exist	278
	Major Labor Pains	286
	Time of Jacob's Trouble	293
IX.	**Breaking Free from Satan**	**301**
	Jesus Alone is LORD	301
	Hell On Earth	308
	Seeing All These Things	315
	Footsteps to the Truth	322

I. RECENT HISTORY

Truth Be Told

No matter who you are in this world, regardless of how much you think you know about things, or how finely tuned your stack of diplomas might be, this book should be permitted to serve as a strong warning and/or a stern wake-up call. There is a world-wide con being waged against humanity by the demonic forces of evil, seeking to defraud mankind of the truth. I define the **demonic forces of evil** as *'anyone who is a follower of Satan, or is controlled by him or his demons.'* I define **truth** as *'God's word to man, defined primarily via the Holy Bible.'* We know from his first mention in the Garden of Eden, Satan or the devil, is working to reduce mankind to ashes. He wants nothing more than to secure our eternal destruction. God said he was *"more devious than any of God's other creations."* [1] The original word used to describe him is **arum** [*aw-ROOM*] which means *'crafty, shrewd, devious.'*

If you are one to deny 1) there are demonic forces of evil, 2) the existence of a Satanic conspiracy against humankind is not real—only imagined, or 3) the Bible isn't the inerrant Word of God; you are already under the demonic influence of Satan. You need to wake up! Unless you heed the words of this book, you will likely

---

[1] Genesis 3:1 "Now the serpent was more crafty than any beast of the field which the LORD God had made."

Jefferson Daniel Seal

remain so until your physical death, followed eventually by your spiritual death. The Hebrew word **Satan** [*saw-TAWN*] means '*accuser, adversary, antagonist.*' The first appearance of the word as a proper name comes when Satan moved against King David, motivating him to take an illegal census, against God's will for Israel. [2] This is precisely how Satan and his army of demons' work. They begin by first seeking to deceive man, via the cloaking of some lie within a carefully chosen dialog of truth. Then, using half-truths they sway man to take the desired step of sin, just as they intended. It was exactly how the Devil first got Eve, and then Adam to fall. He's still diligently working his con against us!

It so happens, the entire platform of the Democrat Party is composed of these sugar-coated lies. At first glance each plank appears reasonable and even looks like the right thing to do. But upon deeper examination using the light of God's word, the hidden evil is quickly exposed. Within the pages of this book we will examine many of the "planks" in detail, carefully aligning them with verses taken directly from the Bible. I offer a prayer of understanding: "Dear LORD, it is my fervent hope and heartfelt prayer those reading the pages of this book will have their eyes opened to the wiles of the demonic forces arrayed against them. Amen."

---

[2] 1 Chronicles 21:1 "Then Satan stood up against Israel and moved David to number Israel."

Allow me just a few quick examples which more than adequately make my point. Do you think abortion on demand should be permitted? In your opinion should gay marriage be legal? Should the LGBTQ lifestyle be embraced as normal and left up to personal choice? Should wealthy persons be taxed at a rate far above the average working person? should corporations be forced to share profits with workers? Should the borders of the United States be open to anyone who wants to come in, illegally or otherwise? Do you believe racism is prevalent across the whole of American society? If you answered yes to more than one or two of these questions, then I guarantee you are living a life entirely influenced by Satan's demonic forces.

There is no other way to say it. God makes it abundantly clear: we are either with Him; or by default, we are against Him. [3] There exists no middle ground. If you are truly filled with God's Holy Spirit, you will be found frequently uttering the word "Amen!" as you read the words on the pages lying before you. Otherwise, you have a demonic being living within you; telling you over and over again, the words before you are wrong! Those are the only two positions. We are not just discussing differences of opinion herein. And please listen carefully to me: God's position is the *minority* position. His policies are

---

[3] Matthew 12:30 "He who is not with Me is against Me; and he who does not gather with Me scatters."

always the least popular and do not conform to social norms or societal favorites. The bottom line: God doesn't care what you or the rest of mankind thinks. He's only interested in getting _you_ to see the truth before it's too late. And time is running out.

On the other hand, if you happen to think the United States is a misogynistic and racist nation, you hate the thought of Israel's right to exist, refuse to accept the Bible as the inerrant word of God, accept God's Ten Commandments are merely "guidelines," believe Jesus was only a great teacher, and accept Donald Trump is somehow a man of pure evil—then again, you are clearly living under the influence of demonic forces. Before you throw this book down and dismiss it as garbage, I want to tell you; "God loves you and wants you to see the truth!" But, doing so will be nearly impossible until we get the demons to leave, drive them out of your head, and away from your psyche, using God's Holy Spirit.

One other point, the fact you attend church regularly or have a long-standing membership in any religious oriented ministry, means absolutely NOTHING! Most of the churches I speak in are filled with non-believers and hypocrites. I define a **non-believer** as '_anyone who has failed to receive Jesus Christ into their hearts as LORD and SAVIOR forever_.' If you are disagreeing with this text, then you are likely yet a _non-believer_. That's a fact. The first step to breaking free of sin is recognition of your condition!

Jesus also told us; "No one can serve two masters."[4] He even spelled out the results for us in black and white. He said we will hate the one and love the other; or be devoted to the one and despise the other. We are seeing this displayed daily across the media on every news channel. It even has a name: "Trump Derangement Syndrome—or TDS." The struggle over ideology has become so fierce; normal decency has taken leave of any political dialog. There is a very good explanation for this, which is detailed later in this volume. If you are suffering from TDS, that's probably your best clue you are living under demonic control. Your thoughts are not your own! You are being deceived! It's time to wake up! Allow me to assure you: once you come to see God's Word for the truth which it is: you will *never* turn back. You will thank Him every day for bringing you His Word. I guarantee it!

Which brings me to the basis for this book. As you can already see, I make frequent use of the dictionary to define words. I want the reader to have <u>zero</u> doubt about what I'm trying to communicate. And when appropriate, I will list a Biblical reference which speaks to the issue being discussed. Notice the reference is printed at the bottom of the page; and not hidden somewhere in the back of the book. I want

---

[4] Matthew 6:24 "No one can serve two masters; for either he will hate the one and love the other, or he will be devoted to one and despise the other."

you to verify using your own Bible the words I am speaking. I've written many books and all of them use these same principles. I want the reader to become arbiter and judge over the words lying before them. Don't take my word for any of this. Go before God Almighty in prayer and ask Him to help you decide. I am just the messenger and <u>not</u> the author. God Himself is the basis for all of my work. I will one day soon stand before Him and give testament of what I have done. My prayer and hope is to stand blameless before Him, in the shadow of my Savior, Jesus Christ.

To the best of my knowledge, I am an ordinary man in every way except one. I'll discuss it in just a moment. But know for now, I'm a sinner, just like everyone else who's ever lived—with the exception of the One who saves us. He is God's only Son, Jesus Christ whom I have committed my life to follow, by making disciples of people from every nation. Like the Apostle Paul, I too am foremost among sinners. [5] And just like the Apostle Paul, I too found mercy, such that Christ Jesus was able to demonstrate His perfect patience through me, as an example for those who might believe in Him for eternal life. [6] You see, God chose me to reveal His prophecy before mankind. To

---

[5] 1 Timothy 1:15 "It is a trustworthy statement, deserving full acceptance, that Christ Jesus came into the world to save sinners, among whom I am foremost of all."

[6] 1 Timothy 1:16 "Yet for this reason I found mercy, so that in me as the foremost, Christ Jesus might demonstrate His perfect patience as an example for those who would believe in Him for eternal life."

this moment in time, I am the only person in modern times, who God permitted to correctly predict a date for the fulfillment of Biblical prophecy well ahead of time.

God allowed me to reveal the date for the affirmation of Israel's sovereignty over Jerusalem and the Temple Mount, nearly ten years before it came to pass. It happened when President Trump moved the U.S. Embassy from Tel Aviv to Jerusalem, on the exact predicted date of 14 May 2018. And even as the date was approaching, many skeptics told me it wouldn't happen! "It takes ten years and a billion dollars to build a new embassy!" they cried. Then, one of Donald Trump's Jewish friends informed him he had an empty building; and for seventy thousand dollars it could be made ready to become the new United States Embassy in Jerusalem. The U.S. was the first nation to officially recognize Jerusalem as Israel's undisputed and undivided capital. This event happened exactly 70 years after Israel's Independence Day, perfectly in line with Daniel's prophecy.

The Library of Congress holds a book I wrote in 2006, which predicted this very event. "The End is Near" was the inaugural book beginning my ministry. This date is just the first of many, which are soon to take place. This is the evidence and proof I am speaking of on behalf of God. Say what you will but NO ONE I am aware of can make the same statement truthfully. I attribute all the Biblical knowledge I have obtained to His holy guidance and teachings. And for those believing I somehow guessed the date; you are completely in error. The long trail of Biblical explanation contained within **The End is Near!** excludes any thought of speculation. There are twelve Biblically derived dates, spread over nearly 2,600 years of Biblical history, which totally substantiate my work. It would be like stating Albert Einstein was guessing when he derived the formula for the Theory of Relativity. You'd be ignoring a lot of his scientific work while making such a statement.

I've also written books detailing many soon coming prophecies to include: the identity of the Antichrist, the starting date of the Tribulation, the date for the appearance of God's two witnesses on the Temple Mount—just to name a few. And just so you know, thus far, God has allowed my determination of those dates from out of Scripture to be perfect—100% accurate. You can reject me as a false prophet or some kind of crazy fraud. That's your choice. The truth is I haven't yet given any incorrect dates for God's prophecies. And, even if eventually I miss one by a day, a week or perhaps as much as a month, I'm still the only person even close to being within the confines of God's Biblical ballpark. So, you can ignore my message, but you do so at your peril.

As you read through this volume, keep in mind you just MIGHT be among those being conned by the

Father of all Lies. [7] At least consider the possibility as you examine each point I make, and CAREFULLY see if what I am saying contains elements of truth. Don't listen to the voice inside your head—he's lying to you! At least give God the benefit of the doubt before you make your final decision. Proof always "trumps" lies. It's up to you to find the truth allowing it to do so. By the way, God has a wonderful sense of humor. Just as you read about "Truth Trumps Lies;" it's no accident President Trump is fighting a staunch campaign against "Fake News." I've been fighting against fake Biblical quotes for many years now. In the same way, God announced four separate times the prophecies of the end times would be locked up until they were "un-sealed." [8] I don't believe it's a mere coincidence my last name is "Seal." My middle name is Daniel, and I was born on 9/27. Go and look up Daniel 9:27, and then decide what the truth might be. If you knew my full history, you'd be slow to make a snap judgement.

And finally, I work for one purpose: To bring Almighty God the King, who is eternal, immortal, invisible, and the only God; all honor and glory forever and ever. Amen! [9] I do not labor for money, power, recognition or fame. The Bible tells us it's physically

---

[7] John 8:44 "Whenever he (the Devil) speaks a lie, he speaks from his own nature, for he is a liar and the father of lies."

[8] Daniel 12:8-9 As for me, I heard but could not understand; so I said, "My LORD, what will be the outcome of these events?" He said, "Go your way Daniel. For these words are concealed and sealed up until the end time."

[9] 1 Timothy 1:17 "Now to the King, eternal, immortal, invisible, the only God, be honor and glory forever and ever. Amen."

Jefferson Daniel Seal

impossible to serve God and wealth at the same time. [10] He laid and made my financial path for me well before I began DWJD Ministries. That's why neither I, nor any family member, friend or relatives have ever received any money or compensation from the Ministry. If anyone inside our familial circle elects to work for DWJD, they do so as an unpaid volunteer. You can trust my words, and you can trust my motivation for putting them out there for public consumption. We do it for the glory of God alone.

God is using me to help spread the word of His soon return and the end of this age. But I am one among many. With all persons claiming to speak for God, please look closely at two things. First, do their words and actions closely match the words printed inside the cover of the Bible. If they don't, then flee such preachers, as they are part of Satan's con. They might be unwitting participants, but participants still the same. Second, tightly scrutinize their apparent motivation for doing their work. If all they seem to be doing is amassing wealth by constructing large buildings and accumulating "stuff" for their ministry, once again, I'd flee such organizations for purer eschatological pastures. If you are considering purchasing this book, buy it right now and read it as soon as you can. I describe such behavior as mandatory. **Mandatory** is defined as '*required by law*

---

[10] Matthew 6:24 "No one can serve two masters; for either he will hate the one and love the other, or he will be devoted to one and despise the other. You cannot serve God and wealth."

Satan Would Be A Democrat

view from your backyard to include a larger sized body of water. So, you and your spouse began searching around your area for the perfect spot.

After a few weeks of looking around the area where you reside, you discover an emerging new housing development, featuring lots laid out along prime river real estate. You discover a perfect plot meeting all of your requirements. It sits directly on a river, giving you the view you've always wanted, with a price fitting just inside your budget. So, you purchase the land in the belief all is well. The development quickly sells out due to popular demand. And so, buyers can now begin their construction process. This all sounds like part of the American dream, right? Well, as Paul Harvey used to say on his radio show; "It's now time for the rest of the story!" As construction begins, an immediate problem arises. The beginning prep work for laying the foundations uncovers a colossal problem. The vast majority of the area of the development is found to be completely unstable and unsuitable for building. You discover the lot you purchased cannot be built upon. Thus, you now own what is essentially a worthless lot. How would such information make you feel?

Most people would be outraged! They would immediately begin efforts to file a lawsuit against the developer, the city planning commission and anyone else having a hand in this deception. Sounds good,

Jefferson Daniel Seal

right? Well, there's much more to the story. It seems you are the final participant—aka "the victim" or the target—in a long-term scam. You are at the end of a con game which originated over twenty years prior. The original owner learned the land was worthless, after hiring an engineering firm to privately assess the property. There was only a limited area available for building, which was not large enough to construct anything of real value. Instead of letting the city know about it, the property owner destroyed the portion of the report detailing the unsuitability of the land. They then paid off the engineering company to keep the information permanently buried. The owner had an idea for a scheme which might net them a large amount of cash. But their malevolent plan would require many years to properly implement.

The first step of their scam involved selling the property to a friend of theirs for a reasonable price, showing plans for a structure built on the land. The friend obtained a low interest loan from a local bank for the purchase of the property. After waiting a year or so, this investor then sold the land, in-turn to a different friend of theirs for a higher price, thus now showing reasonable appreciation. This latest investor obtained another low interest loan, this time from a different bank, expanding the building area on the plot to show a few more structures. Again, nothing was ever built. After another year or so had passed, they then sold the land to yet a third friend for an

Satan Would Be A Democrat

even higher price. The latest purchaser added more potential development to the plans for the property; and like the others before, got a low-interest construction loan from a third bank. The investment was deemed to be a safe investment, due to the property now having a solid history of appreciation. And so, it went, until after twenty years of trading hands twelve times, it was sold to an unsuspecting developer—who was never part of the original owner's circle of friends and business acquaintances.

It was your developer who purchased the land in good faith, with the intent to build a new subdivision along the scenic river. Like the other persons before him, he obtained a loan from a bank, based on the steady appreciation of the land, coupled with the slew of building sites shown on the property plans. Since construction was slated to finally begin, real engineering work was begun, this time by a different firm. But they quickly revealed what was hidden twenty years earlier: the land was unstable and unsuitable for building. Of course, the buyers all try to pursue legal action—but to no avail.

This was due to each previous owner of the land denying any knowledge of the fatal flaw in the property. There was no proof of any conspiracy. Everything had been performed word of mouth. Each person only purchased the land once, using a different bank each time. Their defense was they too relied upon previous reports on the property, just as the developer did. And, when they go back to the original owner, they discover his sale of the land at the time was entirely legal. His proposed building site was sound. The city bears no fault as the sale of the property was properly recorded. No permits were ever issued or previously denied. The banks cannot be sued, as they were swindled; just as the developer and all of the lot purchasers.

The end result is the scam was well orchestrated and legally fool proof. The small circle of friends got away with it scot free. It was only when another unrelated legal case was brought many years later against the original owner; the pyramid scheme and conspiracy was inadvertently revealed. Otherwise, it might have gone undetected forever. Just so you know, a **conspiracy** is defined as '*the act of conspiring together*.' The parties to the conspiracy knew full well what they were doing; along with the harm they were plotting to bring to unsuspecting persons. To **conspire** means '*to join in a secret agreement to do an unlawful or wrongful act or an act which becomes unlawful as a result of the secret agreement*.' Humanity is being targeted by such a conspiracy. And what's perhaps worse for you: You may well be an unsuspecting participant.

The aforementioned conspiracy was assembled for the sole purpose of making money. The money they made was stolen from ordinary, hardworking folks—just like you. The conspirators didn't stop to target anyone specific. No, they didn't care who they stole the ill-gotten gain from. Con artists never do. All they want is the cash. Did you ever stop and wonder why this is true? To begin with, there are a multitude of reasons why people steal from others. A small child will shoplift a piece of candy to satisfy a strong craving. Most kids quickly grow out of this phase. Hungry people will steal food, or items which can be quickly sold, in order to purchase food. When their needs are satisfied, they too will cease stealing. Society tends to judge such persons, who steal to meet basic human needs, quite gently. It almost rises to the level of 'justifiable behavior.' And then there's everybody else.

It's All About Money

Stop for a long moment to consider your thoughts about the cultural use of money. In our society, it's quite difficult to function apart from having cash available. Money can take on many forms—credit cards, currency, electronic credits, etc. It's impossible to live anything close to resembling a normal life in the modern age apart from using money. Those of us who have been so completely broke, we've been forced to wait some number of days for our next paycheck to arrive, before being able to purchase even a stick of gum! Unless you are much younger than about sixty years of age, I tend to doubt you've experienced such a situation. But, even as a modern adolescent, the times spent without dough in your pocket are tough! It means not being able to do almost anything; or go nearly anywhere apart from perhaps biking or walking. Your options are severely limited. When you're used to having "options," time spent without having any money is quite unpleasant. As you will soon see, the con being waged upon you starts and ends with your control over being able to exercise monetary "options."

No true discussion of money can take place without first offering a proper definition. The dictionary defines **money** as '*something generally accepted as a medium of exchange, a measure of value, or a means of payment*.' So, while money can be paper bills and metal coins, it can also take on just about any other form. Anything having some *value* can become money in a black-market economy. The most basic creation of wealth begins with the individual and the labor they produce. The more valuable the person's labor, the higher their wage. My granddad used to advise me to find a job using my head instead of my body. He'd always tell me; "They'll pay a ton more for your brainpower, and you can work a lot longer!" And his advice has proven to be both wise and accurate. A lawyer is paid far more than a ditch digger. And, a lawyer can create billable hours far in excess of a person's endurance to dig ditches! And, an airplane pilot can sit in the cockpit far longer than an installer of sheet rock can hang boards.

Satan Would Be A Democrat

I think we can all agree—having some minimum amount of money is desirable and even necessary to living a normal and productive life. While the Federal Minimum Wage in the United States stands at $7.25 per hour, that's certainly not enough to live on. The minimum wage was never intended to be such. The minimum "living wage" is deemed to be somewhere around $15 per hour for most locations. This equates to a little over thirty thousand dollars annually. Many locales require a significantly higher wage than that. Let me be clear: The Democrats are not interested in taking any of the money from this level of wage earner. No. This is where their bread and butter voters reside. Instead, they are putting their sights on those earners occupying the top half of the Internal Revenue Service (IRS) roles.

So, let's discuss those upper tier people for a moment. Is there anything made worse about people due purely to their earning power? Is it bad to be someone who truly earns a significant amount of money? Are they somehow evil or malevolent? Is somehow becoming rich an evil pursuit? Of course, it isn't—so long as the manner in which the money is earned is inside the law. And, how much does a person need to earn to be considered rich? At what point does a person's income become a threat to another's power? There's a current political party out there, touting their demented ideology which would have the lower earning individuals think so. The truth is, rich people's behavior is no worse or better than poor or middle-class citizens. Sure, a few of them might be caught committing "white collar" crimes at times. But such can be said for all persons, regardless of economic stature. Working hard to obtain more money is <u>not</u> a bad or evil pursuit, so long as your reason for doing so remains untainted by excessive desire.

You've probably been told; "Money is the root of all evil." Well, it's not. And if you've been taught that's what the Bible says, you have it entirely wrong. This is yet another gross misquote of Scripture. The Bible does teach; "The love of money is a root for all sorts of evil." [11] Please take a moment and closely examine the footnote at the bottom of the page. I always display my footnotes there, and not buried someplace in the back of the book. I want you to read them. Primarily to show the full verse; so, you can see I am not "cherry picking" the words of Scripture and twisting them into meaning what I want them to say. I always go back to the root languages shown in the footnotes.

Notice the verse doesn't even state; "The love of money" is even necessarily bad. Clearly, it is for some folks, but not for most. Also distinguish, it doesn't state the love of money is the root of <u>all</u> evil. What it

---

[11] 1 Timothy 6:10 "For the love of money is a root for all sorts of evil, and some by longing for it have wandered away from the faith and pierced themselves with many griefs."

Satan Would Be A Democrat

does say is; "the love of money <u>can be</u> a starting point for all sorts of evil." The love of money by itself is not always bad. Therefore, money cannot be bad. If it were, then the Bible would have said so. Money serves an important purpose in society. It is our prime medium of exchange. Loving money too much will sway some persons to begin walking a path into all sorts of evil. Remember these words. They have been grossly twisted by the master of deception in the con being worked against your life.

The possession of money brings three capacities to the individual. Firstly, money can be used to satisfy our personal desires. We use money to purchase our basic human needs, followed by a hierarchy of assorted desires. The more money we have, the more desires we can thus fulfill. Secondly, money can be used to influence others. This can be accomplished in the form of contributions, investments, donations, etc. Money is a strong and powerful tool in controlling the actions of others. This can include individuals as well as groups, communities or organizations. Frequently, companies will use money (commissions) as a motivation to increase product sales. And finally, money can be used to create esteem, admiration and veneration. It happens all the time around well-known persons of wealth. Many will purchase a book simply because it was written by a celebrity. And they will do it solely for the belief they will discover secret details of how their money was made. It can become the material essence, the animating principle driving force within a person's life. Money can become the sole reason you get out of bed every morning and go to work. This happens when a person places money at the top of their list of goals and achievements.

Money all by itself is not good or bad. It's what money is used for which drives the distinction with a purpose. Money buys power. **Power** is defined as '*the possession of control, authority, or influence over others.*' It's what we do with the resulting power which determines whether we are performing good or evil. It is our desire to obtain such power which lures us away from the principles of our faith and becomes the cause of our troubles. The pursuit of power for the sole purpose of having it is not necessarily wrong. However, those who do chase the aspirations of getting more power rarely have benevolent purposes in mind. And so it is, with the Democrats. Their true motivation for grabbing all available power is driven by the evil force; which has been quietly lying in wait for mankind for the better part of six thousand years. The struggle between the Republicans and Democrats is entirely a political melee over power; and the exercise thereof. The party with the power gets to drive the governmental agenda. And getting this power requires securing a plurality of the votes being cast in the elections. The Democrats can only truly seize power if they can capture all three branches of government.

Satan Would Be A Democrat

The party occupying the White House, the Senate and the House of Representatives has the full authority to push the limits of their ideology on the American nation. And up until lately, it hasn't been even close to a fair fight. To prove my point, just take a good look at the public record on the votes taken on the floors of both the Senate and House of Representatives. Every vote which is critical to the Democrats sees a nearly universal party line vote supporting their issues. The number of times a Democrat has voted *against* their own party can be counted on two hands. When an item essential to the advancement of their stratagem comes to the floor for a vote, they stand in firm lockstep together. Surveying the Republican side of the debate shows much more independent action of the part on their representatives. The real question is why is this unassailable fact proven to be true time and again?

Some might postulate the Democrats are simply more united and stronger amalgamated. Those same persons will then accuse the Republicans of being more fractured and divided, as a group. This is true, but again the real question centers around the word; "Why." The answer to the question is: "Centralized Control." The Republicans are free to vote on each issue as they wish. Most will vote their conscience— reflecting what is best for the nation as a whole. So, they will experience differing votes at times due to diverse views. Whereas, all Democrats vote as an

Jefferson Daniel Seal

unbroken block—reflecting they are doing what is best for the Democrat Party, usually at the expense of the American people. Democrats are serving a sly master, largely hidden from public view, unless one knows where to look. He continues to deceive them about his real and diabolical purpose for their work.

In the United States of America, power and thus control comes from those holding significant amounts of money. The Democrats are the party seeking to remove as much money as possible from the upper echelon of American society (at least the conservative element) and in turn; transfer it to the poorer half. This exercise is nothing more than the indirect purchase of votes, using the money taken from the pockets of the wealthy, and given to the less fortunate, in the sole pursuit of power. This redistribution of wealth can be found in the recent creation of the ideologies of the Communist and Socialist parties.

It should not be surprising to anyone both Carl Marx and Joseph Stalin were Godless men, whose ruthless form of atheism resulted in the modern enslavement of billions of people in the 20th century. The Democrat Party is attempting to do from within the borders of the U.S., what the Communists and Socialists were unable to do from without; take down the powerful citizens of the United States. The prime directive is to gain power over the nation. The first step is removing all the wealth from the affluent.

Seeing is Believing

Even the most impartial observer cannot help but notice the behavior of the modern-day Democrat. They can plainly be viewed behaving like petulant children, nearly everywhere within the public realm when it comes to dealing with " anything Trump." They are throwing what can only be described as an "adult tantrum" on the civic stage of America. After essentially getting their way over the past sixty years, their progressive agenda has suddenly, and quite dramatically been halted. The slow but steady slither of American values, sliding down the slippery slope towards the left side of the political spectrum has been abruptly stopped. The fast-moving socially driven train towards Sodom and Gomorrah has effectively been derailed for the time being. And it all came about with almost no warning.

The Democrat's ride towards the liberal side of the political and social spectrum was unexpectedly ended with the election of Donald John Trump, as President of the United States. The unexpected loss was so unanticipated and unforeseen, the left immediately became unhinged and has been suffering in mental anguish ever since. Every fiber of their being *refuses* to accept such a man could become President of their United States. It remains the mission of every demonically driven Democrat to deny giving one inch of legitimacy to his ascension to the highest office in the land. The Democrats are searching under every rock and bush, looking for the one golden needle in the haystack which will validate their thesis: Trump is a fraud! He won by *cheating* the citizens of the United States! He is an *imposter* who has no legitimacy to remain as President! As you read this book, I'm quite confident their fervent search for some morsel of proof goes on unabated.

While the Democrats are essentially losing their minds, the Christian Right has been continually down on its collective knees thanking a merciful and gracious God, daily with every breath. To them, Trump's victory fully met the definition of being a real and true miracle. Apart from God's mighty and capable hands, the United States might have begun an irreversible slide into the darkness of unabated evil. Another Clinton presidency would have accelerated the movement continued by Obama towards the abyss of iniquity and sin. Appointing two additional leftist leaning Supreme Court Justices would have eliminated all sense of balance on the highest court. Religious liberty, freedom of the press, and gun ownership would have all been quickly stolen from the American people in very short order. Abortion, drug use, and sexual promiscuity would next become the norm for American society.

To the untrained eye, this last election of a president might appear to be nothing more than the mere struggle between political ideologues. Republicans versus Democrats; and left versus right;

conservative versus liberal. Some believe the American election was nothing more than the usual political theater. One side won, and the other side lost. It would appear at first glance this is the simple truth. The Democrats were pouring all of their hopes and support solidly behind Hillary Clinton—a campaign juggernaut who could not lose to any Republican challenger. But lose she did. Apparently against a self-inflated buffoon of a rich man, none-the-less, according to her base supporters. The vast majority of viewers sitting before their televisions on November 8th, 2016 had little doubt who would become the 45th president of these United States. The Democrats were firmly convinced their candidate was set to make history. The Republicans were fearful their candidate would bring too little, too late to the fight, and suffer loss.

As far as contests go, the Democrats firmly believed they had the election in the bag. Most polls showed Hillary Clinton holding a tall lead in every category which mattered. Their confidence was high, thinking they had run the perfect campaign. In total vote count, Clinton was projected to win the popular vote by a margin in excess of five million votes. Most of her staffers were secretly holding out for a landslide victory. Just so you know, there is no legal or constitutional definition of a **landslide victory**. But one generally agreed upon definition is 'when the winning candidate secures at least 375 of the *electoral votes,*' it can be said they had; "won by a landslide." Every Clinton advisor and consultant were promising and proclaiming a landslide victory against the misogynistic Donald Trump. They made their voices heard right up until the reality of Trump's victory silenced them by removing all of the hot air from their lungs.

Clinton's advisors were so confident of victory, they essentially advised her to cease making the more difficult campaign stops in the latter part of her campaign. Thus, they scratched making planned stopovers in many of the smaller cities, lying within the states they expected to easily win. So, Clinton largely skipped going to Wisconsin, Michigan and Pennsylvania. Had she won these three states; she would have sealed the Presidency with a minimum electoral vote total of 274. Instead, the Clinton campaign put most of their final energy into working to flip red states, believed to be close enough to be swayed over to her side. So, they poured their remaining resources into Florida, Ohio and Iowa, where polls grossly underestimated Trump's support. They were striving and reaching for the landslide victory, which appeared to be within easy reach.

It wasn't enough for Clinton to simply win and become the first female president in U.S. History. No, the Democrats wanted a *landslide* victory, thus securing what they were really after: a mandate from the American people! This would give them all the

Satan Would Be A Democrat

more power to inflict their socialist will on the United States citizens. But, Clinton's campaigning in these chosen venues was having little to nil effect as the election drew near. The rumors surrounding her destroyed emails were beginning to attract more negative attention than what was desired. So, they began scaling back Hillary's public appearances at just the time she needed them most. They didn't want her exposed to questions she couldn't effectively answer. We don't know if her sudden slowing of campaigning was due to health problems, simple overconfidence coupled with campaign trail fatigue, or avoidance of probing questions; but the effects were lasting. Simply stated by even her most ardent supporters: Her campaign began coasting to victory far too soon. And breezing along was the one thing which cost her the election.

Donald Trump, on the other hand, as election day drew near, began holding three or four rallies per day, and on some days as many as five in his herculean effort to garner support over to his side. And his campaign was laser focused and concentrated on each of the aforementioned swing states. All of the rallies were wildly popular with his supporters and were all easily attended by crowds in excess of 25,000 persons each. In what would have been unthinkable on the opposite side, many of the rallies didn't even begin until well past 9 PM local time. Trump's message was consistent: "Make America Great

Again!" His message would mean undoing much of the bureaucracy placed on the American people by his predecessors. He promised a return to personal freedom, by eliminating much of the burdensome legislation put in place by the Obama administration. He promised to free us from government overreaching programs—like Obama Care. His promise to bring back jobs was a siren call to the American worker—both union <u>and</u> non-union workshops.

Sitting down to watch the election returns come in on the evening of the 8th of November 2016 found most Christians and Republicans facing an uneasy sentiment. Unlike the Democrats, most republicans already believed most of the polls to be inaccurate indicators of what was going to happen. While the reasons are varied, most polls understated Trump's level of support. Reasons for this range from: 1) The media's left leaning bias, 2) The level of visceral passion displayed on the part of the left, and 3) Something Trump himself referred to as "Fake News." This uneven coverage resulted in many persons either not participating in polls (by refusing to answer any questions) or simply lying to coworkers about their true beliefs and feelings. True scientific polling, unaltered by politics and television, is very difficult to garner in the modern media age. There are just too many opportunities for one side to unfairly influence the outcome of the vote.

Nearly every single poll heavily favored Hillary Clinton. The few polls giving Trump any chance of winning were hardly mentioned in the national news. The media stated Clinton's chances of winning on election night was a seemingly insurmountable 71.4%. Trump was given a mere 28.6% of victory. Thus, Hillary had a three times greater chance of claiming victory than did "The Donald." The real question of the hour was: "Which poll was correct?" Did any of them truly know which candidate was going win? As I settled into my couch for what I envisioned to be a long, painful evening, I realized my fate and faith was not in mankind and his polling abilities; but rather in God Almighty who fully knows the entire future. God foreknew which candidate was going to win. There was never any doubt in His mind. It was always going to be His candidate.

I played sports most of the time while growing up; a practice which continued well into high school, college and beyond. Let me just tell you: I was no kind of super-athlete! It was the love of the game which essentially kept me coming back season after season. The thing about sports which makes such competition special, are the lessons we learn from participation. I'll readily admit the feeling of winning a tough fought contest is rarely bested by experiential feelings found away from sports. And nothing stings as much as losing a game which should have been easily won. Nothing. We've all watched in awe at the miracle comebacks. I still remember the intense thrill while watching the United States hockey team beat the Soviets in the 1980 Olympics. Every pundit said the U.S. squad didn't stand much of a chance. But in the end, they pulled out "A miracle on ice" and won the game!

Now, look at the game from the point of the view of the Russian team. Put yourself in their place for a minute. That loss likely defined the lives of many of those young men. Coming home in shame after having lost to the American Capitalists could never have been easy to accept. The Soviets did go on to finish with the silver medal. But it was only the second time they failed to win gold at the Olympics since their debut in 1956. The loss was made more painful because the Soviets were recognized as the top international team in the world. They lost to an American team composed mostly of university level players. The American team returned home as heroes; having praise and glory heaped upon them. But, for the second place Russians, they had no victory parade upon their return, and only felt nothing but pain and shame. This is exactly how the supporters of Hillary felt on the fateful election evening, after Donald J. Trump took down the mighty Clinton political machine.

As we all watched the unfolding of the election results, Democrats' worst fears were slowly realized as the tally of the votes came in state-by-state. While

Satan Would Be A Democrat

the initial count and exit polls seemed to match the expected Clinton onslaught, the early euphoria was replaced by first quiet anxiety and then outright exasperation. As expected, the vote from the cities came in quicker and much stronger for Clinton, but the outlying more rural areas began to come in slower and later, with a much heavier tilt for Trump than was expected. One by one, Trump carried all of his expected states. The Hillary machine failed to flip a single state over into her category. All of her late effort campaigning was to be for naught.

As the evening wore on, five purple states began a slow turn to red. To the horror of the Clinton campaign and her supporters, Trump began removing bricks from out of the impenetrable Clinton wall. First Pennsylvania, then Ohio. These were followed shortly by Iowa. It was Ohio which was the state sealing Trump's victory by taking him over the 274-threshold needed to win. Towards the end of the evening, Trump removed two more bricks from the vaunted Clinton wall; Michigan and Wisconsin. Once the victory was sealed, the true agony for the Clinton supporters began. We saw television news anchors with tears streaming down their faces, showing their strong left bias. The Democratic convention center was almost deserted by the time the election was decided. Stunned faces, showing pure shock was displayed in our television screens. Even the candidate herself was so upset and shook up; she was unable to sufficiently compose herself to be able to utter even a short concession speech at the end of the evening. For all of those who witnessed the spectacle—seeing is believing.

A Crooked Candidate

No explanation for the outcome of the election will seem plausible apart from some in-depth analysis of exactly what happened in the course of the election. The race was heated on both sides with each candidate having traits and behaviors repulsive to the other party. Hillary carried the baggage of failure to defend Benghazi, the deletion of 30 thousand files off of her personal server, and the corruption associated with the fictitious Steele dossier. Trump endured countless accusations of election tampering, collusion with the Russians and of having affairs with adult movie stars, buying their silence to protect his reputation. Both candidates had high negative polling values.

The differences however; could be laid out in very simple terms. Everything attributed to Trump was largely either hearsay or from his relative distant past. For Clinton, all of her problems were recently self-inflicted, while she was *serving* in government. Only her cunning and deceit kept her far enough ahead of the law to escape indictment. The accusations against Trump have remained largely unproven or have been completely dismissed. A two-year Department of Justice inquiry by a special counsel was forced to admit there was "No Collusion, No Conspiracy." And while the long-anticipated report attempted to avoid giving Trump a clean slate, neither could they charge him with any crime. Hillary on the other hand was forced to destroy a personal server, even going as far as bleaching the hard drive, to ensure she remained out of prison. She avoided submitting some thirty-thousand plus emails, only stating they were of a personal nature. Her staff members destroyed Blackberry devices and cell phones using hammers after they had been subpoenaed by Congressional inquiry. Here could clearly be found both collusion and obstruction of justice.

Nothing which Trump was being accused of was of a criminal nature. Even his payments to an adult movie star, while indicative of less than honorable behavior, were yet legal under the law. Whatever actions transpired between Trump and a supposed woman of ill repute, still did not violate any laws. And, the transaction happened well before Trump began any action to run for public office, taking place well over a decade prior. This was long before Trump made any announcement he was considering running for president. The money paid to Ms. Daniels was for a nondisclosure agreement. She agreed to not discuss details of any dealings with Donald Trump, in exchange for a contractual sum of money. On the other hand, *everything* Hillary was accused of, was allegedly performed as part of her role within the office of the State Department, while she resided as Secretary of State. American voters collectively, have an ability to adjudicate such matters with the ballot. They chose Trump, perhaps seen and judged as a lessor of two evils. I am not defending or justifying any of President Trump's actions, I'm simply laying out the facts before you; being as straightforward as I can.

Nevertheless, the 2016 campaign was a tough fought battle seeing the expenditure of over a billion dollars. While the Democrats maintained control of the cities, the Republicans were able to keep a tight grip on the rural counties. Out of 3,112 counties in the United States, Trump won 2,623, or a staggering 84% of the total. Clinton won just 489 counties. Trump won 30 of the 50 states. While it's likely true Clinton won the popular vote total, the Presidential election is _not_ decided by the popular vote. The candidate with the majority of _electoral_ votes is the victor. In the Super Bowl, the team with the most points wins the contest, not the team with the most yards. President Obama won 701 counties in both of his elections. Donald Trump flipped fully _one third_ of those over to his side. There were 207 other counties where Obama won only one time. Trump flipped _all_ _but_ _thirteen_ of these over to his side. In the 2,200 counties in which Obama _never_ won, Clinton was only able to manage to flip 6 counties. This is clearly the point where the election was lost.

Satan Would Be A Democrat

There is no argument the Democrats suffered an agonizing defeat. The real question remains; "Why did it happen—especially against such high odds of her victory?" Shortly after the Democrats began their primary season, Hillary Clinton's campaign machine took over the Democratic National Committee's funding and day-to-day operations. This was done for one purpose: to undermine her main rival Bernie Sanders. Donna Brazile, the DNC's party chairwoman, stated she discovered an August 2015 agreement between the national committee and Clinton's campaign fundraising arm, which gave Clinton "complete control of the party's finances, strategy, and the entire sum of money raised." This was in exchange for taking care of the massive debt leftover from President Barack Obama's 2012 campaign. "While the move wasn't technically illegal, it sure looked to be highly unethical," Brazile stated.

The usual practice is for candidates to assume control over their respective party's operations *after* securing the nomination. But Hillary Clinton did so almost fifteen months *before* the election. The DNC intentionally rigged the primary system, essentially guaranteeing her a sizeable portion of the delegates beforehand in order to prop up Clinton, thus assuring she became the nominee. The evidence for this first popped up in DNC emails, hacked by the Russians and then published online. They definitively showed former DNC Chairwoman Debbie Wasserman Schultz and others *conspired* to tip the scales towards Clinton versus Sanders. By securing the delegates votes early, it was impossible for Sanders to have ever won, regardless of the vote totals of the individual states. Sander's support might have grown far stronger had Clinton's stranglehold on the delegates not been so fierce and overwhelming.

This episode is just one more proven indicator Clinton would do anything to win—first her party's nomination, followed eventually by the presidency. Just as with the contents of Clinton's email server, all evidence of internal corruption showing the DNC had rigged the system against Sanders, throwing the primary to Hillary, was erased and eradicated. But the staff forgot the one incriminating agreement. Brazile went on to state; "This was not a criminal act, but it totally compromised the party's integrity. If the fight had been fair, one campaign would not have controlled the party before voters decided which person they wanted to lead." Sadly, this discovery was made mere weeks before the election—too late to affect the outcome of the primary.

Conspiracy and collusion—the very things the Democrats accused Donald Trump of doing—were the very tools used to assure Hillary would be the 2016 party nominee. This action was viewed as practically guaranteeing Hillary Clinton would become "the first female president of the United States." Following the conclusion of President

Satan Would Be A Democrat

Obama's eight years in office, there was little doubt she would follow him as the next Democrat President. Even so, they would not take any chances this time. Hillary was the "heir apparent" for the 2012 Democrat nomination, until a relative unknown senator by the name of Barrack Hussain Obama came out of nowhere to defeat her. She had given him a good run during his fight for the nomination—and yet still lost. The party officials were determined to not allow it to happen again. It was decided Hillary would become the Democrat nominee for 2016. They took every possible step well ahead of time to guarantee this time she won.

Please listen to me for a moment. I honestly don't care who you voted for, who you endorsed, nor which candidate you gave money to. Right now, it doesn't matter. You know who you supported, and I'm sure you think you have valid reasons for doing so. So, I'm not asking you to support any political party, agenda or particular candidate. I honestly don't care. Do what you will but realize in the end it just doesn't matter. Each of those selections are up to personal prerogative. I will always tell you to vote your conscience. I'm a huge believer God gave every man a free will. And, most earthly governments allow men to exercise it. But Satan doesn't like us having such power. He takes every opportunity to try and deny us from using it. Just take an honest look at the facts as they have been laid out before you.

Jefferson Daniel Seal

I cannot state Hillary Clinton was Satan's prime candidate choice for the 2016 election, but it certainly appears that way. She was assumed to be the lady in waiting. While President Obama proudly made history as the first black man to be elected President of the United States, Hillary would likewise make history by being the first woman to do so. She was issued a whole slew of ill-gotten advantage. Her long record of being in governmental service was trumpeted over and over again. Successful lawyer, Governor's wife, President's wife, Senator and Secretary of State. A quick glance at her resume looks pretty darn good! But I will plainly tell you, her resume is equivalent to our earlier mentioned "retirement lot." Recall the lot was simply beautiful, with the most amazing view, and it appeared to be the perfect building location! Persons, after taking a quick look, agreed to purchase the land; putting down hard-earned money to secure their space in the development. Not so fast!

Examining Hillary's biography will show you upon closer inspection, she never held any employment not associated with directly working to gain political influence and authority. Her every move following her graduation from Yale Law school in 1973 was motivated by the thought of gaining another step up the political ladder of politics. All of her supposed jobs away from politics were cursory and superficial. She worked as a child advocate court appointed attorney.

Her only case where she actually appeared in court was defending a man accused of raping a 12-year-old girl, in 1975. Rather than see the trial to conclusion, she got her client to plead to a lesser charge. Clinton now claims she was forced to take the case; but there is a taped interview where she clearly states she accepted the case as a favor to a prosecutor. The rape victim herself, at the age of 52, recorded in an interview she still personally blames Hillary Clinton for "putting her through hell." So much for the mantle of child advocate.

In February of 1977, Clinton joined the venerable Rose Law Firm, a bastion of political influence in Arkansas. Her job was focused on patent infringement and intellectual property law. She is not shown to have ever litigated even a single case in court. She upheld the ruse of working, by continuing to claim performing pro bono work in child advocacy. She was appointed as chairman of the board of directors of Legal Services Corporation by President Carter in 1978, as repayment for her serving as 1976 campaign director of his Indiana election campaign. Carter expanded the grant money from $90 to $300 million while she served as chair. Clinton quickly learned the lesson of how to get paid in politics without actually having a real job.

Then, in 1979, just two years after joining the Rose Law firm, Hillary was made full partner. This despite having practically zero trial experience! But she was the governor's wife—which must have driven the decision entirely. Clinton learned favors can be traded away for lucrative paying positions. During this same time period, she supposedly engaged in trading of cattle futures contracts. She allegedly turned an initial investment of $1,000 into $100,000, in just ten months. Experts have said; "Even with perfect knowledge of the future, it was an impossible task!" Hillary now learned the art of accepting bribes via the use of fraudulent investment. Recall the earlier example of the vacation land scam? That was actually performed by Bill and Susan McDougal, with the Clinton's playing the part of purchaser. You shouldn't be surprised. It was just another scam employed by the Clintons in their savage quest for money & power.

Close scrutiny of Hillary Clinton's resume reveals the same results as the land scam. Hillary's job history is a carefully crafted deception, designed to give the appearance of rising experience and increasing responsibility. But in the same way the fact of the vacation land being covered over by twenty feet of water every several years, her resume is a fraud. Everything about her employment chronicle is just about hiding the truth of her real goal: assumption of power over government. Her historical foundation is composed of nothing but deep shifting sand, completely useless for building upon. The deeper one looks; the more corruption is uncovered. I've only given a short summary of a few of the many fraudulent scams she has been involved in. Go and have a look for yourself. I recommend you do so before more of the facts are removed from public access. She is the definition of "crooked candidate."

From Out of Nowhere

I've had many discussions with persons since the election, and the one question I always ask: "At what point did you think Donald Trump would become the Republican nominee for President?" I will ask you the same question. Most persons didn't have any idea Trump would win the nomination, until *after* he captured a sizable lead over the other leading Republican contenders. This didn't happen until fairly late in the race. At the beginning of the campaign season, it was viewed as a wide-open race, with no clear front-runner. The polls fluctuated wildly with potential candidates who were preparing to announce for the two years leading up to 2015. In the year before the start of actual campaigning, a total of seventeen candidates announced their intention to run for the Republican nomination, thus making it the largest presidential primary field in American history. That number has since been eclipsed by the large number of Democrats running for the nomination in 2020 with 24 candidates. But at the start of the Republican campaign season for 2016, very few people gave "The Donald" much of a chance to win.

Examining the list of Republican candidates prior to the start of any campaigning is revealing. The early-on favorite was Florida governor, Jeb Bush (1). He was probably the most organized and best financed before any actual politicking began. Chris Christy (2), the New Jersey Governor, Ted Cruz (3), Senator from Texas, Marco Rubio (4), Senator from Florida, Rick Perry (5), Governor of Texas, Paul Rand (6), Senator from Kentucky, and Scott Walker (7), Governor of Wisconsin, were all clear-cut favorites at the very beginning. Cruz, Rand and Rubio gained a lot of recognition in the Senate for their work with the Tea Party. Ben Carson (8), Carly Fiorina (9), and Mike Huckabee (10) all had very strong name recognition due to previous work performed and jobs held. Rick Santorum (11), Bobby Jindal (12), George Pataki (13), Jim Gilmore (14), John Kasich (15), Lindsay Graham (16) and Donald Trump (17) were all widely known names for assorted reasons. Usually it was due to their presence within the television media. I grouped the candidates by the popularity tier they were in before any stumping began and ordered them by last name. Look who comes out at number 17 – dead last.

By the time the primary season started in early 2016, three candidates quickly emerged as front-runners. Florida Senator Marco Rubio, Texas Senator Ted Cruz and New York businessman Donald Trump were in the lead. Despite Trump's lead in most national polls, the first primary in Iowa was won by

Satan Would Be A Democrat

Ted Cruz. Trump rebounded with strong wins in New Hampshire, South Carolina and Nevada. On Super Tuesday, Trump expanded his lead by winning seven of the eleven states up for grabs. Cruz won Alaska, Oklahoma and his home state of Texas. Marco Rubio won Minnesota. Between Super Tuesday and the beginning of the "winner-take-all" primaries, Cruz stayed neck and neck with Trump, winning four states to Trumps five. Rubio won several smaller contests including Puerto Rico and Washington, D.C. In the first round of winner-take-all contests on March 15, Trump expanded his lead by winning five of six contests. After losing in his home state of Florida to Trump, Rubio suspended his campaign. John Kasich won his home state of Ohio. While Trump was leading in delegates pledged, the race had just only begun, and the fight for the nomination was far from over.

As the primary season entered the spring, the field was now essentially down to three: Trump, Cruz and Kasich. The gap between Trump and Cruz narrowed significantly with Trump doing well in the South, the Northeast and parts of the Midwest. Meanwhile, Cruz performed best in the West. Cruz pulled off an upset win in Wisconsin. Speculation began over whether the Republican convention would be a brokered one, due to no person winning a majority of the delegates. In this scenario, the delegates themselves would choose a nominee. It was rumored the establishment would select a person other than Trump or Cruz, as they were not viewed favorably by the Republican delegates. As April came to a close, Trump won a resounding victory in his home state of New York. Both Cruz and Kasich were mathematically eliminated from winning the nomination outright. But they could still win enough delegate votes to prevent Trump from being able to win a majority. Both men then formed an alliance to block Trump from winning the nomination outright. By working together, they had a good chance at pulling it off.

The race rolled on. Five states in the northeastern corridor of the United States voted on April 26th. Trump swept all five and greatly expanded his delegate lead. In a final push to block Trump's path to the nomination, Cruz sought to capture more of the woman's vote by announcing Carly Fiorina would be his running mate were he to become the nominee. Nevertheless, Trump won the Indiana primary on May 3rd, giving him an inside track to the nomination. Cruz then suspended his campaign, and the Republican national committee chairman Reince Priebus announced Trump was the presumptive nominee. Kasich suspended his campaign the following day. Trump then went on to win all the remaining primaries. Trump did officially surpass the necessary number of delegates to secure the nomination. But he also broke the 2000 campaign record number of popular votes received by the winner of the Republican presidential primaries, by over 2 million votes. This was an increase of 15% over the previous record!

Do you see the huge, glaring even, difference between the Democratic versus Republican races? On the Republican side, there was no cheating, no conspiracy, and no pre-determined candidate. There was no manipulation of the results or forgone conclusions. I'm not saying every possible *legal* effort wasn't made by the assorted Republican candidates to win. Few of the establishment delegates wanted either Trump or Cruz to win. They believed each man would be a failed candidate against Hillary Clinton. And while many efforts were undertaken to try and assure the correct candidate was selected, none of them were illegal or unethical. They fought by the established rules. And in the end, perhaps even if quite reluctantly, they accepted Trump's victory as being legitimate. It was a surprise only God could have seen coming.

Are you aware it is God Himself who selects the government the world resides under? It is absolutely true. The Bible is quite clear on the subject. God always acts with deliberation—as seen throughout Scripture—to both chastise as well as bless His people. He uses many ways in which to act, but perhaps His favorite is to use leaders of the people to do His bidding. God has used Kings, emperors, rulers, monarchs, prime ministers and now presidents, to enact His will over His people. The Bible is very clear on this subject. Take a look at what the Apostle Paul wrote over in Romans:

> "Let everyone be subject to the governing authorities, for there is no authority except that which God has established." [12]

In a nutshell, God is the One who places the authority over mankind. This is how God often controls the meting out of His will. When Israel went astray and needed to be set back on the right track, God used Nebuchadnezzar and the Babylonians as His instrument. I'm sure the Hebrews didn't like it at the time. But no one ever said life was fair. Based on Scripture, the Bible is very clear: mankind pretty much gets the leaders we deserve. The Greek word for authority is **exousia** [*ex-oo-SEE-ah*] and means '*the power to act, conferred power, delegated empowerment.*' And just as He did with Pharaoh and Nebuchadnezzar, God always uses a leader to confer His will upon His people. So, the question before us now is: "Why would God choose a man, of a uniquely outspoken nature, who uses blunt language, combined with inflammatory rhetoric, a man who frequently contradicts the behavior of traditional political candidates, to inflict His will?

---

[12] Romans 13:1 "Let everyone be subject to the governing authorities, for there is no authority except that which God has established. The authorities that exist have been established by God."

The short answer is: "Because He can!" God frequently chooses the *least* likely candidate to do His bidding. When the Hebrew army was facing the Philistines, God chose a teenager to bring a rock to a sword fight to take down the nine-foot-tall Goliath. God chose Noah to build an arc, at a time when the earth didn't even see rainfall. God selected an elderly couple, well beyond childbearing age to produce offspring leading to the nation of Israel. He chose Rahab, a prostitute, to provide refuge for the Israeli spies sent to scout out the Promised Land. Each of these persons seemed at first glance to be unprepared and unworthy to perform Godly work. In the end, God showed us He can use anyone. And so, God chose Donald J. Trump to fulfill His purpose for the United States, and eventually the world. "What purpose?" you ask. The purpose of God bringing reformation and redemption to the earth, via the people and wealth of the United States. Donald Trump's victory was the answer to nearly every person of faith's prayer before the 2016 Presidential election. [13]

It is a fact: God waits until the last minute before bringing judgment down on anyone. This includes the whole of humanity. God is compassionate and gracious, slow to anger, and abounds in loving

---

[13] 2 Chronicles 7:14 "And when My people, identified as those who proclaim My name, humble themselves, and pray and seek My face, and turn from their wicked ways, then I will hear from heaven, will forgive their sin, and will heal their land."

kindness and truth. [14] But He will eventually reach His limits with mankind. God waited until there were only eight people yet following Him before He brought the flood. He waited until Abraham and Sarah were well past childbearing years before bringing the heir through which the Messiah came. And God waited as long as He would before the last great bastion of His people was reduced into sliding down the slippery slope into becoming a modern-day Sodom and Gomorrah. Had God failed to bring us just the right person, imagine where the U.S. would be today.

After a Clinton Presidency would have appointed two more leftist judges to the Supreme Court, the rights of conservative America would disappear faster than a shallow mudpuddle on a hot July afternoon! The right to bear arms, free speech, and control of taxation with representation would all have been effectively ended by mindlessly aggressive legislation. Abortion, gay rights and pornography would have become uncensored and unlimited. If you fail to see how the United States has slid to the left, consider that prior to 1973, abortion was a crime and an illegal act. Now the Democrats are describing it as a right and "a core value" of their party. One of the Democrat candidates running for president is proudly gay and in a same-sex marriage. The right to same-sex marriage did not even exist in this country until the Supreme

---

[14] Exodus 34:6 "The LORD, the LORD God, compassionate and gracious, slow to anger, and abounding in loving kindness and truth;"

Court discovered it a few years ago. As will be shown within this book, all of the planks in the Democrat platform are in direct defiance of the word of God.

Friends, as most of the other books I've written clearly prove; mankind is living within the end times. The Biblically predicted dates are getting closer, with one already coming to pass exactly as prophesied. This alone should be proof enough for you to begin to take action. With the election of Donald Trump as President of the United States, God alone is the One who is going to make America Great Again in His eyes. And He's going to continue to use Donald Trump as His point man. Take a moment and consider the FACTS as they are laid out before you. Donald Trump is no politician. He comes from a business background. This is sort of like picking a teenager to face the giant, isn't it? No armor, no sword, just a slingshot and a few small stones. That's all God needs. And just like David, who one day became leader of the Hebrews, God chose Donald Trump to become President, and He picked him from out of nowhere.

Who's Inside Your Heart?

The most important thing a person can do is allow the Holy Spirit into their heart and life. Barring that, you really don't know who's influence you're living under. That's the reason I'm telling those who are blindly following the Democrat lead; "You are being duped and conned!" That should be a really scary

Jefferson Daniel Seal

thought to you. If you are in mostly full agreement with their agenda; then you aren't inhabited by God's Holy Spirit. Every person born is given freewill. Webster's dictionary defines our **freewill** as '*freedom of humans to make choices which are not determined by prior causes or by divine intervention.*' Notice, the very idea of God giving us our freewill is ingrained into its very definition (divine intervention). Freewill is our most basic human right, given to us at birth by God Himself. You have been given the ability to choose. People get to make all sorts of choices. The job where you work, the car you drive, what you eat for breakfast, etc. Some choices involve coordination with others: who you marry or who you go into business with. The only real choice which counts however; is realized at the end of your life. "Did you choose God—or did you choose someone/something else?" The consequences are eternal.

If you've read any of my books, you know the freewill God granted to us contains three parts. Sigmund Freud identified them as: The Id, the Ego, and the Super Ego. Jesus identified them as: The Heart, the Mind and the Soul. [15] Jesus wasn't just making this up for Sigmund to later copy. No, Jesus was quoting directly from the Old Testament. Read the footnoted verse carefully. Did you notice some of the words of Jesus appear all in large font? That's the

---

[15] Matthew 22:37 "And He said to him, 'YOU SHALL LOVE THE LORD YOUR GOD WITH ALL YOUR HEART, AND WITH ALL YOUR SOUL AND WITH ALL YOUR MIND.' "

Bible's way of showing us the applicable text appears in the Old Testament. [16] Your "heart" represents your bodily desires. Your "mind" reflects your thoughts and beliefs. And your "soul" is indicative of who you worship or revere the most. More specifically, it's symptomatic of who's controlling you from the inside. A basic tenet of freewill is God stays largely away from you until you make the choice to follow Him. There are no Godly jumbotrons in the sky trying to influence your choice. Let's take a close look at **2nd Chronicles 7:14**:

> "And when My people, identified as those who proclaim My name, humble themselves and pray, and seek My face and turn from their wicked ways, then I will hear from heaven, I will forgive their sin, and I will heal their land." [17]

All three elements of freewill are present within this verse. **Heart**: "Turn from their wicked ways." Our bodily desires are reflected and displayed within our daily actions. **Mind**: "Seek My face." The Hebrew word for **face** is frequently translated '*presence*.' To seek God's presence means to meet Him on His terms. We must align our thoughts with what we

---

[16] Deuteronomy 6:5 "And you shall love the LORD your God with all your heart and with all your soul and with all your strength."

[17] 2 Chronicles 7:14 "And when My people, identified as those who proclaim My name, humble themselves, and pray and seek My face, and turn from their wicked ways, then I will hear from heaven, will forgive their sin, and will heal their land."

discover His thoughts to be. **Soul**: "Humble themselves and pray." A person cannot worship anything without first subjecting themselves to it. That's what humility is all about. Prayer is a form of earnest and solemn communication.

God requires His people to perform these three things before they can become His people. When we surrender each element, God does something in response. When we "turn from our wicked ways;" **God hears from heaven**. This opens up the line of communication. If we fail to turn from our wicked ways, our prayers and cries don't get much farther than the ceiling. When we "seek His face (presence), **God** is faithful and **forgives us of our sin**. Submitting to the LORD means we believe Him and accept His Word. When we "humble ourselves and pray;" only then does **God heal our land**. In the case of the United States, God began the healing of our land by sending us His chosen leader—Donald J. Trump.

Look again at **2nd Chronicles 7:14**. It is at the top of the next page. I've highlighted the word **My** and **I** in each place where it appears. Notice each word appears exactly three times. This is not an accident. It was done by design. God is graphically telling us about each part of our freewill. He is instructing us on what we should do; both as individuals _and_ as a nation of believers:

> "And when **My** people, identified as
> those who proclaim **My** name, humble

*themselves and pray, and seek **My** face and turn from their wicked ways, then **I** will hear from heaven, **I** will forgive their sin, and **I** will heal their land.*" [18]

Each word is intentional and specific. Each time we submit a part of our freewill to God, He acts decisively. I want to point out the Hebrew word used for proclaim is **niqra** [*nik-RAW*]. It means '*to proclaim, to call out to.*' It's a verb. This usage is completely consistent with the Apostle Paul's writings in the New Testament. He makes it crystal clear: all persons calling on or proclaiming the name of the LORD will be saved! [19]

I know some Bible translations state: "those who are called by My name." Unfortunately, this is not accurate. That's not what the original Hebrew word means. Think about it: What difference does it make by what name someone calls you? This verse is located in the Old Testament, written at least a thousand years before the birth of Christ. So, it's not talking about being called "Christians." Besides, the simple truth is most people today in America who are

---

[18] 2 Chronicles 7:14 "And when My people, identified as those who proclaim My name, humble themselves, and pray and seek My face, and turn from their wicked ways, then I will hear from heaven, will forgive their sin, and will heal their land."

[19] Romans 10:13 for "WHOEVER WILL CALL ON THE NAME OF THE LORD WILL BE SAVED."

Acts 2:21 'AND IT SHALL BE THAT EVERYONE WHO CALLS ON THE NAME OF THE LORD WILL BE SAVED."

called "Christians" are not worthy of the name. Their lives look exactly like those who aren't followers of Christ. It doesn't matter what metric you use: Divorce, Alcoholism, Gay, Pornography, Drug Use— those calling themselves Christians are equally afflicted as those persons who don't. Their only difference is a visit to church on Sunday morning.

It doesn't matter what name or names a person is called. What matters is who they call upon! The Bible teaches an oral and public confession of Jesus Christ as LORD of your life, while believing in your heart God raised Him from the dead, is what leads to salvation. [20] Nothing else does. And the total surrender of our freewill over to God is the manner in which we appeal to Him. You've heard the phrase: "It's not what you say, but what you do." God requires us to <u>do</u> three things. Now, this "doing" is not about earning or meriting our salvation in any way. This "doing" is all about submission and surrender. Total capitulation before God Almighty. A person surrendering has absolutely nothing to brag about. It is the act of surrendering our freewill which God is seeking. So, how do we do it?

First, we must turn from our wicked or sinful ways. Turning away from our normal lifestyle is an admission. This is an act acknowledging we've been

---

[20] Romans 10:9 "If you confess with your mouth Jesus as LORD, and believe in your heart that God raised Him from the dead, you will be saved."

Satan Would Be A Democrat

walking on the wrong path. Second, we must seek His holy presence. Again, this requires effort. We must study to discover who God is and how to move ourselves into His presence. And finally, we must humble ourselves, followed by prayer. **Humility** is defined as *'freedom from pride and arrogance.'* Again, this is yet another required element of surrender. Only after we've done the first three things do we then pray. Prayer is the last component, done only *after* we've surrendered the three parts of our freewill before God. So, how do you know if you've surrendered your freewill to God and He's now living on the inside? We look at the base of the tree!

Jesus taught "No good tree can bear evil fruit, nor can an evil tree bring forth good fruit." [21] He was laying down the basic premise: what you do is controlled by what's on the inside. Jesus goes on to describe that people are distinguished by what they do. [22] The rest of humanity can plainly see what side you are on. Of course, we are not trees in the sense we shed fruit. No. Jesus went on to explain, a good man produces Godly works from out of the depths of his heart. And in the same manner, an evil man produces evil works from the evil which is located within his heart. Jesus then puts an exclamation point

---

[21] Luke 6:43 "No good tree bears bad fruit, nor does a bad tree bear good fruit."

[22] Luke 6:44 "Each tree is recognized by its own fruit. People do not pick figs from thorn bushes, or grapes from briars."

on His words by telling us; "The mouth speaks what the heart is full of." [23]

So, if your "manifesto" is chock full of ideas and pronouncements which go diametrically opposite to the word of God, what is it saying about you? That's what this book is going to graphically demonstrate: the 2016 Democrat Party Platform is composed of planks (declarations) which are 100% opposite to what the Bible teaches. As you look at the facts laid out before you, you will be forced to admit one of three things. First, if you agree with the word of God, then you likely shouldn't be supporting any ideology which goes counter to His guidance. Second, if you weren't aware of what the Democrat Party espoused in their doctrine, then you have a decision to make. You either embrace their doctrine, try to change it, or flee far from it. And finally, if you see no problem and agree with their platform, then you are among those being totally and completely duped and conned.

There are only two options for what's living inside you. You either have the Holy Spirit—or you don't. As has been pointed out, if you have the Holy Spirit, then the planks of the Democrat Party platform will be seen for the evil which it reflects. If you have the Holy Spirit, your life will put forth good works (as defined by the Bible). If you don't have the Holy Spirit, then

---

[23] Luke 6:45 "A good man brings good things out of the good stored up in his heart, and an evil man brings evil things out of the evil stored up in his heart. For the mouth speaks what the heart is full of."

you are being swayed and influenced by demonic forces. The degree to which you are being swayed is reflected in the degree you align yourself with the Democrat Party. If you have swallowed the Democrat ideology and creed—hook, line and sinker, then you are demonically possessed. The fact is you are being duped and conned. You can refuse to listen to the demons inside you, but it'll be tough to get them out. The important part is determining where you stand.

Look at the facts: Are you a Democrat in name only—or are you fully fledged into the party? If you fail to see any significant difference between the Republicans and Democrats, you are being deceived. If you can't discern the Democrat Party platform runs nearly 100% counter to the Word of God, you are being intellectually swindled. Concentrate for a moment and stop listening to the demon residing inside your brain right now. And forget about the struggle between Democrats and Republicans for the time being. The Bible tells us there is a way which seems right for a man but leads to destruction.[24] So, if you are being tricked by Satan's army into thinking the Democrat way is acceptable, you are on the highway to Hell, my friend. You need to determine the real answer to: Who's living inside *your* heart?

---

[24] Proverbs 14:12 "There is a way which seems right to a man, but its end is the way of death."

Jefferson Daniel Seal

II. DEMOCRAT DEFINED

Followers of Satan

The United States of America is a Republic, just as the framers of the Constitution intended. A **Republic** is '*a state in which supreme power is held by the people and exercised by their elected representatives, and which has an elected or nominated president rather than a monarch.*' Many people think the U.S. is a Democracy, which carries a different meaning than does a Republic. In terms of the actual definition, the U.S. is <u>not</u> a Democracy. A **Democracy** is defined as '*a state in which supreme power is held <u>and</u> directly exercised by the people.*' That is, where the *people* meet and exercise government *in person*. This is commonly referred to as a "direct Democracy." The United States is technically a "representative Democracy," or more correctly a "Constitutional Republic."

A pure **direct Democracy** is '*a political system in which the majority enjoys absolute power by means of democratic elections.*' In such a system, unrestrained by a constitution, the majority can vote and unilaterally impose tyranny on themselves and the minority opposition. **Tyranny** is defined as '*oppressive power over people.*' This form of Democracy can vote in candidates who would infringe upon our inalienable God-given rights. Thomas Jefferson referred to this as "elected despotism" in his work: *Notes on the State of Virginia.* By taking full

Jefferson Daniel Seal

control of the Presidency, the Senate, the House of Representatives, and the Supreme Court, the Democrats would move quickly to destroy this God-blessed nation. America votes in her representatives, who then assemble and administer government, according to the wishes of the people, limited by a constitution. A **constitution** is defined as '*the basic principles and laws of a nation or state, which determine the powers and duties of the government, guaranteeing certain rights to the people within it.*'

Thus, the United States is a Constitutional Republic, who's powers of government are limited and divided to preclude elected officials from being able to impose tyranny upon the people. That's why the founding fathers adopted a constitution with limited enumerated powers, divided and checked across several branches and levels. Our three separate, but equal branches of government were designed to have built in checks and balances to prevent abuse of the people by one branch of government, which unexpectedly became too powerful. Unfortunately, the progressive era of the early 1900's ushered in a wave of attacks on the constitution. At this present time, we see all our founding principles under assault. Our personal liberties are under attack, our social values are being abrogated. Satan's at war with the United States, and he's trying to win without firing a shot.

Satan Would Be A Democrat

The fact is; he's using primarily the Democrats to wage it. Webster's dictionary defines a **Democrat** as *'an adherent of democracy.'* To be **adherent** to someone or something means to *'adhere to it by giving support to a particular cause or by maintaining loyalty.'* Thus, Democrats are the loyal supporters of the Democrat Party. **Democracy** can be defined as *'government by the people.'* To **govern** means *'to exercise continuous sovereign authority over a nation.'* Accordingly, the government is what rules over the people living under its control. Democrats are one of the political parties seeking to exercise that power, and thus control the narrative and agenda for implementation of public policy. This book will prove the Democrats are operating under the influence of Satan. His goal is to destroy America. So, it should not be surprising to discover the work of the Democrats is furthering that effort.

As you read this book, I want to make a few things crystal clear. First, as you have seen, I make extensive use of the dictionary to define words and terms. This is important! The meaning of words is critical to understanding the truth and eliminates most of the confusion about what I am trying to communicate. My goal is to be as precise as the written word will allow. Second, all references are placed at the bottom of the page where they are used, and not hidden in the back of the book somewhere. I *want* you to check my work. There can be no real trust apart from verification. Without trust there will be no acceptance of my words. Third, I make extensive use of the Holy Bible in making my case. There is <u>no</u> other document on the face of this planet having equal qualifications to the Bible. As you study each point, insure you go and read the verses for yourself. This insures <u>you</u> are seeing the word of God with your own eyes. My only goal is to bring honor and glory to God by furthering His truth and wisdom. Let's return to our discussion of Democrats.

Another popular definition of a **Democrat** is '*one who practices social equality.*' The concept of having true **equality** implies '*a state of all being equal.*' In the United States of America, we adhere to the principle of being equal under, or before the law. We hold that each human being must be treated equally by the law. This concept demands all persons are subject to the same laws of justice. But, this in no way assumes or mandates any idea of *social* equality. Every person is entitled to the same legal due process, which we call judicial equality. But, this is not the same as social equality. **Social equality** is defined as '*relating to human society, all members enjoy an equal level of prosperity.*' **Prosperity** is defined as '*the condition of being successful or thriving, economic well-being.*' It is this idea of social equality for everyone which drives the democrats to produce the ideology upon which they stand. But this creed is nothing more than a cover for their true agenda; which is to try and take over the government of the most powerful nation God has ever created on the earth.

The current approach the Democrats are using is nothing new. Satan has been attempting to use this method of class warfare since the invention of Democracy. The first real recorded republic was the Roman Republic, which traditionally ran from 509 BC until 27 BC, when the Roman Empire was established. There were two political parties back then. One was the **Populares**, which means *'favoring the people.'* This political faction favored the cause of the plebeians (commoners). This party attempted to gain power by showing concern for the welfare of the urban poor. Their efforts were directed towards implementing vast social programs comprising a grain dole, assimilating new colonies and a redistribution of wealth. They also drafted laws granting Roman citizenship to large non-Italian populations. And, they used the guise of corruption to reform Roman judicial laws, favoring the lower-class citizens. So, which modern party does this sound like to you? If you said, "Democrat," you would be correct.

The other political party were the **Optimates**. This word means *'good men, or best ones.'* The Optimates represented the conservative political faction of the Roman Republic. They formed in response to the Populares, who's attempt at passing harsh agrarian laws and to implement political reform to the detriment of the Optimates. They were the large landowners and didn't look too keenly on those trying to steal their land via legal means; by attempting to change the law. The Optimates favored the ancestral Roman laws and customs, as well as the supremacy of the Senate over popular assemblies. They also rejected the massive extension of Roman citizenship to outsiders, as advocated by the Populares. They eventually came to even oppose Julius Caesar—himself an Optimate—believing he was planning a coup against the Republic. I think any person of sound mind can see the near total resemblance of the Roman Republic's struggle to today's hotly contested political environment.

The Populares forced the government of ancient Rome to implement a bread dole. They used the term **Cure Annonae**, which means *'care for the grain supply.'* They did this in honor of their goddess Annona, who was the divine personification of the grain supply. Annona is typically depicted with a cornucopia (horn of plenty) in her arm. But the reality was this program was nothing more than controlling the food supply to the poor. Once more, control over the food supply means control over those who are being fed. Today we can equate the vast food stamp program with the Roman bread dole. Make no mistake: neither program is about feeding people. Rather, both programs were about control and securing the votes of those being fed.

In the same way, the Populares supported the redistribution of land to the poorer persons of the empire. The confiscated family-owned property of the wealthy was stolen from the citizens which rightfully owned the land. They used various "legal" means to accomplish the taking of the land, to include laws mandating "agrarian reform." This was nothing more than wealth redistribution. Anytime a tax burden is placed on the wealthier citizens, without having it apply to all citizens, wealth redistribution is the result. Taxing the wealthy to pay for national defense, roads and highways, schools and hospitals and for the administration of regulation (public safety) and judicial systems is not wealth redistribution. Most of the US social programs—such as section 8 public housing, food stamps, Earned Income Credit, Medicaid, Headstart, etc., are all forms of wealth redistribution. The list goes on and on. These are all forms of social welfare. As you will see in a coming section, regardless of how the reasons are made to sound, or what rationalization is used for justification, the concept of social equality sails opposite to the Word of God.

The Populares also were responsible for drafting laws granting Roman citizenship to large non-Italian populations. Back then, as now, there are strong benefits granted to those who are legitimate citizens. Roman citizens had the right to vote, the right to land ownership, and were protected by the Roman judicial system. The massive influx of persons who were not loyal to Rome greatly diluted the advantage held by Roman citizens. For example, Roman citizens were not subject to capital punishment. So, the Populares drove the reform of Roman judicial laws, in favor of the lower-class citizens. Today, we see the Democrats using the very same tactics to give full citizen rights to illegal aliens. Since these illegal immigrants are not legally entitled to public services, they assume a superior position by displacing US citizens rightfully eligible to use those services. And when the right to vote is conferred on the newly minted "citizens," the electorate is unfairly swayed over to the side of the political party allowing them in.

The struggle faced by Rome, mirrors the current political situation being faced by the United States. In the Roman Empire, the division between the two political parties was acrimonious and hostile. The reason was each side sought diametrically opposed goals. When one party is demanding reforms, which would lead to the effective dissolution of the other party, there can be no compromise. Just as with the Palestinian's demands, which include the destruction and elimination of the nation of Israel, how can there ever be a Peace deal achieved? In the case of Rome, the power of Rome was degraded until a series of civil wars erupted between the two parties. The policies of the Populares greatly weakened the Roman Republic, leading to her demise.

Satan Would Be A Democrat

History does indeed repeat itself. This is largely due to the entity who is driving human activities while attempting to negatively influence history in efforts to degrade God's plans for humankind. Satan sinned against God and was removed from his place in glory. Now, he wants nothing more than to prove God Almighty wrong just one single time. Lots of major events were precipitated by the hands of Satan and his demons. The Great Flood, the destruction of the Roman Empire, the Holocaust are just a few examples of Satan's attempts at thwarting God. He uses the same tactics, just disguised slightly differently each time he tries them. He does it by getting into the hearts and minds of a group of people and motivates them to do his evil will.

The proof is all around you. Open your eyes wide and take a look at what the Democrat Party actually stands for. Oh sure, they appear to the be champion of the poor. But, close examination of the inner cities controlled by leaders from the Democrat Party tells an entirely different story. Epic poverty can be found in all the large cities run by Democrats. This is what drives all of their efforts directed at stealing power from the wealthy and giving it to the poor. They are also the Party of wide-open borders, extreme taxation of the rich, and for the confiscation of second amendment protected firearms. Once more, all their gun laws try and remove and restrict gun ownership for law abiding citizens. They are doing nothing to protect the thousands killed by Democrats living in their inner cities. They pretend to be the party of inclusion, until a Godly group wants to be included. They will kill an innocent baby, even after birth, but refuse to execute a mass murderer. Using such examples, it is easy to show being a Democrat is equal to being a follower of Satan.

Silencing the Demons Inside

The Democrat Party lays claim to favoring the rights of the common man over those of the more wealthy and elite in society. This mirrors exactly the quest of the Roman Republic **Populares**. The Republican Party supports protecting the status quo of government, as well as the standing of the persons upon whose backs the country was built. It also works on behalf of those citizens who contribute the most to the daily operation of the government, via the paying of taxes. This reflects the purpose of the **Optimates** of ancient Rome. The Democrat Party seeks to control the functions of government to directly facilitate subsidizing those making up the lower economic class of persons, via the detriment of the wealthier class. The Republicans are fighting to maintain the current role and scope of government, preserving the built-in protections as guaranteed by the Constitution. Most people pass off the differences between the two parties as merely a variance in ideology. Nothing is further from the truth.

Satan Would Be A Democrat

The way Satan and his demonic crowd work is they first try and control the social dialog. This is necessary due to the prerequisite of wrapping their perverted lies in sweet sounding words, thereby hiding the corruption lying within. In the same way God is unchanging, Satan seems to be bound by a matching principle; "A leopard cannot change his spots." We know from early in the book of Genesis, Satan is described as "crafty." [1] The Hebrew word used is **aruwm** [*aw-ROOM*] and means '*crafty, shrewd, sly, subtle and sensible.*' The definition gives us an excellent description of the exact way in which he works. At some point in the Garden of Eden, Satan approached Eve with an intentional, and deviously worded question: "Are you *sure* God said, 'You can't eat from *any* tree of the Garden?' " [2] The first thing Satan did, was to waylay the only person who'd not heard God speak the actual words concerning the rules about which trees in the Garden could be eaten from. That's Satan's first move: get people to question the **status quo**. It's a phrase which comes to us from Latin, meaning '*the current state of affairs.*'

Satan's next move is to gently twist the words of the original rule(s) so as to bring them into question. Satan's query to Eve was nothing more than a simple set up. Satan knew precisely what God had said. But,

---

[1] Genesis 3:1 "Now the serpent was craftier than any beast of the field which the LORD God had made."

[2] Genesis 3:1 "And he said to the woman, "Indeed, has God said, 'You shall not eat from any tree of the Garden?' "

by deliberately placing a negative in his wording, he was able to introduce doubt. Note: God told Adam; "From any tree in the Garden you may *eat freely*;" [3] Notice Eve's reply to the Devil was *almost* perfect: "From the fruit of the trees of the garden we may eat; but from the fruit of the tree which is in the middle of the garden, God has said, 'You shall not eat from it or touch it, or you will die.' " [4] Did you catch Eve's mistake? She did exactly what most people do today; she <u>added</u> to God's words. Eve incorrectly inserted the false requirement of not touching the tree or its fruit. God never said such a thing to Adam. But, by doing so, she unwittingly created an opening which Satan could make use of against her; which he quickly used to his advantage.

I am comfortable with the idea Adam repeated to Eve, everything God had said to him regarding the tree of the knowledge of good and evil. After all she correctly quoted God's words. But I think Adam's mistake was to inadvertently add to God's words, by perhaps telling Eve something along the lines of; "We are not to ever touch it." While this seems to be good advice on the surface, it deviated from what God had

---

[3] Genesis 2:16-17 "the LORD God commanded the man, saying, "From any tree of the garden you may eat freely; but from the tree of the knowledge of good and evil you shall not eat, for in the day that you eat from it you will surely die."

[4] Genesis 3:2-3 The woman said to the serpent, "From the fruit of the trees of the garden we may eat; but from fruit of the tree which is in the middle of the garden, God has said, 'You shall not eat from it or touch it, or you will die."

Satan Would Be A Democrat

actually said. Satan must have heard Adam speak the error to Eve; which explains why he sought to exploit man's mistake. The reason we are delving deeply into man's first encounter with the Devil is simple: Satan is pulling the exact same stunt with mankind today! And he's managing to achieve the same results. As I go through all the planks on the Democrat Party platform, you will quickly learn to recognize Satan's ploy to deceive persons into unwittingly doing his evil, all in the guise of "doing the right and sensible thing." The only problem is those so deceived will not be doing good, but rather performing evil in the sight of the LORD.

Satan saw his opening and immediately took it. Once more, Satan knew merely *touching* the fruit or the tree was not forbidden—nor the slightest bit harmful. So, I can imagine him then walking Eve over to the tree of the knowledge of good and evil, so she could see it with her own eyes. The Bible tells us the tree was absolutely beautiful! [5] It's not recorded directly in Scripture, but Satan must have convinced Eve to touch the tree by perhaps having her pick some of the fruit. That's why he said to her; "You surely will not die, from just touching the tree or its fruit!" [6] And when she didn't immediately die after touching it, Satan had her right where he wants us all—firmly in

---

[5] Genesis 3:5 "When the woman saw the tree was good for food, and that it was a delight to the eyes,"
[6] Genesis 3:4 The serpent said to the woman, "You surely will not die!"

Jefferson Daniel Seal

the palm of his hand. Eve might have sought clarification, by asking of Satan; "Why would God seek to prevent us from eating from this beautiful tree?" Satan had his next lie ready to go; "For God knows in the day you eat from it, your eyes will be opened, and you will be like God; knowing good and evil." [7] The trap was now fully set. Satan had Eve on the doorstep of doing exactly what he'd planned all along.

Satan has been seeking to destroy humankind since the day of our creation. Nothing about this has changed over the entire time of man's history. He uses misinformation and lies to get man to stumble and fall time and again. With Eve now holding the fruit of the tree of the knowledge of good and evil in her hand, it was easy to now believe God was somehow holding out on them. From such a shaky point of trust, it was a simple decision for Eve to disobey God's Word and eat from the tree. [8] She didn't die, and instead had her eyes opened. This happened just as Satan told her. So, she convinced her husband to do the same—doubtless using the same arguments brought by the evil one—which Adam then did. The biggest lesson from the study of man's fall from perfection, is to *not* rely on the words

---

[7] Genesis 3:5 "For God knows that in the day you eat from it your eyes will be opened, and you will be like God, knowing good from evil."
[8] Genesis 3:6 And that the tree was desirable to make one wise, she took from its fruit and ate; and she gave also to her husband with her, and he ate."

of others *alone* when learning the word of God. We must ourselves be diligent students of the Word, by continually seeking to verify its truth, using our own eyes. Remember one of my first quotes: "There can be no real trust apart from verification." This goes not only for my words, but anyone's words. Do not trust what they say until you have meticulously checked their accuracy against the Word of God.

Friends, this is exactly how the demonic playbook works. Take a large piece of attractive truth, mix in a little, seemingly insignificant lie, along with some misinformation, and it's fairly easy to fool someone. All that's required is the skillful introduction of doubt into the situation. Satan used the misinformation concerning touching the tree would result in death, to cast doubt on the word of God. By the way, God's words and warnings always have two components. When God told Adam he would surely die, God was telling the truth. After eating of the tree, both Adam and Eve died. God never said the tree was poisonous and would quickly kill them. But that's exactly what the serpent implied. Adam and Eve both were placed on the pathway to two deaths. The first death would be the passing of their physical bodies. For Adam, this happened some 930 years later. The second death would be the demise of their soul, at some point after the Great White Throne of Judgment, an event yet to come in mankind's future.

Jefferson Daniel Seal

Satan's goal has not changed. His tactics are the same ones he's used before. So, if you fail to see what is happening right before the eyes of the world; there can only be one explanation. You are being conned and deceived! The only solution for those being fooled is to examine <u>all</u> the evidence closely. I'm going to postulate a common scam being waged right now, all over the United States, Canada, England and Australia. The scammer's goal is to separate you from a sizable chunk of your money.

Imagine someone came to you with a briefcase full of money, claiming they found it. They might even use an accomplice to create a staged event for you to see the briefcase fall out of a moving car, get left at a bus stop bench, etc. They will use you as a co-witness to the event and make a claim about wanting to return it to the rightful owner. Sound's reasonable, right? They will allow a cursory inspection of the money, but only a brief look. There might be some twenty- or hundred-dollar bills wrapped around stacks of cut newspaper. It will appear to be a lot of cash. They will suggest the money be taken to the police station; usually explaining the cops will give the money to those who found it; after some stated waiting period. Or, if the true owner returns, they surely will give a sizable reward for the demonstrated honesty. Next, they will state they need your help due to some reason they themselves are unable to return the money. They might say there's a warrant out for their

Satan Would Be A Democrat

arrest due to false charges brought against them by an ex-wife, business partner, etc.

What has just happened? A person asked you to do what is unquestionably an honorable thing to do: Assist in the return of lost cash. You can't argue with such honesty and logic. Next, they suggest taking the money to the police station just around the corner. Again, what better solution would there be than to deposit all the lost money into the hands of the proper authorities? Finally, they will ask <u>you</u> to take the money to the cops, as they are unable to do so. But, before they give you the bag, they ask for some collateral from you, as a good faith measure, so they know they can trust you. After all you just met. They might take the cash in your wallet, or ask you to withdraw some funds from a conveniently situated near-by bank or ATM. So, let's say you agree and take the suddenly locked briefcase to the police station. The problem with the "reasonable" story is there never was any lost cash. By the time the scam is discovered, it will be too late. You will be holding a briefcase full of newspaper and the thief will be long gone.

Satan works the same way. The "genuine" issue he will use on you will revolve around some form of social inequality. One of his demons will watch you closely until they figure out which concern will be best to use on you which will most likely draw you in. It might be gun control, abortion, gay rights, welfare, etc. They will get you to begin supporting the issue in some way; financially, volunteer work, campaigning, caucusing—a whole myriad of avenues are available. They will get you entirely focused on what appears to be some form of social injustice. They will tell you it's blatantly unfair; and will work very hard preventing you from hearing God's word on the subject. The demons will use every tool at their disposal to insure you don't go near any preacher or church. They will lie and tell you "churchgoers are nothing but hypocrites." "Those holy rollers don't care about the victims of social injustice!" "They only care about the money and the prestige of being seen in church!" "They are a cult, just trying to draw people inside where they can then be brainwashed!" "All they are is a bunch of racists!" The lies will never stop. They've all been spoken about me. I am none of those things. All God is asking you to do is *closely examine* the supposed "social injustice" by using His Word. What have you got to lose? Your soul for one. But to accomplish at least hearing God's side of the story, you've got to work at silencing the demons inside you first.

Who's Your Daddy?

I will not ever seek to lie to you. Everything written herein is the best information I have been given. My prime reference is the Holy Bible, as taught to me under the guidance of the Holy Spirit. My only purpose is to serve Jesus and God the Father

Satan Would Be A Democrat

honorably, to the very best of my ability. I am just a weak vessel, made strong by God, so He alone may be glorified. Listen friends, I already know the demons will use every possible lie and trick in their demonic book to keep you away from the truth. "So, what is truth," you ask. The answer is simple: Jesus said <u>He</u> was the truth. All you need do is get to know Jesus, and you will have a ready conduit to the truth. When Jesus was speaking to those who believed in Him, He told them; "If you continue in My word, then you are truly disciples of Mine." [9] The Greek word for continue is **meinete** [*MAIN-et-tay*] and means '*stay, abide, remain*.' So, if one continues to study and adhere to the Word of God—the Holy Bible, then they are true disciples.

A disciple in the Biblical sense is equivalent to being a full-time college student. If one isn't spending a significant amount of time studying God's word— then they *aren't* His disciple. They are merely someone just hanging around the Temple, feeding off the crumbs of bits of conversation heard. So, to silence the Demons, one must <u>first</u> become a disciple. It's not an easy thing to do. If a person wants easy, all they need do is just stick with what they are doing now. Keep listening to the lies of this world and the

---

[9] John 8:31 So Jesus was saying to those Jews who had believed in Him, "If you continue in My word, then you are truly disciples of Mine."

Jefferson Daniel Seal

demons. That's the easy way. [10] Jesus described it as "a highway to hell." Broad, comfortable, with a downslope—about as easy as it gets.

If one is to become a disciple, Jesus explains they will know the truth, and it is that truth which will make them free. [11] The rationale is simple; by becoming a disciple of Jesus, He will enter a person's heart and drive away all the demons residing there. The demons will never be able to enter again. God will open their eyes to the truth (Jesus) and He will set them free. They will now be able to see the evil in the world for what it is. And with Jesus comes freedom. Freedom from the penalty of sin. No longer will one live under the threat of eternal damnation! As a child of the King, they will be heaven bound. As you will soon discover, following the Democrat Party makes one a disciple of Satan. The religious Jews attempted to refute the words of Jesus by claiming to be Abraham's descendants. They claimed they were never enslaved to anyone. [12] You might be thinking along the same lines; "I'm my own person. No one tells me how to think!"

---

[10] Matthew 7:13 "Enter through the narrow gate; for the gate is wide and the way is broad that leads to destruction, and there are many who enter through it."

[11] John 8:32 "And you will know the truth, and the truth will make you free."

[12] John 8:33 They answered Him, "We are Abraham's descendants and have never yet been enslaved to anyone; how it is that You say, 'You will become free?'"

Satan Would Be A Democrat

Jesus issued them a direct response; "Truly, truly I say to you, everyone who commits sin is the slave to sin." [13] Jesus is not talking about just any old sin. He's discussing the sin being performed intentionally while following the influence of Satan and his evil disciples. If one is listening to them, and doing what they say, then they're a slave to Satan. Jesus then warns us: the door to heaven will not remain open forever. Once Satan has used someone up for his purposes, they will be discarded. Jesus will never discard His disciples. We will remain within the house of Heaven forever. [14] So, if the Son (Jesus) sets one free, then they will be free indeed! [15] If you're drinking the Kool-Aid the Democrat Party is feeding you, then you aren't free. You're still a slave to Satan. Jesus isn't finished speaking about the subject yet. Now He gets to the proof of one's particular discipleship.

Jesus begins by affirming their earlier statement: "I know you're Abraham's descendants." [16] That's His way of saying; "Working as a Democrat, I know you *think* you mean well." Jesus then drops the first bomb; "Yet, take notice of your attempts to kill Me. This is due to My word having no place inside you." [17]

---

[13] John 8:34 Jesus answered them, "Truly, truly, I say to you, everyone who commits sin is the slave of sin."

[14] John 8:35 "The slave does not remain in the house forever; the son does remain forever."

[15] John 8:36 "So if the Son makes you free, you will be free indeed."

[16] John 8:37 "I know that you are Abraham's descendants;"

[17] John 8:37 "Yet you seek to kill Me, because My word has no place in you."

I know Democrats aren't actively seeking to kill Jesus. But, by their stated party platform and manifested actions, they <u>are</u> seeking to kill the *message* of Christ. And, it's all due to the lack of God's word inside them. Jesus next drops the second bomb, when He said, "I speak the things which I have seen with My Father; therefore, you also do the things which you heard from <u>your</u> father." [18] His point is crystal clear: The Democrat Party message and associated actions come straight out of Satan's playbook. That's why they're doing them. They're just following the actions heard by the demons telling them what to do.

The Jew's answer to Jesus was; "Abraham is our father." [19] That's equivalent of the Democrat's saying; "We're only doing what's good for humanity!" Jesus replied; "If you're Abraham's children, then do the deeds of Abraham. But as it is, you are seeking to kill Me—the man who has told you the truth, which I heard from God. This is something which Abraham never did." [20] So, if the Democrat Party is spouting a message which consistently goes directly against the word of God—then who's message are they promoting? Jesus essentially said, "If you want to do what's best for humanity, then do it!" But, since the

---

[18] John 8:38 "I speak the things which I have seen with My Father; therefore; you also do the things which you have heard from your father."
[19] John 8:39 They answered and said to Him, "Abraham is our father."
[20] John 8:39 - 40 Jesus said to them, "If you are Abraham's children, do the deeds of Abraham. But as it is, you are seeking to kill Me, a man who has told you the truth, which I heard from God; this Abraham did not do."

Satan Would Be A Democrat

Democrat Party message is all about silencing His message, which I clearly can read in the Bible, then it's obvious the Democrats aren't doing what's best for humankind. "You are doing the deeds of your father," Jesus told them.

The answer Jesus gave them, must have caught them off guard, for they were clearly offended. In the same way, if one's been heeding the words of a demon, they too will be highly insulted at the words written here—and for the same reason. [21] The Jews responded by directing a strong insult back towards Jesus. They insinuated He was the bastard in the conversation. The Greek word used for fornication is **porneias** [*por-NEE-ee-as*] and means '*fornication, whoredom, pornographic.*' The root idea of the word connotes the selling off of one's sexual virtue or purity. That they would stoop to leveling such a horrific charge against the most innocent person who ever lived! They claimed instead to be those who hold God as their Father. I want you to pay special attention and take notice at how any Democrats respond to information somehow suggesting they are in the wrong. They immediately begin throwing verbal barbs at the person making the comments, by accusing them of some cultural or racial bias. Anyone who's spent any time watching the news media knows this to be true.

---

[21] John 8:41 "You are doing the deeds of your father." They said to Him, "We were not born of fornication; we have one Father: God."

Jefferson Daniel Seal

Jesus debunked their accusation by gently breaking their argument. Notice He didn't stoop to their level of name calling. "If God were your Father, you would love Me, for I have come from God, because He sent Me." [22] In the same manner, God motivated me to write this book for the very same reason. Jesus loves mankind and wants them to become His disciples. He next asks them; "Why do you suppose you fail to understand what I am saying? He then answers His own question; "It's because you are totally unable to hear My words. [23] The Greek word for hear is **akouein** [*ak-KOO-ein*] and means '*to listen, comprehend or understand*.' It's the same way with Democrats reading this book; unless they cease listening to the demons, they too will totally miss the point Jesus was making and fail to comprehend the message of this book. Are you with me so far?

Jesus then cuts to the chase by telling them; "You are of your father the devil. And as such, you want to fulfill the desires of your father. [24] Now, let me plainly ask: Who's desires are the Democrat Party fulfilling? As this book conclusively proves; the Democrat Party platform goes completely and totally against the Biblical sound doctrine of God's word. So clearly, they

---

[22] John 8:42 Jesus said to them, "If God were your Father, you would love Me, for I proceeded forth and have come from God, for I have not even come on My own initiative, but He sent Me."

[23] John 8:43 "Why do you not understand what I am saying? It is because you cannot hear My word."

[24] John 8:44 "You are of your father the devil, and you want to do the desires of your father."

Satan Would Be A Democrat

aren't following God. Who's left? If you said, "Satan," you are correct. You are also on the right path to figuring this whole thing out. Jesus then brings forth His proof: "Satan was a murderer from the beginning and does not speak the truth—because there is no truth in him." [25] The devil is a murderer due to his diabolical actions which directly led to the physical deaths of Adam and Eve—as well as the rest of humanity. But that's evidently not good enough. Satan is now seeking the *spiritual* deaths of all mankind by denying them the information they need to find eternal redemption. That explains why the Democrat Party is against any and all efforts to spread the genuine message of the Gospel of Jesus Christ!

The Bible plainly teaches Jesus is the Truth. So any effort at discrediting Jesus, must therefore be a lie. This is very simple logic. Jesus affirms such logic when He said; "Whenever Satan speaks a lie, he is speaking from his own nature." [26] The Greek word for nature is **idion** [*ID-ee-on*] and means '*particular to an individual, uniquely one's own*.' Jesus then clarifies His words by saying; "For Satan is a liar and is the father of all lies." His meaning is as plain as the actions of any liars: your father is the devil. Going back to our fictitious scam for a moment. How could a person stop from becoming part of a con? For starters, they

---

[25] John 8:44 "He was a murderer from the beginning, and does not stand in the truth because there is no truth in him."

[26] John 8:44 "Whenever he speaks a lie, he speaks from his own nature, for he is a liar and the father of lies."

Jefferson Daniel Seal

could refuse to stop and talk to the perpetrator. They could just keep walking. Okay, let's say they did stop. How could they then foil the con men? Another suggestion is to ask to see the money—all of it. Not just a quick glance inside the briefcase. It's unlikely the frauds will ever allow someone a good look inside. What next? The person could of course refuse to transport the money to the police. And finally, they could refuse to surrender a thin dime of "collateral" to the perpetrator.

My argument here is quite simple; any of the mentioned actions would quickly defeat the swindlers by beating them at their own game. True information is power, in the same way manipulated and controlled use of words is weakness when believed. Cheats and frauds all use the same approach, they promise *'the delivery of something good.'* That's what they use as **bait**. They offer an item or concept which sounds good on the surface, but upon which they can never supply. Satan does the same thing. He offered Eve the chance to be like God—something he couldn't deliver. They will then seek to get you to place something you have as a guarantee against what they are offering. The Democrat Party is using an identical approach: they are promising a better nation and world, if we only do things their way. We must first surrender to them the power to do it, and then they will bring in the good life.

Instead, the Romans discovered Satan's playbook brought civil war and steady degradation down from the high-quality life they once enjoyed. The Populares *never* delivered on their high promises. Rome was destroyed as a nation and found itself on the scrapheap of human government. If the Democrat Party manages to gain power in the near future, I can see the United States going down the same path as the Roman Republic. What does it hurt to critically examine the purposes of the Democrat Party from a Biblical perspective? If you are a person being honest with themselves, the answer is "nothing." But, if you refuse to weigh the goals of the Democrat Party against the word of God, there's an altogether different question which you will one day be required to answer: "Who's <u>your</u> daddy?"

God is Never Ridiculed

The basis of the efforts of the Democrat Party playbook centers around one central thought. It is the first phrase from the 2016 Platform Preamble: "Out of many, we are one." For those history scholars out there, they will know it's a twisted definition of "**E pluribus unum**." This classical Latin phrase, emblazoned across the Great Seal of the United States, means '*Out of many, one*.' The meaning of the phrase originates from the concept that out of the union of the original Thirteen Colonies emerged a single nation. It's a phrase most commonly associated with the money supply of the United States, appearing on the one-dollar bill, and all of the coins. The actual meaning refers to the combining of separate parts together, thereby making one. The term is never historically used in the context of *individuals*. *People* cannot be combined into one person and still exist. I know this might seem like a small distinction, without a purpose; but it's not. The Democrat Party is clearly speaking about people's wealth—and not just people themselves. It's their driving intent to "level the economic playing field, regardless of the cost." All one need do is study their platform to prove this statement.

One of the earliest phrases used in the 2016 **Democrat Party Platform (DPP)** sums up the true motivation of the Democrat Party perfectly:

> *"Too many Americans have been left out and left behind."* [**DPP** pg. 1]

They want to implicate those having wealth are somehow conspiring against those who don't. Another quote shows their true motivation:

> *"As working people struggle, the top one percent accrues more wealth and more power."* [**DPP** pg. 1]

First off, does this statement sound more like coming from a socialist government, or some form of communism, rather than a Free Enterprise driven economy? And secondly, when did it become a crime or somehow wrong to be good at making money?

Satan Would Be A Democrat

Where is it written rich people are required to share their hard-earned wealth? Would it surprise you to learn this principle, as espoused by the Democrat Party goes *against* the Word of God? Read on for the proof you should now be earnestly seeking!

The Bible is very specific, "Whatever a man sows, this he will also reap." [27] This is sometimes described as the law of farming. But the verse is merely an analogy for the actions of a person. The ground represents a person's life. The seeds represent a person's deeds performed during their life. The Bible is expressing a very basic truth: whatsoever you do is going to eventually come up in the form of lasting consequences. This is a simple prophecy. And, as I've stated before, this verse has two parts to the meaning. The near, or smaller part, informs the person that what they do has consequences in this lifetime. If you make a habit of stealing, you will eventually be caught, and go to prison. But the prophecy also pertains to the next life. If you fail to secure Jesus as LORD and Savior, you <u>will</u> spend eternity in the Lake of Fire. In either case, there's no escaping the consequences of <u>your</u> actions.

The Democrat party seeks to subsidize the poor by taking from the rich. Do you know what the Bible calls taking something for which you have no right to? Stealing! The eighth commandment states: You shall

---

[27] Galatians 6:7 "Whatever a man sows, this he will also reap."

not steal. [28] The word "shall" is used in laws, regulations or directives to express what is *mandatory*. By these words the right of owning wealth and property were formally acknowledged by God, with a protest made in anticipation against modern socialists. Instinctively man knows that some things become his by the toil he spent obtaining them. God defined our duty to respect our neighbor's life, spouse, property, honor, and trust in God. Our social order is built upon these principles. As you will see, the Democrat Party is seeking to undermine all of these tenets of social harmony. Government exists mainly for the security of men's lives and property; not for the dilution of them. Here's another statement from the **DPP**:

> *"We believe that today's extreme level of income and wealth inequality makes our economy weaker, our communities poorer, and our politics poisonous."* [**DPP** pg. 1]

My first question is: how does a wealthy man create a weaker economy? The insinuation is the wealthy man earned the money at the expense of the poorer man. Anyone who understands anything about obtaining wealth knows this is patently false. It is a well-known fact—the wealthy are the job creators—and not the other way around. The Democrats state; "the majority of the economic gains

---

[28] Exodus 20:15 "You shall not steal."

Satan Would Be A Democrat

go to the top one percent and the richest 20 people in the nation own more wealth than the bottom 150 million persons. So what? Where is the sin or the crime? If you want to know what the Democrat Party truly believes, just look at the next statement from the preamble of the **DPP**:

"We firmly believe that the greed, recklessness, and illegal behavior on Wall Street must be brought to an end. Wall Street must never again be allowed to threaten families and businesses on Main Street." [**DPP** pg. 3]

So, by the preceding rhetoric, I ask you; "Who's fostering an environment of poisonous politics?" Anyone breaking the law on Wall Street goes to jail when caught, regardless of who they are. Ever heard of Bernie Madoff? But, by trying to lump all wealthy persons together by calling them greedy, reckless and lawbreakers is highly inflammatory. Saying such persons are somehow a threat to families or small businesses is outright irresponsible! God's principle of sowing and reaping is intact: the activities we participate in with our lives directly affects what we obtain. If one works hard and sticks with the school program or curriculum, they will fare far better than the person who does not.

In my own experience, I grew up in a lower middle-class upbringing. I went to generally poorer schools, with classmates who were from lower blue-collar neighborhoods. I can plainly tell you those students who did the homework, studied and worked hard fared much better than the students who didn't. No person was held back or down due to the color of their skin, religious beliefs or gender. We all were given the same opportunity. Did some kids fare better because their parents were highly educated or more wealthy? Sure! But never at the expense of the other kids. We accepted some kids were just going to have it better than us. In the same way, a few kids had it worse than the rest. That was just life. Those who sowed hard work and studied, earned better grades than those who chose not to do so. This eventually turned into increased scholastic opportunity; just as prophesied by God.

Were you aware the verse concerning sowing and reaping comes with <u>two</u> preambles? A **preamble** is defined as '*an introductory fact or circumstance.*' It's used to clarify the reasons for and intent of the verse. The first thing God warns us about is being deceived. [29] The apparent question is "Why?" The obvious answer is God knew someone was going to try and pass off a different principle to fool humankind. And that person is Satan. The second thing God says is He is not mocked. The word for mocked is **mykterizetai** [*mook-ter-RID-ze-tie*] and means '*to turn the nose up or sneer at.*' Another way of saying the verse is; "Do

---

[29] Galatians 6:7 "Do not be deceived, God is not mocked; for whatever a man sows, this he shall also reap."

not be deceived by those contemptuously rejecting God's Word; stating your deeds do not have immutable consequences." In a nutshell, this is the policy of the Democrat Party. Everything they do is an attempt to bypass God's law of reaping and sowing, by mitigating the consequences for persons due the recompense of their actions.

The Bible teaches us: "If you aren't willing to work—then you don't eat, either!" [30] This is another Biblical principle totally ignored by the Democrat Party. The latest round of Democrat presidential candidates are on record as stating they are in favor of paying people a living wage—even if they refuse to work! I know what you are likely thinking—everyone has a right to eat. No, they don't! The Bible is clear— a person who is unable to work can still be fed, so long as they are *willing* to work. The Bible shows during the Exodus of the Hebrews from Egypt, God provided manna. It was delivered every morning (except the Sabbath) and came and went with the dew. God was explicit: if you didn't get up early enough to go and gather it—you went hungry. There was <u>no</u> allowance made for gathering it for someone else. In a clear picture of wealth, each gathered what they wanted. For those who gathered little—God said it would be enough. And for those who gathered a lot, God said it would not be too much.

---

[30] 2 Thessalonians 3:10 "If anyone is not willing to work, then he is not to eat, either."

Jefferson Daniel Seal

By the way, the phrase "E Pluribus Unum" was never codified into law. While it remains on the Presidential Seal, it was always considered a de facto motto of the United States. The truth is it was never formally adopted. At the height of the Cold War, the phrase was seen as being too near the objective of Communism. So in 1956, the United States Congress passed an act adopting the phrase "In God We Trust" as the official motto. This is the true and entire point made by **Galatians 6:7**. God is telling us the reward for sowing to His knowledge and truth will lead to the reaping of the rewards of living a good life. Our trust is not then placed in a government which is willing to steal other's wealth, for the purpose of providing for those deemed to be "less fortunate."

In God's eyes, there's no such thing as being "less fortunate." We each have access to our God guaranteed potential. All we need do is tap into it. It is certainly true there are those who sow seeds only to things other than what God would have them do. These persons make themselves less fortunate—by the very labor, or lack thereof, of their own hands. They will reap what they have sown. Just as the United States put "In God We Trust" on its money supply, we should see the statement for the truth for who it stands. God is the guarantor of our effort and work; regardless of who and what we work towards. Our failure to perform the deeds which are acceptable to God are what opens us up to the wiles of the Devil. We've been warned. So always remember the law of sowing and reaping; keeping in mind God is never ridiculed.

Corruption Leading to Destruction

There are those Democrats who will attribute their push for social equality to being part and parcel aligned with Biblical doctrine. Their attempt is to tie the principles of "progressive collectivism" to God's Word. They will attribute the root of their ideology as being espoused and even advocated within the pages of Scripture. They will usually point to the book of 2nd Corinthians as their proof. *"God mandates that from our abundance, we must supply the needs of others; that there may be equality."* At first glance their words sound pretty definitive, right? I mean, who can argue with the Bible? Let me tell you, this is the same old Satan, asking Eve "Did God not say, 'You must not eat from any tree in the Garden?'" This is a gross misquote of Scripture. It twists God's Word to say what they want it to. This is why being a disciple of Christ is so very important! Take a moment and examine **2 Corinthians 8:14**:

> *"At this present time your abundance being a supply for their need, so that their abundance also may become a supply for your need, that there may be equality;"*

As an astronaut once said to NASA; "We have a problem, Houston!" I will plainly state: "God's Word in no way ever speaks about there being a requirement—or even a goal, of people becoming social equals." In the New Testament of the Bible, there are exactly two passages mentioning the word **equality**. And both mentions are indeed located in the book of 2nd Corinthians, chapter eight. [31] The Greek word used for equality is **isotes** [*ee-SOT-ace*] and means '*fairness, proportionality.*' The word is not discussing social equality, but rather promoting God's desire for the equality of *treatment* for all His children. God recognizes we each have different requirements. As a result, we are each supplied with sufficient support to meet our needs. And, God at times uses others to assist Him in dispensing that support. Take a moment and read the entire 8th chapter of 2nd Corinthians. Note there is not one mention made of money, wealth or riches.

This is due to the Apostle Paul not discussing social equality, but rather God's Grace (vs 1). Paul is teaching God's followers, there is merit in suffering great ordeals on behalf of Christ. He describes doing so results in an abundance of joy, overflowing any deficiency with an affluence of <u>virtue</u> (vs 2). His discussion is all about sharing the good, as well as the

---

[31] 2 Corinthians 8:13 "For this is not for the ease of others and for your affliction, but by way of equality. At this present time your abundance being a supply for their need, so that their abundance also may become a supply for your need, that there may be equality."

bad, with other believers. Even as God has blessed us with abundant faith, knowledge and teaching, we still need to experience suffering to fully understand grace (vs 7). Helping others is not a command, but rather an opportunity to express our love for others (vs 8). Paul makes it clear: this is not a directive, but rather guidance to prove the earnestness of our Christly love to others.

Paul then goes on to state in verse 15, *"HE WHO GATHERED MUCH DID NOT HAVE TOO MUCH, AND HE WHO GATHERED LITTLE HAD NO LACK."* He was quoting from the Old Testament, Exodus 16:18. The context for the verse reflects the plight of the Hebrew people during the Exodus, who were told to go out and gather manna every morning. They were advised they could pick up as much as they wanted. Manna was the daily food God provided the Israelites, while they were marching out of Egypt to Mt. Sinai. There was no limit placed on how much they could gather. God used the daily manna to show them He could be trusted to provide for their daily needs. This idea is the genesis for the basis of the United States official motto: In God We Trust!

The God-given manna was in actuality a promise; as well as a prophecy. Recall every prophecy has two parts. The first part fed man's physical needs on a daily basis. The manna appeared every day it was supposed to, without fail, right on schedule. It was designed such that our reliance on God is to be a daily occurrence. The second part was a detailed picture of God's coming grace, where there would always be sufficient available for each and every person. [32] The death of Jesus was sufficient to pay everyone's sin debt. The point is this; God gave the Hebrews the amount of food daily to sustain them without want. They were free to take all they wanted. But they did have to get up early enough in the morning to get it. If they waited too long, the manna would evaporate along with the dew, in the heat of the sun. In turn, God gives us the exact amount of grace—all we desire in fact, carefully measured out to be sufficient so every person is satisfied. [33] God uses our weakness to demonstrate His strength; in the process making us strong. Contrast that with Satan's goal of stealing from our strength to make us weak!

The Democrat driven agenda of today can be simply stated as: "The transfer of total power to the Democrat Party by the use of any means necessary." As I go through each of the planks of the platform, it will be quickly revealed to even the most casual observer there is a strict agenda being followed. The evidence points undeniably to the **DPP** having a most sinister element interwoven throughout the planks. The common theme reflects a diabolical taint to their overall plans. **Diabolical** means *'of, relating to, or*

---

[32] 2 Corinthians 8:13 "For this is not for the ease of others and for your affliction, but by way of equality."
[33] 2 Corinthians 12:9 "But he said to me, "My grace is sufficient for you, my power is made perfect in weakness."

characteristic of the devil, Satan.' As is being clearly shown, the entire manifesto of the Democrat Party is riddled with anti-Biblical dogma. This cannot be by accident. Therefore, it must be by design.

Every person commences their life with a God-given freewill. God will not force you to do anything. In the same vein, Satan and his demons cannot *force* men to do their bidding. The hand of God prevents men from having their freewill stolen. But, just as with Eve, people can become unwitting pawns of Satan. I believe the true root of the problem with the vast pool of supporters of the Democrat Party, is they are not even aware they are being deceived. But, as observed in the warning at the start of Galatians 6:7, neither does God view such ignorance as a valid excuse. At the end of the day we are each held liable for what we do—whether we were tricked and/or hoodwinked into doing something or not. The Law of Sowing and Reaping remains in firm effect. God holds us responsible for the information we've been given. The Bible is available to nearly anyone on the planet. Therefore, we are each responsible for its content. Again, becoming a disciple of Jesus is key.

Thus, the definition I am using as to what constitutes being a Democrat, revolves around the personal actions of each person. If someone is working to further the agenda of the Democrat Party—then by definition; they are a fully-fledged Democrat. If your regular habit is to vote straight down the ballot along Democrat Party lines, then you too are a Democrat. If the weighted majority of your financial contributions go to Democrat Party candidates—whether they get elected or not; you are a Democrat. It doesn't matter you're being duped and swindled. The fact each of the Party's prime goals are wrapped up tightly in flowery language, hiding sugar-coated lies, doesn't change the outcome. Every person is still responsible for their actions. This book proves Satan fully intended to disguise the rotten and baleful truth woven throughout the Democrat Party message. His lies are cleverly hidden underneath esoteric sounding words. As with the first humans in the Garden of Eden, it just doesn't change God's opinion—you are yet on Satan's hook. But you should know by now, that's how the Father of All Lies operates.

So, God gave us a litmus test we can use to discover whose side we're really on. A **litmus test** is '*a test in which a single factor is decisive*.' Look at **Galatians 6:8**:

> *"For the one who sows to his own nature will from his nature reap corruption, but the one who sows to the Holy Spirit will from the Holy Spirit reap eternal life."*

If every plank of the Democrat Party goes opposite to the teachings of the Bible; is their philosophy aligned with the Holy Spirit or with human nature? Correct! "Human nature" is the right answer. The Greek word

Satan Would Be A Democrat

for **human** **nature** is sarka [*SAR-ka*] and means *'corruption, destruction.'* The word for **corruption** means *'a departure from the original or from what is pure or correct.'* As this book will clearly show, the planks of the **DPP** all deviate from the word of God. They follow a path which sows to man's own sinful nature. Therefore, by definition, they are corrupted from the truth. There can be no escaping the obvious; following the Democrat Party's corrupted principles must lead to destruction.

Following the truth of God leads to real inner peace and lasting satisfaction. [34] The only way to achieve this level of contentment is to plant our lives in accordance with God's Holy Spirit. This requires we first seek God. We do this by studying and learning God's ways, by studying the Bible. As we slowly assimilate His truth inside of us, we will then naturally begin adhering to those teachings. You won't be able to stop the transformation—nor will you want to. Democrat's will never be satisfied, because Satan can <u>never</u> be satisfied. As the end of time rapidly approaches, The Bible says he will become all the more agitated. [35] So, which seed are you going to plant with your life? The seeds which sprout mercy, leading to eternal life? Or the seeds of human endeavor leading to eternal damnation in the Lake of

---

[34] Galatians 6:16 "And those who will walk by this rule, peace and mercy be upon them, and upon the Israel of God."

[35] 1 Peter 5:8 "Your enemy the devil prowls around like a roaring lion looking for someone to devour."

Jefferson Daniel Seal

Fire? The choice is yours alone to make. Choose carefully, but please do not be deceived. Satan is planting seeds of corruption leading to destruction.

III. DEMONIC PREAMBLE

The Party of Conflict

One of the first items seen in the preamble of the Democrat Party Platform (**DPP**) is the statement: *"Cooperation is better than conflict, unity is better than division."* [pg. 2] "Well, of course it is!" you say. "Cooperation is always preferable to conflict, and unity beats division every time!" I couldn't agree more. But, that's not the real result of what we see happening in the daily realm of politics. Following the election of Donald Trump as President, any rational observer of the interactions between Democrat and Republican lawmakers can plainly see cooperation does not exist on any meaningful level. The Democrats are behaving as total hypocrites. They have become the party of division. The Republicans tried to negotiate in good faith and "meet the Democrats in the middle" over the past 40 years. But a trend developed—it was a slow and steady slide away from Biblical doctrine. Thus, the problem remains: The United States has been constantly and consistently pulled to the left side of the political spectrum as the direct result of this "spirit of compromise" nonsense.

The election of Donald Trump stopped this slide towards evil in its tracks; and even began a strong reversal of demonic gains. In perhaps one small indication of this, the nation heard President Trump say; "We're going to start saying Merry Christmas again." There is zero doubt the United States founding fathers were overwhelmingly Christian. This is reflected time and again in their writings. So, why has the U.S. seen an unrelenting attack on our long-held celebration of Christmas? The left has made every attempt to eliminate religious displays on municipal land. They've attempted to replace saying "Merry Christmas" with "Happy Holidays." It was not good enough for the Democrats when the courts said those honoring other faiths could likewise place displays in municipal spaces. No. The only compromise on the part of the left was to eliminate any locale displaying a manger scene or Christmas tree on public land. Time and again, they use the courts to try and force their way; up to and including the Supreme Court.

The world was witness to the recent Kavanaugh hearings for his confirmation to the Supreme Court. Let me ask out loud and clear: "Where was any sign of cooperation from the Democrats in those proceedings? Was there any snippet of unity seen in the hearings?" Absolutely none was observed, my friends. It was pure and total divergence. The Democrats threw in every charge and issue they could manufacture in attempt to bring down an innocent man. They brought conflict to the chambers of Congress, unseen in the history of the U.S. government. The reason they did so is very simple:

Satan Would Be A Democrat

They would be unable to further their agenda without control over the Supreme Court. This was supposed to have been guaranteed with the election of Hillary Clinton. They pulled out every stop to prevent his admission to the court, and Satan was defeated by God once more. There are many more examples I could present; and unfortunately, the left will create many more such unfortunate situations in the future by their simple refusal to negotiate and cooperate. They choose conflict every time with Donald Trump. So, why is this true?

The Democrat Party is currently living in fear of having a lot of their legislative gains reversed by a conservative President and Supreme Court. Perhaps the most visible issue is they are afraid the court will find reason to overturn Roe vs. Wade; the ruling making abortion legal in the United States. Now, is there any more of an *innocent* person in the world than a new-born baby? No, of course there isn't. But the Democrats are willing to put even a fully birthed baby to death, under the guise: "It's a woman's right to choose!" And in the same breath will fight to prevent the legally sanctioned execution of a serial murderer on death row. How can such diametrically opposed viewpoints be reconciled? There is <u>no</u> way to merge these two viewpoints apart from demonic influence. There is no unity of purpose present even in their dogma. The Democrat Party supports the wanton death of the innocent; yet refuses to legally

Jefferson Daniel Seal

execute the guilty. And, despite all the turmoil, Roe vs. Wade has not yet been overturned.

The Democrats will use <u>any</u> tool at their disposal in pursuit of achieving their goals. They are only in favor of cooperation and unity when as a tactic it suits the advancement of their cause. Otherwise, they quickly resort to using conflict and dissension. Jesus prophesied His message would bring division and conflict—and not cooperation. Jesus said, "Don't suppose I have come to bring peace to the earth." [1] Yes, that's exactly what He said—read the verse in the footnote. "Why did Jesus say that?" you might ask. It's because Jesus understood there's a spiritual war being waged over the souls of men. And the truth is: there's zero common ground upon which to negotiate or cooperate. Those doing the bidding of Satan and his demons are seeking to achieve only one thing: the demise of Christianity <u>and</u> its message. That's why Jesus said He didn't come to bring peace, but instead carries a sword! The question before us now is; "Why did Jesus bring a sword?"

It's due to His knowledge the resulting fight over good versus evil was going to be brutal. Jesus said His message would split families apart, making enemies out of members of one's own household. [2] This

---

[1] Matthew 10:34 "Do not suppose that I have come to bring peace to the earth. I did not come to bring peace, but a sword."
[2] Matthew 10:35 & 36 "For I have come to turn 'a man against his father, a daughter against her mother, a daughter-in-law against her mother-in-law—a man's enemies will be members of his own household.' "

message goes right back to when Jesus said, "You are either with me, or against me." There is no compromise of God's message. This was the first principle discussed back on page 3 of this book. And this isn't because Jesus is some kind of killjoy. Friends, we are fighting a <u>war</u> between good and evil. A person can only be aligned with one side or the other. If on God's side, a person is aligned with the **principle spirits of God**, which are: *'wisdom and understanding, counsel and fortitude, knowledge, piety and a healthy respect for the LORD.'* [3] This is a picture of the one who faithfully is following the teachings of Jesus and the Bible. If on the other hand one is **aligned with Satan**, then they will be *'displaying foolishness and indifference, censorship and weakness, ignorance, wickedness, conflict and division, and no respect for the LORD.'* Each person can only sit in one of the two camps at a time. No exceptions.

In the summer of 2000, President Clinton tried to move heaven and earth to create a legacy. His desire was to create a place in history for himself. He sought to do something no President before him had done; bring lasting peace to the Middle East. So, he invited the prime minister of Israel, Ehud Barak, and Palestinian Authority chairman, Yasser Arafat to

---

[3] Isaiah 11:2 "The Spirit of the LORD will rest on him—the Spirit of wisdom and understanding, the Spirit of counsel and strength, the Spirit of the knowledge and the fear of the LORD."

Camp David, Maryland. The summit took place over two weeks between the 11th and 25th of July 2000. Clinton pressured the Israeli leader to make a generous offer, by getting them to agree to submit to nearly 95% of Palestinian demands; in exchange for the creation of a stable and secure two-state solution. The only major item refused was the Palestinian "Right of Return."

This particular item called for every refugee displaced during the 1948 first Arab-Israeli war, to have the **right of return**. This means *'each refugee from 1948 would be granted the option of returning to their home, with full property restored, and receipt of compensation from Israel for all pain and suffering.'* Israel's position was this 'right of return' would invalidate the need for a separate Palestinian state. Israel would be forced to accept over four million Palestinians into the nation, fundamentally altering the demographics, jeopardizing its Jewish character and eventually Israel's existence as a whole. Not to mention, the cost of reparations would exceed ten years of Israel's total annual government budget! So, despite the dimensions of the Israeli offer and intense pressure from President Clinton, Arafat simply walked away without even offering any kind of counteroffer. Apparently, the only thing which Arafat would agree to was the demise of the Jewish state.

This example highlights two important points. First, did you notice the principle effect of the "right

Satan Would Be A Democrat

to return?" It was essentially the opening of Israel's borders to a huge influx of persons not loyal to the state of Israel. It would have the same effect the Populares' action had on the Republic of Rome. The Israeli citizens would have their vote, power and wealth gravely diluted by the influx of poverty-stricken aliens. This is the same tactic being attempted against the United States today. Even the call for United States reparations by Democrats for members of the black community due to their roots in slavery, stinks of the same evil rhetoric. No person alive in the United States today was ever an African slave. And neither were any of their fathers or mothers. The United States has invested over four trillion dollars in our black communities over the past 40 years, financing improvements to raise their standing in American society. It's impossible to argue the effort wasn't successful as we've had our first black president. Therefore, slavery is no longer a valid argument.

My second point is; there exists exactly zero desire on those following Satan to effectually cooperate or unify at any level with Republicans. If they can't gain the upper hand in any negotiation, then there's never an agreement. We see this happening in all Satan controlled entities. If the disagreement centers around the furthering of Satan's agenda, then there can be no real compromise. They always choose conflict over cooperation, and division over unity. So,

Jefferson Daniel Seal

the statement in the preamble of the DPP is an outright lie. Just watch the news channels, the print media and digital outlets, listening closely to the words of the leaders of the Democrat Party. They all reflect the true characteristics of the one they are following. If one has no respect for the things of the LORD, their willful ignorance leads to foolishness and indifference against Godly wisdom. Their refusal to acknowledge God's truth will lead to censorship and loss of self-control. This explains why Democrats are in actuality the "Party of Conflict." They are only pretending to make use of cooperation in order to gain their demonic objectives. They call for unity only when it means moving over to their point of view; all the while acting as the party of conflict.

There is Virtue in Success

The Democrats plainly state the following in their preamble:

> "Democrats believe we are stronger when we have an economy that works for everyone—an economy that grows incomes for working people, creates good-paying jobs, and puts a middle-class life within reach for more Americans." [**DPP** pg. 1]

On the face of the foregoing statement, who can argue with their beliefs? I mean, who doesn't want an economy where everyone can have a well-paying job? The American dream is for all persons to be at least in the middle-class. Okay, so the real question is: "How do we achieve good-paying jobs with increasing wages?" Their answer is: "We are going to spur more sustainable economic growth." "Oh yeah? How?" The vagueness of their answer only spurs the next question. "Now, tell me specifically how you're going to achieve it?" I've carefully studied the entire **DPP** and can tell you there's not *one concrete* proposal within the entire document based on economically sound principles. These statements are nothing more than sugar-coated words used to hide the ugly truth lying underneath the real demonic motives.

Instead, everything they discussed involves thoughts concerning esoteric values such as; "economic fairness, sharing rewards broadly—and not just those at the top." The Democrats are *not* seeking to improve the economic well-being of all Americans via the proven avenues of hard work and sweat equity. No, they are making the usual Satanic promises of getting something for nothing. They seek to create class warfare by insinuating the only reason there's a lower class in the first place is because of the miserly and tightfisted rich people at the top. Their true desire is to take from those 'greedy and wealthy snobs' at the top and give it to the 'unfortunate poor.' They lie and say it was the evil actions of the wealthy which created the poor. Look at the direct quote below if you have any doubt about what I'm saying.

> *"We believe that today's extreme level of income and wealth inequality—where the majority of the economic gains go to the top one percent and the richest 20 people in our country own more wealth than the bottom 150 million—makes our economy weaker, our communities poorer, and our politics poisonous."* [**DPP** pg. 1]

From the quote above, it's obvious the Democrats are only interested in initiating class warfare. Wealth inequality has been around since whenever the first person managed to earn enough to be considered rich. And how do they think the wealthiest people got to be rich? Oh, they will quickly explain; "It was on the backs of the poor." Well, that's just not true. People aren't poor just because others are rich! It's been proven time and again; it's the wealthy people investing in business which is the job creating engine of <u>any</u> nation. When the wealthy put their money at risk by investing in companies, businesses and enterprises, only then are jobs created. And, if all goes well, the investor makes even more money than when they began. If things go south, they might lose part or all of their investment. That's how real business works. Let's now see what Jesus taught on the subject of investment.

Jesus told a parable about a man who was going on a long journey. He called his slaves together to divide his wealth among them. They were entrusted

Satan Would Be A Democrat

to care for it while he was gone. [4] The use of a parable was the method Jesus used quite often to educate His followers. A **parable** is defined as '*a short story used to illustrate universal truth.*' It sketches a setting, describes an action and gives the result all within a few short sentences. Oftentimes there's a character facing a moral dilemma who has a difficult choice to make. The tale concludes with the person facing the consequences for their actions. Jesus explained how the rich man's wealth was split three ways amongst his slaves. One received five talents, another two talents and one slave received one talent; and the man then went on his journey. [5] This was the situation as Jesus described it.

The parable goes on to explain the person given five talents, immediately went and traded, and doubled the number of the talents entrusted to him. In the same manner the one who was given two talents, gained two more. And the one who was given one talent, went and buried it in a hole; hiding his master's money. [6] The talent being spoken about in

---

[4] Matthew 25:14 "For it is just like a man about to go on a journey, who called his own slaves and entrusted his possessions to them."

[5] Matthew 25:15 "To one he gave five talents, to another, two and to another one, each according to his own ability; and he went on his journey."

[6] Matthew 25:16-18 "Immediately the one who had received the five talents went and traded with them and gained five more talents. In the same manner the one who had received the two talents gained two more. But he who received the one talent went away and dug a hole in the ground and hid his master's money."

the parable has different meaning today. Back then, the talent was the largest denomination of money. A **talent** was actually *'a measurement of value by weight.'* Scholars have estimated a talent was equal to 188 pounds, or the equivalent to a full-grown man's body mass. Therefore, a talent of gold, for example, would be worth a whole lot more than a talent of bronze.

There is some uncertainty about the actual worth of a talent. It has been estimated that one talent was worth an amount equal to what the average person could earn in a lifetime. As we observed in verse 15, the master awarded talents based on a man's ability. The Greek word used for **ability** is **dumanin** [*DUNE-a-min*] and means *'God's power, miraculous power.'* The idea is not that the slaves themselves had miraculous power, but rather it was God's miraculous power which gave each man his relative ability to perform. So, if you were a King, or large landowner, God gave you the ability to earn such that your talent might be made of gold or platinum. The amount this person could generate in their lifetime was huge! For a profession with a lower earning potential, their talents might be composed of silver—and so on. This makes the most sense when the meaning of the parable is brought out.

Jesus went on to explain; after a long time, the master of those slaves returned and settled accounts with each of them. The one who received five talents

Satan Would Be A Democrat

and doubled his master's investment was thus commended. Since he was faithful over a few things, he would be placed in charge of many things. He was permitted to enter into the good graces of his master. [7] Notice, there was no condemnation from the master for the slave earning additional wealth. It was just the opposite. He was commended for his work and allowed to enter into the master's good graces. It was likewise with the slave who was given two talents. [8] I want you to notice this slave received the *same commendation and reward* as the slave who earned five talents. The reward was based not upon the amount earned, but rather on the use of one's ability which they'd been given. The final slave who was given one talent, returned the talent to his master, with the explanation he knew the master was a hard man, reaping where he did not sow and gathering where he scattered no seed. That was why he was

---

[7] Matthew 25:19-21 "Now after a long time the master of those slaves came and settled accounts with them. The one who had received the five talents came up and brought five more talents, saying, 'Master, you entrusted five talents to me. See, I have gained five more talents.' His master said to him, 'Well done, good and faithful slave. You were faithful with a few things, I will put you in charge of many things; enter into the joy of your master.' "

[8] Matthew 25:22-23 "Also the one who had received the two talents came up and said, 'Master, you entrusted two talents to me. See, I have gained two more talents.' His master said to him, 'Well done, good and faithful slave. You were faithful with a few things, I will put you in charge of many things; enter into the joy of your master.' "

Jefferson Daniel Seal

afraid and went and hid his talent in the ground. [9] He made no effort nor did any work.

Recall the discussion regarding the willingness to work and being subsequently fed. God said the one not willing to gather manna would go hungry until they changed their mind and went to work. When we discuss the rest of this parable, I want you to see there is incredible harmony contained within the Word of God. The master's reply to this slave was predictable based on what was told to the other slaves. He was described as wicked and lazy. Clearly God makes a distinction between those willing to work vice, those who do not. The slave was told he could have put the money in the bank and at least made some interest. This is how we know the Bible's discussing money and not God-given faculty. [10] The master took the talent away from the slave and gave it to the slave with ten talents. Jesus announced; "Everyone who has, more will be given more, and they will have an abundance. And it will come from those who don't have; even

---

[9] Matthew 25:24-25 "And the one also who had received the one talent came up and said, 'Master, I knew you to be a hard man, reaping where you did not sow and gathering where you scattered no seed. And I was afraid and went away and hid your talent in the ground. See, you have what is yours.' "

[10] Matthew 25:26-27 "But his master answered and said to him, 'You wicked, lazy slave, you knew that I reap where I did not sow and gather where I scattered no seed. Then you ought to have put my money in the bank, and on my arrival I would have received my money back with interest."

what they do have will be taken away." [11]

Contrast the message of this parable, direct from the lips of Jesus Christ, with the proposed agenda of the Democrat Party. The Democrats are working to do exactly the opposite of what Scripture demands! They are the party who wants to take from those who have in abundance; and instead give it to those who's means are scarce. The master ordered the worthless slave to be thrown into the outer darkness; a place of weeping and gnashing of teeth." [12] That phrase is Biblical language for "The Lake of Fire" or eternal damnation. These are pretty strong words for those unwilling to work. It becomes very clear the Democrat Party's goals run counter to God's Word. As the parable of Jesus Christ clearly shows; there is virtue in success.

Use a Stick Vice a Carrot

The Democrats do suggest one method for how they will employ their agenda in the preamble. They want to use the power of the President, combined with the power of the purse, to reward only those companies bending to their will:

---

[11] Matthew 25:28-29 "Therefore take away the talent from him and give it to the one who has ten talents. For to everyone who has, more shall be given, and he will have an abundance; but from the one who does not have, even what he does have shall be taken away."

[12] Matthew 25:30 "Throw out the worthless slave into the outer darkness; in that place there will be weeping and gnashing of teeth."

Jefferson Daniel Seal

> *"Democrats support a model employer executive order or some other vehicle to leverage federal dollars to support employers who provide their workers with a living wage, good benefits, and the opportunity to form a union without reprisal."* [**DPP** pg. 3]

Once more, the words on the surface appear to sound reasonable and sensible even. Everyone should have a job providing a living wage, with good benefits. I don't disagree. And, neither does the Word of God. The difference occurs with how the result is brought about and for what purpose.

The Federal government uses its power of the purse to bring about certain behaviors within its populace, by making such behaviors more attractive financially. For example, it is in the best interest of the nation to grow a larger population. All of our models for continued fiscal solvency revolve around a growing base of taxpayers. As the current generation reaches retirement age, there needs to be a large pool of taxpayers to absorb the cost of Medicare, Medicaid, and other retirement programs, such as Social Security. So, the government allows a tax break for those having children over those who do not. The more kids one has, the better, until the maximum benefit is reached. The same program rewards those who care for children through adoption and foster

Satan Would Be A Democrat

care programs. The Government uses its power as a carrot—all to entice couples to have more children.

The Democrat Party wants to use the power of the purse as a stick—forcing companies into raising wages and providing benefits. Here is the next sentence in the preamble:

> *"The one trillion dollars spent annually by the government on contracts, loans, and grants should be used to support good jobs that rebuild the middle class."* [**DPP** pg. 3]

Well, the Democrats will say their proposed program would be offered in the form of enticement as well. They will say their only goal is to support good paying jobs, which will have the effect of rebuilding the middle class. Okay, once more it seems fair. But, if their idea has such merit, why implement it via executive order? It was Congress who brought Social Security into existence. Why not use them again? The simple answer is the Democrats learned during the Obama administration Congress can be bypassed via the President with the stroke of a pen. It offers a quick shortcut to implementing their agenda. Implementing legislation is slow—as it was designed to be. The more complex answer is the Democrats know they will be unlikely to hold the Senate for many years to come. That means no socialist legislation through the Congress, as the American people at large, are never in support of it.

So, the Democrats always insert backup plans into their program. Did you notice the mention of "forming unions without reprisal" in the quote on page 116? Unions have long been an instrument in the Democrat toolbox. A **union** is defined as '*a confederation of independent individuals for some common purpose.*' Teachers, auto workers, pilots, steel workers, are all examples of union workers. The percentage of the workforce represented by unions peaked in 1943 at 33.4%, when manufacturing was the main harbor for American workers. Today, the percentage is around 11%. This is due primarily to the loss of manufacturing jobs overseas. The factor driving jobs overseas was the cost of labor in the U.S. became too high, making foreign labor much more attractive. The unions used strikes and associated work actions to drive wages and benefits to an unsustainable level. The companies involved were either forced into bankruptcy or required to move overseas in order to survive. The end result was a burgeoning of the *lower class,* as jobs disappeared or moved away. Unions were the direct cause of what is referred to as: "The American Rust Belt."

The idea of a union sounds great, that is until the union abuses its power by demanding wages and benefits which exceed those which can be reasonably absorbed. Forcing companies to pay inflated wages violates the principle of supply and demand. Something's only worth what someone else is willing to pay for it. **Free Enterprise** depends upon 'free' conditions in which to operate. View its definition:

"Freedom of private business to organize and operate for profit in a competitive system without interference by government beyond regulation necessary to protect public interest and keep the national economy in balance."

When someone forces you to do something you don't want to do, you no longer have freewill. This is a God guaranteed right. While free enterprise is not a God guaranteed right, it does form the basis for the United States economic model for business and commerce.

Unions have always been a stronghold for the Democrat Party. And did they contribute to increasing the middle class? Perhaps in the short term they did. But in the longer term, they caused more loss of good paying jobs and were responsible for creating economic wastelands in areas of the country. Plus, anyone who's worked in a union environment will tell you conditions are lamentable. The result is far too many workers are paid for not working. In the auto industry in 1981, a janitor was paid $27 per hour to sweep floors in the plant. The other issue with unions is their complete intolerance for those who are non-union members. They go to great lengths to exclude those who are not of the same mindset. The Democrat Party talks of tolerance for all—until a

Jefferson Daniel Seal

person chooses to not align themselves with them. Ask any worker who fails to agree with the union about their working conditions. Their answer is always the same: the endurance of much persecution and pain for going against the union. Thus, Democrats are liars. There is no truth in them. Let's examine what Jesus said about the work environment and regulation.

There are essentially four components to the parable we discussed. If you laid them out in the form of a math equation, it might look like this:

$$\text{Talent} \times \text{Labor} \times \text{Time} = \text{Profit}$$

The **Talent** portion of the equation we already identified as a person's God-given ability. The effort made to invest and make use of the God-given talent we will describe as the **Labor** component. Jesus said the master went away for a long time on a journey, so **Time** will represent the mathematical element of a person's life spent working on the job. When the master returned, the first thing he did was settle their accounts. The Master is God Himself. We will each be held accountable for what we did with our God-given ability. Clearly, there is an expectation for us to have turned some level of profit based on what we have been ceded. There is a day of accounting coming for us all.

The reality is; God cares nothing about money, gold or even physical wealth. These are nothing more

Satan Would Be A Democrat

than measures which can be used by humans to assess levels of success. The Bible says God already owns the cattle on a thousand hills. [13] God is not interested in wealth or "stuff." The thing God is most interested in, is obedience to His Word. And that obedience can only come from knowledge of what's written in the Bible. The Bible describes such knowledge as "light." It says every man has been given some light. [14] Light equates to essential truth. God tells us light has been implanted within our conscience. Just as the slaves in the parable, we are each given some amount of the knowledge commensurate with our ability to manage it. The slave knew 'the master was a hard man, reaping where he did not sow.'

That explains why the slave who returned only what he was given was punished. He did nothing to increase his master's investment. He failed to make good use of the talent he'd been given. God is going to inquire of each of us: "What did you do with the knowledge of good I gave you within your life?" Those who expanded upon it will be rewarded, and those who hid it will instead be banished. The profit the parable speaks of is indicative of the success we

---

[13] Psalms 50:10 "For every beast of the field is Mine, the cattle on a thousand hills."

[14] Romans 1:20 "For since the creation of the world, His invisible attributes, His eternal power and divine nature, have been clearly seen, being understood through what has been made, so that they are without excuse."

created within our lives using the knowledge we'd been given. The act of hiding our God given knowledge is equal to surrendering to the demons who twist Godly principles to suit Satan's purposes.

Once more, God awards those who diligently follow His lead and punishes those failing to do so. Why do the Democrats seek to mitigate any reprisal against the formation of a union? Again, it's in their DNA. Unions are not illegal. But their activities are harmful. Thus, Democrats always seek to eliminate or alleviate natural consequences of their actions. They prefer to offer demonic shortcuts via the use of the stick against successful persons and offer the carrot to those who prefer to pursue sloth.

Big Promises Make for Big Lies

The Democrats clearly like hearing the sound of their own words. They issue promises like giving away candy to kids, using words which are just like sugar to the tongue; they are most pleasing to the ear. Study the following quote:

> *"Above all, Democrats are the party of inclusion. We know that diversity is not our problem—it is our promise."* [**DPP** pg. 2]

The word **inclusion** is defined as '*the act of taking in others to comprise them as a part of the whole.*' It means regardless of who is left out of the group, they should be welcome to join and become a desired member of the Democrat Party. Sounds fantastic,

Satan Would Be A Democrat

right? The problem is the Democrats don't mean what the dictionary definition says. What they are actually offering is *conditional* inclusion. So long as one's viewpoint is tightly aligned with the Party's position, they are indeed most welcome. Everyone else will be excluded. So, who are those persons with the misaligned viewpoints? Most typically, it's those persons holding tightly to Judeo-Christian beliefs! As I've shown time and again, anyone with a Biblical perspective on life are decidedly unwelcome within the Democrat circles.

In case you are wondering, I'm *not* talking about the generic lukewarm pew warmer from the local Christian church. No, these people are like the masses of people who came to see the miracles performed by Jesus and partake of a free meal. Identifying such persons is simple. All that's required is a simple question: "Do you see the conflict between the tenets of the Democrat party and the Word of God?" Their answer speaks volumes about who they really are. If they see acute conflict, then they likely aren't a hypocrite. However, if they see absolutely nothing wrong with the stark differences, then they are merely warming up a seat in the sanctuary. Just like the masses who flocked to see Jesus, they aren't there to hear God's true message. By the way, that's why Jesus spoke most of His sermons in parables. He didn't want those present out of mere curiosity to

Jefferson Daniel Seal

become guilty of rejecting Him. **15** Jesus was seeking to lessen their chances of winding up in the place of torment. **16** Did you see the similarity of this verse to the other verse I used back on page 114, while discussing the penalty for the lazy? It's the same for those who reject God's Word.

The first example I offer centers around the LGBTQ+ movement. In case you aren't aware, the acronym stands for **L**esbian, **G**ay, **B**isexual, **T**ransgender and **Q**ueer or **Q**uestioning. The plus symbol (+) is used to indicate the countless groups of sexual and gender minorities being added which would make the acronym too long to be of any practical use. At last count, the acronym had twenty letters and was still growing. The group includes essentially any person who does not adhere to the Biblically stated sexual relationship of one man and one woman. There is also the letter "A" in the acronym, standing for 'Ally' meaning any person who considers themselves a friend to the LGBTQ+ community. Obviously, people disagreeing with their "lifestyle" are not welcome into the group. If you wish to participate in a very loud and heated argument, challenge the legitimacy of any person claiming to be

---

[15] Matthew 13:13 "Therefore I speak to them in parables; because while seeing they do not see, and while hearing they do not hear, nor do they understand."

[16] Matthew 13:12 "For whoever has, to him more shall be given, and he will have an abundance; but whoever does not have, even what he has shall be taken away from him."

LGBTQ+ by using the Word of God. Were I you; I'd bring earplugs along.

Listen friends, please allow me the courtesy of making the Biblical case _before_ you decide to disagree. The Bible teaches **ALL** persons are welcome to come to Jesus Christ; this includes _everyone_ from the LGTBQ+ movement. [17] The Apostle Paul in Acts was quoting from Joel 2:32; hence the capitalized text in the reference. Christians are taught and know full well all persons are welcome to come to Christ and accept Jesus as their Savior. The problem arises when those persons seeking to embrace the Word of the LORD, also wish to retain their sinful lifestyle. We each must arrive before God just as we are; no matter our level of sin. This is because our actions and behaviors could never be made good enough to be presentable to the LORD. We arrive in our sinful state at His feet, and through the miracle of His power, we _eventually_ are made whole. [18]

The act of coming before Christ has a strong element of regret and repentance contained within the approach. We are seeking redemption from our fallen state. Calling on the name of the LORD is a basic element of salvation and presupposes some level of faith; otherwise why would someone do it? God's

---

[17] Acts 2:21 "AND IT SHALL BE THAT EVERYONE WHO CALLS ON THE NAME OF THE LORD WILL BE SAVED."

[18] Isaiah 1:18 "Come now, and let us reason together," says the LORD, "Though your sins are as scarlet, they will be as white as snow; though they are red like crimson, they will be like wool."

Jefferson Daniel Seal

promise for salvation is for those who, in faith, petition Him by invoking His name. To call upon His name indicates we know who He is and are seeking a way to connect. There's a difference between knowing *about* God and knowing Him *personally*. Calling on Him shows personal interaction and a desire for a relationship. To do otherwise, totally negates the need for God altogether.

This is where the Democrats get it completely wrong. God requires each person to renounce their sinful ways. He doesn't allow us to *remain* as we are. We must accept His teachings; admitting *any* sexual relationship outside of one man and one woman goes directly against Scripture. [19] In the verse in the following footnote, Jesus was quoting directly from the book of Genesis. There's been no change—God created every person either male or female—with no exceptions granted. Our DNA and chromosomes are definitive and do not lie. Jesus goes on to clarify: When we grow up and go off to live our own lives, the aforementioned male and female shall become as one in the flesh. [20] This is Biblical talk for "having a sexual relationship." This is the 'God approved' way we were created. Man doesn't get to redefine God's design because he wants to do something different.

---

[19] Matthew 19:4 And He answered and said, "Have you not read that He who created them from the beginning MADE THEM MALE AND FEMALE,"
[20] Matthew 19:5 and said, "FOR THIS REASON A MAN SHALL LEAVE HIS FATHER AND MOTHER AND BE JOINED TO HIS WIFE, AND THE TWO SHALL BECOME ONE FLESH."

Satan Would Be A Democrat

[21] There's been no change in what God created right at the beginning.

The Democrats state they are in favor of embracing differences among people; regardless of whether those dissimilarities are right or wrong. Instead they go even further, stating they venerate those variations.

> *"As Democrats, we respect differences of perspective and belief, and pledge to work together to move this country forward, even when we disagree."* [**DPP** pg. 2]

The word **respect** is defined as *'high or special regard.'* They couch differences among people; including LGBTQ+ as necessary and even desirable diversity. The word **perspective** means *'a mental view.'* Essentially, it doesn't matter what a person believes, so long as they embrace the Democrat way of thinking. They see the Christian rejection of such principles as holding the country back. The nation needs to discard such antiquated beliefs, to move the country forward. They tack on the phrase; "even when we disagree." Again, anyone who has witnessed when others 'disagree' with the Democrats, knows there's no respect for such persons. They are instead met with contempt and insolence; and are insulted and disparaged at every opportunity. Say it ain't so!

---

[21] Matthew 19:6 "So they are no longer two, but one flesh. Therefore, what God has joined together, let no man separate."

Jefferson Daniel Seal

The Bible is very specific, teaching such doctrines would be slipped surreptitiously into the church of believers. He describes such principles would be slipped in by persons creeping into the church "unnoticed."[22] The Greek for unnoticed is **pareisduno** [*par-ice-DOO-no*] and means '*to enter secretly, slip in by stealth.*' Prior to the recent age, those persons were recognized for what the Bible said they were: "marked for condemnation." So, those persons kept their lifestyle a secret and infiltrated church circles by staying 'in the closet.' One of the 2020 Democrat Presidential candidates did this very thing. Presently, he and his partner are openly living in a homosexual marriage and proclaim being gay is completely acceptable within the Christian church.

However, Jude takes strong exception to those thoughts. He says these "ungodly persons turn the grace of God into licentiousness." The Greek word used in the verse is **aselgin** [*as-ELG-gin*] and means '*unbridled lust, wantonness, outrageousness, insolence.*' That's how God describes any person who prefers to live, by remaining in their sin. Another way to say it is: "Total and complete disrespect for God's Word." That's why the Bible calls them "unholy." Our holiness comes only from our willingness to adhere to God's Word. The Holy Spirit knows the true status of

---

[22] Jude 1:4 "For certain persons have crept in unnoticed, those who were long beforehand marked out for this condemnation, ungodly persons who turn the grace of our God into licentiousness and deny our only Master and LORD, Jesus Christ."

Satan Would Be A Democrat

our heart and imputes that holiness to us. [23] As I've said, we are in war with Satan and his demonic army. They were unable to defeat the Church from the outside and so switched their tactics to one which is tried and true: infiltrate the body of believers; then dilute the moral vote. Do you recognize the same tactic as being used against Rome? And today, the same tactic is being employed against the United States.

The Democrats will tell you they are not merely seeking common ground with all people. Read the sentence from the preamble yourself:

> *"With this platform, we do not merely seek common ground—we strive to reach higher ground."* [**DPP** pg. 2]

They go on to claim their purpose is to move the United States to a *higher* plain. The implied assumption is their way is an advanced position. But Jude defined this kind of talk for what it is: blasphemy. **Blasphemy** is defined as *'the act of insulting or showing contempt or lack of reverence for God.'* That's the same thing as "denying our only Master and LORD, Jesus Christ." A person cannot have it both ways: pretend to be a follower of Jesus Christ, while living a life which goes against the teachings of the

---

[23] 2 Peter 1:3 "Seeing that His divine power has granted to us everything pertaining to life and godliness, through the true knowledge of Him who called us by His own glory and excellence."

Bible. The Democrat Platform claims as its highest purpose in the preamble:

"Above all, Democrats are the party of inclusion." [**DPP** pg. 2]

The word **inclusion** means *'a relationship between two classes that exists when all members of the first are also members of the second.'* To determine what the dictionary is telling us, we begin by defining the two classes of persons:

> Class 1: Members of the Democrat Party
> Class 2: Satanic controlled Persons

The rules of logic apply here. All the members of the first class, must therefore be members of the second class. So, that means all Members of the Democrat Party must be under Satanic control, but not all Satanic controlled persons are members of the Democrat Party. Lots of people are under Satanic control. Plenty of Republicans, Independents, Libertarians, etc. They are not all Democrats. But every Democrat must be under the control of Satan, using the **DPP's** own language and admission. Satan would have it no other way.

The evidence is clear: The Democrat Party employs tactics long used by their master and leader, Satan. Go and read the full preamble of the 2016 Democrat Party Platform (**DPP**). There you will find a whole bunch of flowery words with lofty sounding goals and

Satan Would Be A Democrat

aspirations. There isn't space here to go through each line of the preamble. Do some homework and check it out for yourself. You'll see the same old approach employed by Satan's demonic soldiers regardless of which sentence you choose to study. Suffice it to say, from the lofty sounding rhetoric to the talk of occupying the moral high ground, it's all just a bunch of big promises; which can never come true. The reason? Every one of them fly directly opposite to the truth as contained within the pages of the Bible. Once a person understands the scheme being used against them, it becomes clear; every tactic employed by the Democrat Party to win the Presidency, originates straight from the mind of Satan. Are you beginning to see you've been duped? The Democrat party makes big promises; and big promises make for big lies.

Jefferson Daniel Seal

IV. A BRAWL OVER POWER

Unionize then Demonize

Just like God tells us via the Bible, Satan too has commandments which he demands of his followers. The Democrat Party's policies and strategies reflect these commandments. The first commandment is: "Thou shalt use all available tactics to steal the wealth from those above you." Of course, they don't say that out loud. Instead they carefully hide it in their **DPP**:

> *"Democrats believe we must break down all the barriers holding Americans back and restore the basic bargain that built America's mighty middle class: If you work hard and play by the rules, you can get ahead and stay ahead."* [**DPP** pg. 3]

Once again, we read flowery words about a supposed covenant between America and her middle class. Working hard and playing by the rules, guarantees one can get ahead and stay ahead. Interesting, as God Himself promises the very same thing! It's the principle of reaping what one has sown. When we put our God-given talent to good use, we will prosper.

The problem is the Democrat Party isn't advocating Godly pursuits. Instead, they are using words and language to make it seem so. They are merely cloaking their true diabolical agenda. The Democrat Party cannot deliver on such a promise;

Jefferson Daniel Seal

and neither can Satan. So, they seek another route. Look closely at the first sentence. Notice, it's nothing more than a thinly veiled indictment of the American Free Enterprise system. The Democrats see invisible barriers where there are none. And it's these supposed obstructions which are holding Americans back. God says nothing about such barriers. His Word guarantees His process will gain a person prosperity, regardless of their situation or plight. The only requirement is we must each get up, six days a week, going about our work of sowing seeds of success, by utilizing our God-given talent.

Satan knows full well the lower class is the subordinate faction of American society for good reason: they do not follow God's guidance. Therefore, they reap what they have sown. Satan uses the same tactic as always: "bait and switch." Presenting the thought that achieving a middle-class lifestyle is possible; is the bait. All one need do is vote the straight Democrat ticket. That's the solution to getting to become a member of the middle class. "You deserve it," they say. The problem for the Democrats then is to try and figure out a way for the lower class to achieve middle-class status without actually doing the required work.

They need to somehow find a way to beat the system. Simple Watson—just blame the system! Look at the next line in the **DPP**:

Satan Would Be A Democrat

"The system is not working when we have a rigged economy in which ordinary Americans work longer hours for lower wages, while most new income and wealth goes to the top one percent." [**DPP** pg. 3]

They accuse America of having a rigged economy! "Oh Really? By whom?" The U.S. has a long history of having <u>both</u> Democrat *and* Republican Presidents. Control of both houses of government frequently switch between the Democrats and Republicans. States and municipalities have a regular habit of selecting a diverse assembly of executives and legislators from all parties to lead them. And this leadership was elected by the majority of voters. So, who exactly is rigging the economy against the middle class? Read on...

"Republican governors, legislatures, and their corporate allies have launched attack after attack on workers' fundamental rights to organize and bargain collectively. Too many Americans are living paycheck to paycheck, and hallmarks of a middle class life—owning a home, having access to affordable and quality childcare, retiring with dignity—feel out of reach." [**DPP** pg. 3]

"It's the Republicans! Of course! And they've done it by attacking the worker's fundamental rights." I do hope you can see the sheer idiocy of their claim. As I have already shown, union membership numbers fell due to the *elimination* of the union jobs themselves. Nothing was rigged against any workers. The system worked as advertised. Unprofitable corporations do not long survive. The result saw <u>both</u> political parties passing laws, putting in some basic controls, reigning in the power of the unions. This was done to prevent even more jobs from either being lost or shipped overseas.

The reason itself was straightforward: The influence of the unions eclipsed the power of companies and local governments, forcing them into paying unsustainable wages and benefits. The result was companies either moved overseas or faced bankruptcy. More and more local governments are facing the specter of bankruptcy, due to unions driving wages too high. In December of 2015, the city of Stockton, California became the largest city in United States history to declare bankruptcy. The reason was very simple: wage and benefits for city workers became too large to sustain.

The Democrats will never accept blame for the result of their policies. Instead they use the media to assign blame elsewhere. They faulted Stockton's bankruptcy on falling revenues from the 2010 housing crisis and poor municipal investment returns. The truth is; the city council was estimating future revenues based on models using numbers which were far too optimistic. "Hey, we'd all like to make a double-digit return on investment!" But city planners had to create such high projections—otherwise they were unable to show future budgets were balanced. When the economy tanked in 2010, the over inflated wage and benefit payments "came home to roost." As the economy slowed, companies failed or were forced to cut back the number of jobs and wages. And, while plenty of lower-class folks achieved home ownership, as soon as the local economy floundered, they quickly became unable to pay for them when government assistance dried up. All the government funded programs allowing less-than-qualified folks to purchase homes were eliminated to reduce costs.

Stockton and other cities were essentially forced to take such action based on generous wage and benefits being paid to municipal employees. Social programs now consume well over 50% of city budgets. Over the years, unions in Democrat led states have foisted upon municipalities, costs which are too generous to be sustainable. The laws of bankruptcy permit civil entities to restructure their debt, including the forced reduction of wages and benefits to more reasonable levels. The state and local governments were forced to use the power of the court to put expenses back in balance. Many lost homes due to elimination of subsistence programs. God's law of sowing and reaping couldn't be circumvented by public or government policy.

The Biblical view of man is work-oriented. It affirms man was created in the image of God.[1] And we know God is a worker—as Scripture plainly says He is.[2] Logic dictates if God Almighty is a worker, then surely so is man, who was created in His likeness. God put man on the earth to fill it up with people while subduing it.[3] The word for **subdue** is **kabash** [*kaw-BOSH*] and means '*to conquer and bring into subjection.*' There is virtue in completing an honest day's work for a day's wage. Genesis 1:28 affirms man was placed on the earth for the glory of God. This same command was affirmed again after the Great Flood to Noah and his sons.[4] Man is to define himself via theocentric labor. **Theocentric** means '*having God as the central interest and ultimate concern.*' That means we each must work, and all of our work must be honorable and bring glory to God.

In Genesis, God defined the work week as lasting six days.[5] God then pronounced His work as; "It was very good." The Hebrew word used for good is **towb** [*towve*] and means '*pleasant, valuable, bringing prosperity and happiness.*' This sets the bar regarding

---

[1] Genesis 1:26 Then God said, "Let Us make man in Our image, according to our likeness;"

[2] Genesis 2:2 By the seventh day God completed His work which He had done, and He rested on the seventh day from all His work which He had done.

[3] Genesis 1:28 God blessed them, and God said to them, "Be fruitful and multiply, and fill the earth, and subdue it;"

[4] Genesis 9:1 thru 7 Please read the passage from out of your own Bible.

[5] Genesis 1:31 God saw all that He had made, and behold, it was very good. And there was evening and there was morning, of the sixth day.

Satan Would Be A Democrat

man's work. It must be honorable labor and meet the requirement of being worthy. When performed properly, it will bring a level of bounty to the worker. Otherwise, it will fail to be "good" seed. Any attempt to perform work which is not honorable in its nature will not bring forth good results.

When man sinned, God redefined the terms of his workday. [6] God cursed the ground, commanding that toil would now be required to scratch out a living. The earth untainted by sin would have given up great yields for the work done by the hands of man; but no longer. "By the sweat of your face you will eat bread, till you return to the ground." [7] Unquestionably, God ordained man must work much harder in order that he might eat. The Democrat Party has other thoughts:

"It's no wonder so many Americans feel like the deck is stacked against them. The Democratic Party believes supporting workers through higher wages, workplace protections, policies to balance work and family, will help rebuild the middle class for the 21st century." [**DPP** pg. 3]

---

[6] Genesis 3:17 Then to Adam He said, "Because you have listened to the voice of your wife, and have eaten from the tree about which I commanded you, saying, 'You shall not eat from it,' Cursed is the ground because of you; in toil you will eat of it all the days of your life."

[7] Genesis 3:19 "By the sweat of your face you will eat bread, till you return to the ground, because from it you were taken; for you are dust, and to dust you shall return."

The Democrat Party is attempting to thwart God's punishment of the lower class by promising they too have the <u>right</u> to achieve middle class living. The American middle class remains solidly right where it's always been. The real problem is many persons who once belonged to unions fell out of the middle class due to large scale elimination of good paying jobs. When those opportunities disappeared, there was nowhere for many to go besides down. The Democrat Party has now set its sights on removing those protections lawmakers put in place to preserve the middle class by defanging the power of unions. The Democrats are seeking to remove those protections.

> *"We will continue to vigorously oppose those laws and other efforts that would eliminate dues check-off procedures, roll-back prevailing wage standards, abolish fair share requirements, restrict the use of voluntary membership payments for political purposes, attack seniority, restrict due process protections, and require annual recertification efforts. We oppose legislation and lawsuits that would strike down laws protecting the rights of teachers and other public employees."* [**DPP** pg. 5]

The bottom line is it's not each man's right to work; rather it is their *duty*. Honorable work, or the willingness to work, is required of *every* person. Each person has a lawful right to compete for the job they want, not a right to it. In the same way, companies can compete for the labor services they wish to purchase. No one has a right to their job—just the right to fairly compete for it. And the rules surrounding all jobs must be fair and reasonable for both the company and the worker. The work itself must be honorable and moral. Otherwise the law of sowing and reaping will not apply. Satan hasn't changed his tactics. He is still seeking to upset the balance established by supply and demand. He uses the power of unions to usurp an unfair share of pay and benefits from companies and municipalities. The result is nothing more than a forced transfer of wealth from those who earned it over to those who are told the lie they deserve it. Not all unions are bad. Just the ones which unionize the workforce and then demonize the host organization or company, by using ignominious tactics of coercion.

God's Power is Always Good

If you think the Democrat Party is *not* waging a war against the wealthier citizens of American society, then you haven't done your homework. All one need do is read the **DPP** from beginning to end to see the irrefutable evidence of the Democrat plot against more affluent voters. Here is their opening statement on this topic to their party faithful:

Jefferson Daniel Seal

"To restore economic fairness, Democrats will fight against the greed and recklessness of Wall Street." [**DPP** pg. 11]

The rationale and justification for their beliefs are once again centered around reasonable sounding language, carefully crafted to foster class warfare. They seek to demonize those who have rightfully earned their money in the stock market—aka "Wall Street." They couch the terms of their fight as being a *benevolent* battle to restore economic fairness. So, ask them to show you anywhere it's written in any of the founding documents where *economic fairness* is part of either the Bill of Rights <u>or</u> the Constitution. And they cannot say such justification is part of Scripture, as it clearly has been shown it's not there.

Make no mistake, this war is over which party occupies the highest seats of power in the United States government. He who controls that power, controls the direction of the agenda. And in order to obtain that power, they must somehow get a majority of the vote. Satan already controls a sizeable component of the voters. But he lacks a simple majority. He needs to gain additional votes to turn the tide. Those pursuing Godly principles are the toughest to turn. They are also the wealthier of society—as per the law of sowing and reaping. If this were not true, Satan would have declared victory long ago. So, he must go after the poor. But even poor people must be enticed to come over to his side. And fighting a war is an incredibly expensive proposition. The money must come from somewhere, and the poor are not the ones who have it.

In conventional warfare, the goal of each side can be stated very simply: "Reduce the enemy's ability to wage war." This includes attacking not only the enemy's military forces, but also those government and civilian activities which directly support the military. So, the satanic driven forces are going after the wealth of those who oppose them. This is the easiest way to reduce the power of those not sharing their viewpoints. Cash is the equivalent to the military forces in the war over control of the vote. The voters themselves represent the territory over which the war is being fought. At the end of the day, the side holding the most votes wins. So, to attack the wealthy by accusing them of being "greedy and reckless" is highly problematic. This is true first of all, because the Bible teaches Godly principles are required to create wealth and then keep it. Secondly, it's a problem because the Democrats want the same thing!

I'm not saying all wealthy people are good and all poor people are somehow evil. That's not the point of the law of sowing and reaping. I'm just pointing out those persons pursuing goals in life via the use of Godly principles—whether they be followers of Christ or not—yields a better life than those who do not. Clearly, the rich can be adherents to Satan, yet still observe Godly economic principles in attaining wealth. The point is those controlled by Satan eventually reach a point where their evil sowing will begin to reap malevolent rewards. So, to demonize the wealthy for getting rich by accusing them of using principles of greed, self-indulgence and recklessness is highly hypocritical. Let's now examine what Jesus had to say concerning this topic.

Jesus was out one day during His ministry when He came upon a man who was unable to speak. Jesus ascertained the man was possessed by **a mute**, this was '*a demonic entity which causes muteness.*' Jesus cast out the demonic mute and the man was then able to speak. [8] Those watching were quite amazed at what they observed, saying, "Nothing like this has ever been seen in Israel!" [9] After witnessing the miracle, the astonished crowd began to question; "This man cannot be the Son of David, can He?" [10] By asking if Jesus was the Son of David, they were in essence asking; "Is this man the long-expected Messiah?" It was then the Pharisees straightway began casting dispersion upon Jesus. They accused Him of casting out demons via the power rendered

---

[8] Luke 11:14 "And He was casting out a demon, and it was mute; when the demon had gone out, the mute man spoke; and the crowd was amazed."

[9] Matthew 9:33 After the demon was cast out, the mute man spoke; and the crowds were amazed, and were saying, "Nothing like this has ever been seen in Israel."

[10] Matthew 12:23 All the crowds were amazed, and were saying, "This man cannot be the Son of David, can he?"

Satan Would Be A Democrat

only from Satan and not God. [11] They sought to deny a solid Biblical principle: The power to do good things must come from God alone.

By describing those who amass wealth as being somehow evil and underhanded, the Democrats are alleging the same thing as what the Pharisees did. They are attributing what is clearly a virtue (the honest earning of money) over to Satanic moralities. The Bible tells us Jesus knew their thoughts and told them; "Any kingdom divided against itself is laid waste; and a house divided against itself falls." [12] This wasn't just merely a morsel of truth directed at them. It was also a prophecy. Satan and his kingdom will one day soon fail and be laid to waste. Jesus went on, "If Satan is then divided against himself, how will his kingdom stand?" [13] It was a solid argument and the Pharisees knew it. Today, Jesus would be asking the Democrats, "If money's so terrible, why are you seeking to gain more of it?"

Jesus wasn't finished with them yet. "For you say I cast out demons by using the power of Satan. If that's true, then by whom do <u>your</u> sons cast them out?" [14] Certain members of the clergy and religious elite

---

[11] Matthew 12:24 But when the Pharisees heard this, they said, "This man casts out demons only by Beelzebub the ruler of the demons."

[12] Luke 11:17 But He knew their thoughts and said to them, "Any kingdom divided against itself is laid waste; and a house divided against itself falls."

[13] Luke 11:18 "If Satan is also divided against himself, how will his kingdom stand?"

[14] Luke 11:18-19 "For you say that I cast out demons by Beelzebub. And if I by Beelzebub cast out demons, by whom do your sons cast them out?"

were able to cast out demons as well. But the Pharisees weren't attributing *their* power over to Satan. By pointing out the hypocrisy, Jesus was in essence asking the Democrat Party; "If making money is such a terrible thing, then how did those rich Democrats supporting you obtain <u>their</u> money?" Jesus understood there was only one power which was able to cast out demons—and it wasn't demonic. In the same way certain principles are required to amass and retain wealth. The rules of sowing and reaping mandate virtuous activity and there is only one source for such benefit. Jesus told the Pharisees, "One day your sons will be used to indict you for what you are doing." [15] Jesus knew the Pharisees were an evil lot with a future day of Judgment coming.

Jesus next, as He always did, closed off the argument with His signature checkmate answer. "But if I cast out demons by using the finger of God, then you *must* admit the Kingdom of God has come upon you." [16] It's the same way with Donald Trump and the Republican Party. If their policies and strategies are successful in raising the economic state of the nation, the Democrats can no longer legitimately describe such as being attributed to evil means. If the people of the United States are following Godly principles, then success of the nation cannot be accredited over to greed, unfairness, materialism or unethical

---

[15] Luke 11:19 "So they will be your judges."
[16] Luke 11:20 "But if I cast out demons by the finger of God, then the kingdom of God has come upon you."

behavior. Success and abundance are virtues. Calling them anything else is meaningless.

The use of disparaging language by the Democrat Party doesn't remove the wealth from the wealthy. But what it does do is serve as the convenient lie to tarnish those who have wealth. These lies are then used to garner support from those of lessor means. It's all about garnering necessary votes to steal the wealth using legal schemes. Since the Democrats cannot simply rob the wealthiest Americans at gunpoint, they seek alternate ways to pilfer the money from them. Use of the tax code is the primary tool they utilize to transfer the wealth.

> *"At a time of massive income and wealth inequality, we believe the wealthiest Americans and largest corporations must pay their fair share of taxes."* [**DPP** pg. 12]

Do you see what they are doing by implying income and wealth inequality is somehow evil? It's all part of their larger strategy to remove the wealth from the top earners in American society. They wish to put in a multimillionaire surtax.

> *"We will ensure those at the top contribute to our country's future by establishing a multimillionaire surtax to ensure millionaires and billionaires pay their fair share."* [**DPP** pg. 12]

Jefferson Daniel Seal

The Democrats intentionally ignore the fact the top 20% of Americans earn 52% of the total U.S. income, but pay 87% of the total income tax. On Federal tax returns, more than half of all Americans pay zero income tax at all. This means the bottom 50+ percent of the workers already pay no federal income tax! But that's not good enough for Uncle Satan and his "Demoncrats."

"In addition, we will shut down the 'private tax system' for those at the top." [**DPP** pg. 12]

The tax system in the United States is already designed to be progressive; meaning those with higher incomes are already asked to pay a larger percentage of the total tax bill. Those with relatively low incomes, see the standard deductions and exemptions quickly lower their tax burden to zero. Of the lower 50% of Americans who pay no federal income tax, roughly half simply don't earn enough money. The other half don't pay because of special provisions in the tax code benefiting certain taxpayers; notably the elderly and working families with children. So, I ask you; "Which half of the taxpayers have a private tax system—if there indeed is one?"

Jesus was accused of using the power of Satan to cast out demons. The Democrats accuse the Republicans of creating tax laws which create millionaires by using a private tax system to benefit the wealthy. In both cases, at the end of the day truth wins out, exposing the demonic lies for what they are: illegitimate attempts at wiping away Godly virtue by casting dispersion on those persons utilizing virtuous pursuits. There already are provisions in the tax code doing exactly what the Democrats are calling for. But it's not in actuality what they are truly seeking. Despite having the bottom 50% of income earners paying zero Federal tax, they are still unable to unseat those wealthy persons sitting at the top of the tax code. It doesn't matter what the Democrats try and do, they will never win. Until God removes His Spirit restraining evil in this world at the time of the Rapture of His church, Satan and his minions will be destined for repeated failure. Thus, despite all the lies and deceit Democrats will be unable to override the fact God's power is always Good.

A Most Wicked and Odious Sin

It's interesting to note Democrats were among those drafting the tax laws currently in force. Despite attaining their initial goal of having the lower economic half of American workers pay zero taxes, they are no closer to getting the wealth believed to be necessary to achieve victory. Thus, the demonizing of the wealthy has largely turned out to be an idle threat. When a Democrat is President, income taxes tend to go up, targeted to the wealthier citizens. But when Republicans fill the office, tax breaks are delivered to Americans, largely undoing the previous increases. Raising taxes on the rich has proven to be

Jefferson Daniel Seal

a mostly unsuccessful pursuit for the Democrats. While they are certainly not giving up on stealing the wealth from the rich, they are adopting tactics to garner as much wealth for their side as possible. As usual, they start their quest with words fitting of God:

> *"Democrats believe that everyone deserves the chance to live up to his or her God-given potential."* [**DPP** pg. 13]

Amen! This is a moral lesson taken directly from the parable Jesus taught on the use of our talents. The Democrats next step is to find or create a cause which can lead to more benefits for their constituents. So, in order to get more assistance for the minority populations, they placed inflammatory language in the **DPP** concerning what they refer to as "institutionalized and systemic racism."

> *"Democrats will fight to end institutional and systemic racism in our society. We will challenge and dismantle the structures that define lasting racial, economic, political, and social inequity."* [**DPP** pg. 14]

Racism is defined as '*a belief that race is the primary determinant of human traits and capacities and that racial differences mark an inherent inferiority of a particular race.*' Use your common sense on this one. The most recent leader of the Democrat Party was a member of the black race. He was elected and then reelected by a clear majority of the American people.

Satan Would Be A Democrat

This despite him being leader of a political party which nearly half the population does not support.

Therefore, America is hardly a racist nation. Were that true, Mitt Romney and John McCain would have become president, and not Barrack Obama. Our governmental institutions have outlawed racism in any form and put in place programs to advance the cause of all minorities. One example is, the United States uses the power of the purse to award contracts only to those companies with a sufficiently diverse workforce. We've opened access to our institutions of higher learning to minorities via the use of affirmative action. We've granted over a trillion dollars of public assistance to those Americans of lower economic means. Once more, Satan is using an empty argument in an attempt to foster division and discord.

The Bible does speak specifically concerning racism. God commands His followers to <u>not</u> show favoritism to *any* group for <u>any</u> reason. In fact, God forbids favoritism in *any* form: either positive or negative. [17] The word used in the verse for **favoritism** is **prosopolempsiais** [*pros-oh-pol-emp-SEE-as*] and means '*partiality, inclined to show favor of one group over another.*' Favoritism rises to the level of discrimination when showing partiality for one group over another. Read the full text of chapter two of the footnote. The Bible teaches a very poignant lesson

---

[17] James 2:1 "My brothers and sisters, believers in our glorious Lord Jesus Christ must not show favoritism."

involving two men who come into an assembly of believers. One is clearly a rich man, wearing a gold ring and dressed in the finest clothes; while the other is a poor man dressed in dirty clothes. The rich man is invited to sit down in a place of honor, while the poor man was told to go stand somewhere in the back, or perhaps sit on the floor. [18] Today, we'd describe this behavior as racism, especially were the poor man to belong to a recognized minority.

This is precisely what the Democrat Party is doing. Instead of venerating the rich, they are showing favoritism to only potential voters and their supporters. They are seeking to discriminate under the guise of helping out "those poor and oppressed citizens of color." God already foreknew their reasons for doing so. He says; "Have you (the Democrats!) not created differences among yourselves (alleged racism) for a specific purpose, and thereby become judges possessing evil motives?" [19] When the Democrats create issues over economics and race, they are breaking people out by class and thus are creating artificial distinctions within society. The Bible is clear: showing *any* degree of favoritism, is an evil sin. Why? It's not that helping others is a bad thing.

---

[18] James 2:2 & 3 For if a man comes into your assembly with a gold ring and dressed in fine clothes, and there also comes in a poor man in dirty clothes, and you pay special attention to the one who is wearing the fine clothes, and say, "You sit over here is a good place," and you say to the poor man, "You stand over there, or sit down by my footstool,"

[19] James 2:4 "Have you not made distinctions among yourselves, and become judges possessing evil motives?"

No. It becomes evil behavior because the Democrats have a malevolent reason for doing so. They are being driven by evil motives. It makes solid sense: Satan is orchestrating the Democrat agenda via the use of evil motivation. A **motive** is defined as '*something (such as a desire) which causes a person to take action.*' So, an *evil* motive triggers a person to undertake *immoral* action. It worked on Eve in the Garden of Eden; and Satan is having spectacular success duping those within the Democrat Party.

The Democrats will state they believe the United States criminal justice system is seriously flawed. Their position is the U.S. imprisons too many people, as compared to the rest of the world. Their solution is to reduce the numbers of persons the U.S. incarcerates. They will state the reason for the prison population being composed primarily of minorities is due to police racial profiling. Democrats will tell you the "War on Drugs" has disproportionally singled out people of color, leading to higher prison incarceration rates. They want to remove the requirement where a convicted felon must openly disclose they have spent time in prison. And they want all persons who've been in prison to have their right to vote restored. Does this tactic sound reasonable to you? The Democrats say they want research and evidence to guide criminal justice policies:

Jefferson Daniel Seal

> *"Research and evidence, rather than slogans and sound bites, must guide criminal justice policies."* [**DPP** pg. 15]

Okay. Let's do a little investigative homework. On the list of the crime rate by country, the U.S. ranks 49th out of 150, with a crime index of 46.73. Taking the 1,000 most populous cities in the U.S. and comparing each by its associated crime rate, shows a direct correlation between crime rate and percentage of minority populations. The higher the percentage of minorities living within the city, the higher the crime rate. The evidence is straightforward. While I'm not saying all police are perfect, I'm saying their charge is to investigate crimes based on *available* evidence. The arrest records reflect the result of persons caught perpetrating a crime, and not who racist cops *think* they should detain and arrest. If all crime committed by black Americans were eliminated from the United States crime rate, the nation would have the crime rate of Finland. Finland sits 112th on the list with a crime index of 22.75. And if the crimes committed by <u>all</u> minorities were excluded, the U.S. would have the crime rate of Liechtenstein, who is at the bottom of the list with a crime index of 11.25!

The law of sowing and reaping requires law abiding citizens to not only obey the law, but to enforce it as well. [20] We are not permitted to show *favoritism* to any group, regardless of their plight or

---

[20] Exodus Chapter 21 Please read the passage from your Bible.

social conditions. The Democrats don't wish to blame the crime on the criminals; instead they seek excuses by which to ultimately blame others. "Oh, it's not the drug user's fault they do drugs. It's the fault of the city or state for keeping them in repugnant living conditions." Satan is well aware of those persons from whom he can obtain votes. All he needs to do is get them out of jail and prison and give them back the right to vote. There is a huge problem with the Democrat approach to solving the crime rate. It doesn't revolve around Democrats attempting to forgive persons of their crimes and reducing their sentences. No, it interferes with God's Law.

The law of sowing and reaping is alive and well and cannot be supplanted. God says He is; "A jealous God, punishing the children for the sin of the parents to the third and fourth generation of those who hate me." [21] This means the parent who willingly sins against God will have the effects of their iniquity carried down to his grandchildren (3rd generation); and even his great grandchildren! (4th generation) Satan and his followers all hate God, so the recompense for their sin is carried forward to subsequent generations. It may not seem fair, but it's what the Bible says. The word **jealous** means 'hostile towards a rival, intolerant of faithfulness.' While we commonly think the word

---

[21] Deuteronomy 5:9 "for I, the LORD your God, am a jealous God, punishing the children for the sin of the parents to the third and fourth generation of those who hate me."

pertains only to romantic rivals, clearly it extends over God's rivals as well; Satan and his followers. That's the reason it's so tough for those caught in the trap of sin and the resulting consequences to get away from misconduct, thereby breaking the chain of poverty. God doesn't want the chain broken. Remember: God is not ridiculed! "A person WILL reap what they have sown!"

The only true hope and help available for the poor living in crime riddled cities is for them to individually turn to the love of God. God tells us His love abounds for those who love Him by making effort to keep His commandments. [22] The only resolution available for those children whose parents are living a life of sin, is for those parents to seek the love of Jesus Christ and repent of their life of sin. Continuing to hate God is counterproductive to getting out of the lower-class economic lifestyle. There is no other way out! But so long as one listens to the voice of the demon inside their head, whispering the same mantra spoken by the Democrat party, they will remain on the highway to hell. [23] While these words are not perhaps what anyone necessarily wants to hear, they are none-the-less the truth of God.

---

[22] Deuteronomy 5:10 "but showing love to a thousand generations of those who love Me and keep My commandments."
[23] Matthew 7:13-14 "Enter through the narrow gate. For wide is the gate and broad is the road that leads to destruction, and many enter through it. But small is the gate and narrow the road that leads to life, and only a few find it."

Satan Would Be A Democrat

The apex of the Democrat rhetoric for reforming the justice system in America speaks volumes about who they really serve. The Bible clearly mandates the punishment fit the crime. For example, should you murder someone, then you too shall be executed. [24] The Democrats have a different idea:

"We will abolish the death penalty, which has proven to be a cruel and unusual form of punishment. It has no place in the United States of America. The application of the death penalty is arbitrary and unjust." [**DPP** pg. 16]

Once again, the Democrat's ideas flow directly opposite to the guidance of the Bible. They willingly will permit the execution of the most innocent of humanity (unregulated abortion), while in the same breath oppose the lawful execution of those who are most guilty. And there is even a more relevant example which can be used to prove this point.

On the last night of His life, Jesus was brought before Pontius Pilate to be judged. Pilate was well-aware Jesus was innocent of all charges and the Jews were stimulated by evil motives. [25] And so, Pilate looked for a way to set Him free. It was the governor's custom to release one prisoner chosen by the crowd

---

[24] Exodus 21:12 "He who strikes a man so that he dies shall surely be put to death."

[25] Matthew 27:18 For he knew it was out of self-interest that they had handed Jesus over to him.

Jefferson Daniel Seal

during Passover. [26] Pilate gave them a choice. He brought before the crowd a notorious terrorist by the name of Jesus Barabbas. [27] He then asked, "Which one do you want me to release to you: Jesus Barabbas, or Jesus, who is called Messiah?" [28] One man was clearly guilty and the other was completely innocent. The Bible says the Chief Priests and elders persuaded the crowds to ask for Barabbas; and to put Jesus to death. [29] "Barabbas," they answered. [30] What shall I do, then, with Jesus, who is called Messiah?" Pilate asked. They all answered, "Crucify Him!" [31]

The leaders of the Democrat Party are the modern-day equivalent of the chief priests. They are the ones lying to the party faithful about what's really going on. They are aware they are pushing their self-interest over what is Godly, reasonable and good. The leaders of the Democrat Party are calling for the crucifixion of the innocent via scalpel, and in the same breath are demanding the guiltiest among us be set

---

[26] Matthew 27:15 Now it was the governor's custom at the festival to release a prisoner chosen by the crowd.

[27] Matthew 27:16 At that time they had a well-known prisoner whose name was Jesus Barabbas.

[28] Matthew 27:17 So when the crowd had gathered, Pilate asked them, "Which one do you want me to release to you; Jesus Barabbas, or Jesus who is called the Messiah?"

[29] Matthew 27:20 But the chief priests and the elders persuaded the crowds to ask for Barabbas and to put Jesus to death.

[30] Matthew 27:21 "Which of the two do you want me to release to you?" asked the governor. "Barabbas," they answered.

[31] Matthew 27:22 "What shall I do, then, with Jesus who is called the Messiah? Pilate asked. They all answered, "Crucify Him!"

Satan Would Be A Democrat

scot free. Thus, the favoritism shown by the Democrats is truly a most wicked and odious sin.

Granting Wrong Rights

The Democrat Party Platform states the high goal of never giving up the fight to ending discrimination in America. Once more, the words they write sound really good on the surface.

> *"Democrats will always fight to end discrimination on the basis of race, ethnicity, national origin, language, religion, gender, age, sexual orientation, gender identity, or disability."* [**DPP** pg. 16]

Of course, such fights waged by the Democrats always come with a very high price tag. As has been discussed, the Democrat Party believes most racial discrimination is the direct result of people of color living in poverty. For the Democrats, they see poverty as a root cause, with discrimination following along as the final outcome. And their solution for eliminating poverty is the same as most of their government programs—throw lots and lots of money at it.

> *"We reaffirm our commitment to eliminate poverty; by focusing on communities suffering from persistent poverty,"* [**DPP** pg. 18]

Instead of admitting poor people are likely impoverished due to their own behavior; they seek to shift blame elsewhere. Instead of building programs targeted at altering the conduct which puts and keeps people in poverty; they instead seek to apply a fix without first attempting to eliminate the root cause of the problem. This explains why poverty has persisted within black communities for multiple generations. The Democrat Party is still looking to throw more money at the problems by dramatically increasing government assistance. Programs such as food stamps, Earned Income Tax Credit, Child Tax Credits and Affordable Housing Programs would all be greatly increased were the Democrats to have their way. Of course, all this extra money has to come from somewhere. And we know it will come in the form of a vastly increased tax burden on the upper half of the U.S. taxpayers. The Democrats have struggled for decades trying to implement their plan with little to no success.

> *"Democrats have a comprehensive agenda to invest in America's cities, grounded on the premise that local leaders are best equipped to create a better future for their residents."* [**DPP** pg. 20]

The reality is the top ten worst cities in America for poverty and crime are led by Democrat mayors and Democrat controlled city councils. Their plans always fail due to the insolvency of their economic model. Throwing money at poor people doesn't solve the root cause of their problem; always due to personal behavior. The social programs all attempt to mitigate

Satan Would Be A Democrat

the consequences of evil behavior—which goes directly against Scripture. And the communities just become even poorer, as what little tax base present at the start continues to dissolve over time. The Democratic solution to this continuing mess? Dramatically increase federal funding to fix crumbling infrastructure.

> *"We will dramatically increase federal infrastructure funding for our cities."* [**DPP** pg. 20]

The Democrats are telling the rest of America their plan: "Use more of your money to fix *our* problems caused by Democrat programs."

A cursory examination of the discrimination in America as seen by the Democrat Party reveals a consistent agenda which flows diametrically opposite to the Word of God. In the next quote from the **DPP**, notice how *they* highlight their *real* agenda, by specifically numerating the real focus of their schema. The numbers in brackets are mine:

> *"We know that there are barriers standing in the way of that goal, from the enduring scourge of systemic racism* [1] *to our deeply broken immigration system* [2] *to discrimination against people on the basis of sexual orientation* [3] *or gender identity* [4] *and religious freedom* [5] *— and we are committed to facing those problems and fixing them."* [**DPP** pg. 14]

Jefferson Daniel Seal

We've already discussed their plan for what they describe as systemic racism [1], so let's continue with discrimination based on national origin [2]. The Democrats would have us believe such discrimination is rampant throughout the nation.

> *"Democrats believe we need to urgently fix our broken immigration system—which tears families apart and keeps workers in the shadows—and create a path to citizenship for law-abiding families who are here, making a better life for their families and contributing to their communities and our country."* [**DPP** pg. 16]

The truth is Democrats are only talking about people who have come to America *illegally*. Once more, their only desire is to decriminalize and absolve people who came to America without authorization. Say it any way you wish, but such persons committed a crime the moment they crossed the border illegally. It actually speaks volumes about the patience and goodwill the United States has shown towards such persons. As a nation we've generally looked the other way while illegal aliens utilized government benefits and health care; to the detriment of needy American citizens. So, to state the U.S. discriminates against their undeniably criminal behavior is the height of duplicity and hypocrisy. We are just seeing Satan use the same tactic he used against Rome by the efforts of the Populares.

Satan Would Be A Democrat

Other selected behaviors the Democrats chose to describe as being affected by rampant racism is sexual orientation [3] and gender identity [4].

"Democrats applaud last year's decision by the Supreme Court that recognized that LGBT people—like other Americans—have the right to marry the person they love." [**DPP** pg. 18]

Once again, the Democrat Party is trumpeting a Biblical sin as being honorable behavior, due to a flawed decision made by the Supreme Court. The nation's highest court, "recognized marriage as a fundamental right because it supports a two-person union unlike any other in its importance to committed individuals." [32] They went on to say in their 5-4 decision that, "Same-sex couples have the same right as opposite-sex couples to enjoy intimate association, a right extending beyond mere freedom from laws making same-sex intimacy a criminal offense." So, the Democrat Party uses this as their justification for recognizing LGBT marriage as legal. However, using the Supreme Court as justification for going against the Bible can <u>never</u> be a valid reason.

As discussed in a previous section back on page 126, God is crystal clear: marriage is a <u>God</u> ordained institution; one He defined as being comprised of *one* man and *one* woman. [33] As far as intimacy being a

---

[32] Supreme Court United States Syllabus No. 14-556
[33] Matthew 19:4 thru 6 See the footnotes on page 126.

Jefferson Daniel Seal

fundamental right between <u>any</u> two individuals, regardless of sex or gender, as opined by the Supreme Court; God has an altogether dissimilar outlook on this particular subject, which is very specific: "A man shall not lie with a man as one lies with a woman." [34] God describes such an act as an *abomination*, worthy even of death! The word **abomination** is defined as *'something regarded with extreme disgust or hatred.'* God only describes certain things in Scripture using the word "detestable:" idolatry, homosexuality and blasphemy are the main three. My purpose herein is not to debate whether Gay Marriage should or shouldn't be legal in the United States. My point is the Democrat Party can be shown once more to be endorsing policy which flies in the face of sound Biblical doctrine.

The Democrat Party dare not attack the word of God directly, as there are far too many Americans who would not stand for it. So, they instead seek an end around run by condemning Bible preaching Christians as "misusers of religion for the sole purpose of discriminating." [5]

"We support a progressive vision of religious freedom that respects pluralism and rejects the misuse of religion to discriminate." [**DPP** pg. 17]

---

[34] Leviticus 20:13 "If there is a man who lies with a male as those who lie with a woman, both of them have committed a detestable act; they shall surely be put to death."

Satan Would Be A Democrat

The word **progressive** means '*the effort to advance new ideas, findings, or opportunities*.' Well, there are no new ideas when it comes to the word of God. The cannon of Scripture was closed around 90 AD when the last Apostle died. The Democrat Party states they respect pluralism. **Pluralism** is defined as '*holding two or more positions or stances (such as religious theology) at the same time*.' Essentially, the Democrats accept any and all religions, so long as it isn't "intolerant" Christianity. But once more the truth is; there is but one God, and only one mediator between God Almighty and men, the man Christ Jesus.[35] While I selected one verse for the footnote reference, there are over fifty verses in the Bible which specifically state there is one God and one mediator. There are no other positions which can therefore reflect reality. To postulate such is both misleading and deceptive; something the Democrat Party is willing to do as part of their plan.

One consistency in the Democrat Party approach to implementing their plan, is they use lots of high sounding and flowery language to sell their message. They never want potential followers to dig down too deeply when reading their missive. The real problem is their rhetoric fails when closely matched up against the Word of God and/or a dictionary. So, they deflect attention away from what they are really saying by

---

[35] 1 Timothy 2:5 "For there is one God, and one mediator also between God and men, the man Christ Jesus."

Jefferson Daniel Seal

creating artificial divisions. Those being targeted by the con are told instead to focus on the supposed enemies of the Democrat Party. These adversaries are called terms such as; "a basket of deplorable's, misogynistic, homophobic, racists, intolerant, white supremacist, etc. for the purpose of creating division between the electorate. The Democrats don't need their followers to trust them, they just need to make the voters believe they are entrusted by the Party.

In the world of con artists, frauds, swindlers and cheats there is one iron-clad rule: "Always show the targeted "mark" how much you trust them!" By the swindler showing trust in the mark, it's much easier to have them accept the surrounding circumstances. There are many ways to do this, but the most common method employed is to pretend to seek another person's help. Con men ply their trade by appearing to require assistance with some task; which they will sell as being critically important. The reason they do it so often—is because it works. The Democrat Party will shout to all who will listen; "The future of America as a free nation is at stake. Donald Trump must be stopped at all cost!" They will say they can't do it alone. They require the help of all people to get out and vote against the Republican agenda. Democrats repeatedly tell their voters it's up to them.

"This election is about more than Democrats and Republicans. It is about who we are as a nation, and who we will be in the future." [**DPP** pg. 4]

Satan Would Be A Democrat

The ability to fool mankind begins within the realm of the mind. The human brain produces oxytocin when we are put into a position whereby, we have the ability to help others. Oxytocin has a positive effect on the brain and makes us feel really good. Thus, the key to a successful con is not making the target trust the conman himself; but rather have the swindler convey the appearance <u>he</u> is the one who trusts the mark. They will put forth a situation calling for action based on common sense. What the victim doesn't realize at the time—is the situation being presented has been built by the charlatan.

Con men ply their trade by appearing to be someone in a precarious position in need of our help. That shifts our focus away from being on them over to the circumstances before us. Circumstances, which can be easily manipulated to look like almost anything the con desires. And due to the effect oxytocin has on the human brain, we typically don't dig too deeply when faced with being asked for help. We naturally feel good when we help others. This is what forms the basis for domiciliary connection to family and friends. And is the driving force for allowing cooperation with strangers. The words; "I need your help," is a potent stimulus for action.

Satan understood this principle well when he went before Eve, feigning ignorance. He went to her seeking help with understanding the word of God. "Hey woman, I have a question, I'm at a complete loss to answer." Satan said, showing need to Eve. Then he asked. "Did God really say, 'You can't eat from any tree in the garden?' " [36] The trap was laid. Satan sought help with a question to which he already knew the answer—just like a con man would do. Eve didn't have to trust Satan. She just had to believe he trusted her. And when she did, the devil stole man's innocence, damning him to the Lake of Fire.

It's the exact same scenario with the Democrats. They will continue saying they need every voter's help saving the nation. Then, just like the swindler flimflam man, they will steal our freedom, damning the U.S. to the ash heap of history. It happened to the previous empires which led the world, and it will happen to us. As of the publication date of this book, the world is less than fourteen years from the start of the Tribulation. A revived Roman Empire will be coming back for a dreadful period of seven years. It will be the worst time in man's history. And the man indwelt by Satan will use as his main tool, control over the world's money supply. No one will be able to buy or sell without having his mark. But first, he must take control of the world's money supply. Only then can he move to seize control of world. And he'll do it by granting all the wrong rights to the common people, something already started by Satan and his demons.

---

[36] Genesis 3:1 Now the serpent was more crafty than any beast of the field which the LORD God had made. And he said to the woman, "Indeed, has God said, 'You shall not eat from any tree of the garden?' "

V. STEALING THE VOTE

The Guise of Protection

Just like any swindler, the Democrat Party must first manufacture a crisis before they can come to the American public asking for help. That's how tricksters operate: they create a situation which seems to require some assistance with obtaining a resolution. That's the point at which they will try and get a potential victim involved. So, the Democrats began their scam by affirming the fundamental and sacred nature of the American right to vote:

> "Democrats know that Americans' right to vote is sacred and fundamental." [**DPP** pg. 23]

Once more, notice the straightforwardness of their language. Who'd argue against such sentiment? The word **sacred** means 'regarded with great reverence and respect.' The word **fundamental** means 'forming a necessary base or core; of central importance.' Both of these words reflect the American approach to the right to vote. Okay, so the next step is to directly link the right to vote to the Democrat Party:

> "The Democratic Party was founded on the promise of an expanded democracy. The right to vote is at the heart of our national vision." [**DPP** pg. 23]

Well, truth be told, the previous statement of the Democrat Party being founded on "the promise of expanded democracy" is highly misleading. The Democrat Party was founded in 1792 by supporters of Thomas Jefferson and James Madison. The party split away from the Federalists because the Federalists were pushing for too strong a central government and a nationally consolidated banking system. Jefferson and Adams opposed the move due to fear the government would gain too much power—the very reason the colonialists left England. The new party they formed was known as the Democratic-Republicans, which favored limited and decentralized government.

The Federalist Party began an immediate decline, fielding their final presidential candidate in 1816. They ceased to exist shortly thereafter. Less than a decade later, in 1828, the Democrats split off from the Republicans, once again forming their own party. Interestingly enough, they began almost immediately mirroring the policies of the now defunct Federalists. They targeted the voters of the South, who were much poorer and less educated than northern voters. So, who does the Democrat Party of today most resemble? You are correct if you said; "The Federalists." There have always really only been two parties in politics: The Populares (Demonic) and the Optimates (God favoring). The Democrats have

Satan Would Be A Democrat

changed their name over the ages many times, but their Satanically driven tactics have remained intact.

The quote on the bottom of page 171 does indeed reflect the true purpose of the modern Democrat Party. They are working very hard at expanding the vote to include <u>everyone</u> who will possibly vote for them. This list includes all the people of color living in the United States legally; as well as inviting in hordes of others who come here illegally. They will expand the vote regardless of who they lure in or bribe using largesse from the U.S. government treasury. The effort reflects the goal of diluting the true vote of American citizens by bringing in large numbers of others who have no stake in the American dream. That is precisely what the *Populares* did back in the Roman Republic. It worked then and it can work today. All that need happen is for Americans to turn a blind eye to what is actually being done; and instead focus on the words of what is being said:

> *"It is a core principle of the Democratic Party to maximize voter participation for all Americans. Our democracy suffers when nearly two thirds of our citizens do not or cannot participate, as in the last midterm elections."* [**DPP** pg. 23]

First, they advocate "maximizing voter participation." Again, that's a good thing. Both sides of the political isle are working very hard to get out

Jefferson Daniel Seal

the vote. The Republicans are acutely aware the actual number of Democrat voters exceeds those on the right. So, the biggest obstacle for the Republicans is reducing voter apathy, as it's generally true; off year elections do not see turnout much above about one-third of registered voters. The Democrats have an even harder time overcoming voter lethargy. Despite having larger numbers of available voters, the Democrats experience a significantly lower turnout than do the Republicans. The Republican voters largely see the threat being posed by allowing the Democrats too much power; and subsequently will go and vote. This was the direct result which led to the victory by President Trump in 2016. Democrat voters in general lack the zeal of the Republicans to get out and vote for their side. They must be enticed and exhorted to make the effort.

The Democrat Party would have us believe it's "too difficult" for a large block of their voters to go and vote. Did you see the excuse in the last quote stating, "many of their voters didn't vote because they *cannot participate*?" The Democrats again won't place blame where it belongs, choosing instead to indict the system. But, by doing so, they are showing their hand as to what they are really up to.

> *"Democrats believe we must make it easier to vote, not harder."* [**DPP** pg. 22]

They begin by telling the electorate their vote is under assault and needs protection. They first blame those bad corporations for exercising undue influence over elections.

> *"We believe that we must protect Americans' right to vote, while stopping corporations' outsized influence in elections."* [**DPP** pg. 23]

Notice if you will, no specifics are given about how the evil corporations are accomplishing their feat. It's due to the fact the accusation is demonstrably false. Corporations are composed of people—Republicans, Democrats and Independents. All seek to create legislative environments where their business can survive and thrive. Lobbying Congress is done by all groups and is part and parcel of both sides of the isle.

Next, Democrats blame Republicans for disenfranchising people of color, low-income people, as well as young people.

> *"We will stop efforts by Republican governors and legislatures to disenfranchise people of color, low-income people, and young people, and prevent these voters from exercising their right to vote through onerous restrictions."* [**DPP** pg. 21]

The word **disenfranchise** is heard frequently within Democrat circles today and means *'to deprive someone of the right to vote*.' Notice, the Democrats are listing their primary block of voters as being the sole targets of such activity. They make the claim such

Jefferson Daniel Seal

actions being performed by Republicans have prevented these people from voting; through the creation of *onerous* restrictions. Okay, fine. Just tell us how they do it.

Anyone who is of the age eighteen or older can go down to the department of motor vehicles and register to vote. It's usually automatically offered when a person obtains a driver's license. The percentage of Americans who have a driver's license has been steadily increasing since 1960, when 57% of the population had them. The trend has gone up following increased ownership of automobiles. Today, 68.1% of U.S. citizens have one. When you consider the bottom 22.4% of the population isn't old enough to vote yet, we've just accounted for over 90% of the population. Add in a portion of the elderly, some of whom are unfit to drive, those persons with a handicap severe enough to preventing them from driving, and the prison population (including felons who have lost the right to vote) the total now includes 97% of Americans. The remaining percentage of Americans who are left, is less than 3% of the total population. So, Democrats: "Who are you talking about that's being disenfranchised?"

They won't state any specific examples, because they cannot. But they will continue to wail loudly by pointing out the supposed "gutting of the Voting Rights act."

"We must rectify the Supreme Court decision gutting the Voting Rights Act, which is a profound injustice." [**DPP** pg. 23]

"Hey, aren't you the same folks who just praised that very same Supreme Court for their decision to allow gay marriage? Oh, I see. You only complain when you don't get your way. Got it!" Again, the truth is, The Voting Rights Act of 1965 was signed into law due to African Americans in the South facing tremendous obstacles to voting, including poll taxes, literacy tests and other bureaucratic restrictions denying them the right to vote. They technically had the right given to them upon the end of slavery, but they still endured harassment, intimidation, economic reprisals, and physical violence when they tried to register to vote. It took one hundred years to happen, but the Voting Rights Act was signed into law in 1965.

I want to point out a few glaring omissions of history the Democrat Party will not tell you. Although the Democrats held a two-thirds majority of the seats in both chambers of Congress after the 1964 elections, they would not have been able to pass the voting act legislation without strong Republican support. President Johnson (a Democrat) worried his party would not do so based on Southern Democrats would filibuster the legislation, as they were **opposed** to civil rights. He needed at least 67 Senators to guarantee overriding a filibuster. The Senate passed the bill by a 77-19 vote. [Democrats voted 47-16, and

Jefferson Daniel Seal

Republicans 30-2]. The <u>only</u> Senators voting *against* the measure were from Southern states. Just as with the issue of slavery itself, it was the Republicans who had the backs of the African Americans. The Voting Act of 1965 has since been readopted and strengthened five times.

As far as the Supreme Court gutting the Voting Act of 1965; this is patently untrue. What the Supreme Court has allowed; is for states to tighten up the voter identity verification requirements, thus insuring only persons who are eligible to vote in elections can do so. Lately, many swing-state jurisdictions have seen a large influx of cases where people who no longer live local, are taking advantage of voting loopholes by voting in elections where they do not reside. I voted in the last presidential election and was surprised to discover the majority of license plates in the parking lot of the polling station were from Mississippi, when the polling station was located in Memphis, TN!

The Democrats insist the system is rigged against the minority vote:

> *"We will ensure that election officials comply with voting protections, including provisions mandating bilingual materials and voter assistance."* [**DPP** pg. 23]

The Supreme Court has allowed states to adjust some voter registration requirements. For example, a state or local government can shut down early voting sooner, allowing more time for the verification of voter identities. The elimination of same day voter registration is allowed for the same reason. And, finally the Court allowed the implementation of more stringent voter identification requirements, to include requirements for a photo ID. Currently, the move towards employing all of these measures are aimed at reducing election fraud and not suppressing minority voters. It's a fact; the Black population in the South enjoys a higher voter registration percentage over white voters.

Clearly, there's no voter suppression crisis and the Voting Act of 1965 is not under attack; so, what's the problem? The truth is there's no crisis. Take a look at a quote from Rahm Emanuel, President Obama's White House Chief of Staff:

> *"You never let a serious crisis go to waste. And what I mean by that it's an opportunity to do things you could not do before."*

Since there is no voter crisis, the Democrat Party is seeking to create one by using false facts and inflamed rhetoric. Their efforts are to manufacture a serious crisis any way they can, to keep the doors open for voter fraud. There is no other rational reason for them doing so. The only voting being suppressed is that which is illegal or fraudulent. But, under the guise of voter protection, the Democrat Party continues to run its con on the American People.

Jefferson Daniel Seal

Campaign Mis-Finance

Any manufactured crisis, in order to be more believable, must have a malevolent antagonist, whose actions are best described as those belonging to the enemy of the cause. As has already been detailed, the Democrat Party wants their electorate base to believe their very freedom to vote is under direct assault. The named nemesis is predictable: the wealthier citizens of the United States. The Democrats have identified their legalized method for infusing limitless amounts of money into elections: The United States campaign finance system.

> *"And we will fight to reform our broken campaign finance system, which gives outsized influence to billionaires and big corporations."* [**DPP** pg. 23]

The Democrat Party attests in their platform the campaign finance system is defective, thereby giving a whopping level of influence over to billionaires and giant corporations. Here's another attack on the wealthiest Americans to back up their claim those persons having lots of money are somehow wicked. Thus, the enemy must be defeated so control can be given back to whom it truly belongs: The American people.

> *"It's time we give back control of our elections to those to whom it belongs—the American people."* [**DPP** pg. 23]

Satan Would Be A Democrat

Their attack is quite disingenuous. To assert <u>all</u> billionaires and big corporations are somehow responsible for stealing enough of the vote to control the outcome of elections is ridiculous and completely unsubstantiated. First of all, fully 60% of the top 25 billionaires in the United States are on record as *primarily* supporting the Democrat Party. They already own the majority of such persons. So, are the Dems just talking about the 40% of billionaires who *don't* support them? What about the billionaires who give donations and support to Democrats? As we've seen time and again, the facts don't seem to slow the Democrat Party down from distorting their version of reality.

"Big money is drowning out the voices of everyday Americans, and we must have the necessary tools to fight back and safeguard our electoral and political integrity." [**DPP** pg. 22]

While there can be no doubt the party spending the most money on advertising during a campaign frequently wins—it's *never* a sure thing. Certainly, advertising and such information can create power via name recognition. But the tactic works as well for Democrats as it does for Republicans. Either way, large numbers of all voters will recall the publicized names on election day; and then vote without always knowing how the candidate stands on the important issues. Negative ads can also be an effective means of running a smear campaign against an opponent. As

I've said all along, money is power; and Democrats want enough of each to seize total control.

The question remains: whatever happened to "One Man, One Vote?" The system is still intact. The problem is the threat of one side disproportionally swaying the election is always present. The truth is the United States Congress has already taken concrete steps to prevent big money from overly influencing elections. They passed such legislation nearly fifty years ago with the Campaign Finance Act of 1971. This Act essentially sought to regulate certain aspects of Federal political campaign spending and fundraising.

As was the desire of Congress, the Act instituted more stringent disclosure requirements for candidates for federal office, political parties and Political Action Committees (PACs). The law originally focused on increased disclosure of what contributions were being made, and by whom. Government subsidies for federal elections began as part of the Law, as Congress established the income tax checkoff to provide for financing of Presidential general elections and national party conventions. In 1974, the Act was amended to place legal limits on campaign contributions and expenditures, creating the Federal Election Commission (FEC).

The fact is Democrats got most of what they wanted in the legislation, but as usual; it's never good enough. They are now again throwing the Supreme

Satan Would Be A Democrat

Court under the bus because the Act didn't do more of what they were seeking:

"Democrats support a constitutional amendment to overturn the Supreme Court's decisions in Citizens United and Buckley v. Valeo." [**DPP** pg. 24]

After passage of the Act, American citizens themselves (and not politicians) believed certain parts of the legislation went too far. So, several individuals and groups sued in Federal Court to have the offensive portions of the Act changed. Two of the cases went all the way to the Supreme Court. In 1976, the Supreme Court sided with them and ruled certain provisions of the Campaign Finance Act were indeed unconstitutional, and violated the First Amendment, which guarantees and protects free speech.

Not all the news was bad for the Democrat Party. The High Court upheld the limits on political contributions. But they felt the Act went too far on limiting expenditures by the candidates themselves. This was an unnecessary suppression of free speech. The opinion of the High Court held discussion of public issues, and debating the qualifications of candidates, is integral to the operation of the system of government as established by our Constitution. Sounds reasonable to me. But the Democrat Party will not tell you those facts. Instead they state:

"We need to end secret, unaccountable money in politics by requiring, through executive order or legislation, significantly more disclosure and transparency—by outside groups, federal contractors, and public corporations to their shareholders." [**DPP** pg. 24]

As I said, the Court upheld strict limits on contributions to candidates. For example, the maximum <u>any</u> individual can contribute to a Federal Candidate is $2,800. Corporations and Unions are *prohibited* from contributing directly to candidates; as are Federal Contractors and foreign nationals. Any cash donations are limited to $100. Giving in another person's name is also prohibited. Besides checks and currency, the FEC considers anything of value given to influence a Federal election to be a contribution. So, donations of food, beverages, office supplies, furniture, printing or other services, etc. are considered "in-kind" contributions, so their value counts against the individual limit. The only exclusion is a person's time spent volunteering; so long as they are not being compensated for it. A person is free to volunteer all the time they wish to do so.

The Court did strike down limits on how much a candidate can spend on their campaign. The candidate is limited on where they get the money, and how much from each source, but not the total expenditures. The High Court also eliminated restrictions on how much independent groups can

Satan Would Be A Democrat

spend during an election cycle. That's entirely the right of independent groups to decide how much they wish to spend. But the Court did uphold mandatory disclosure and reporting provisions; so, the source of all monies being spent can still be seen and examined.

And finally, the court eliminated the manner in which the commissioners to the FEC were appointed. Previously, the members were appointed by Congress directly. The High Court felt this created a poisoned vote by allowing a direct relationship between the regulator and the regulated. Therefore, they ruled there could be no direct link between commissioners and those who they are limiting. The commissioners are now appointed by the President and confirmed by the Senate to six-year terms. So, billionaires can contribute all they wish to independent groups, but their level of support must still be disclosed.

Thus, there are no covert stashes of secret money being clandestinely spent on political campaigns. And if there are, then they're breaking the law and working very hard to stay below the radar of the FEC. Now, what the Democrat Party is really seeking is limits on how much each candidate can spend on their campaign—a clear limitation on Free Speech. Just as Satan experienced with Eve, there is a natural limit to how long and far his lies can travel before being exposed. Eventually, the truth of the light of day will become known to the masses.

Jefferson Daniel Seal

The Democrats are at a huge disadvantage when it comes to their bottom-line message. Their missives cannot long stand up to the full scrutiny of illumination over time. In the same way Satan deceived Eve when she was not in the presence of Adam, he attempts the same thing with the undereducated and unknowing voter. As I've said all along, the Democrat voter is not a bad or terrible person. They are just regular folks who are ill-informed and lacking some of the facts, which are preventing them from getting the total picture which only the truth can deliver.

> *"Our vision for American democracy is a nation in which all people, regardless of their income, can participate in the political process and can run for office without needing to depend on large contributions from the wealthy and the powerful."* [**DPP** pg. 24]

I hate to be the bearer of bad news to the Democrats, but the above statement is already true. Every legal person, who properly registers to vote can participate in the political process; and can do so, regardless of their income. And, they can run for any office which they choose. Sure, it's unlikely they will win a top political office; but it's possible. Look at Alexandria Ocasio-Cortez. She was a bartender who won the 14th congressional seat from New York and made it to Congress. So, we must ask the question: "What is it the Dems are really seeking?"

Satan Would Be A Democrat

They are seeking to deceive the American voter by telling them their votes are being diluted by money from billionaires and big corporations. They won't tell you it's already against the law for corporations and unions to make donations directly to candidates. They fail to mention fully 60% of billionaires are giving to the Democrat Party. The American people are being deceived. So, God commands we be at least as wise as serpents; using the most innocent behavior when dealing with such persons. [1] Otherwise, the Satan led rhetoric will deceive you, saying it's all the fault of government, and flawed judges, who's corrupt actions and faulty decisions have led to intentional campaign mis-finance.

Outright Lying Hypocrisy

In the verse listed in the footnote below, notice what the words of Jesus advises us to do: *"Be as shrewd as serpents and as innocent as doves."* When fighting against the wiles of the Devil, it's best to be as shrewd as possible to avoid being swindled. The word **shrewd** is defined as *'having or showing sharp powers of judgment, being astute.'* So, we must carefully study the tactics and words of the enemy if we are to remain unaffected by them. But, be forewarned; as there is a cost for such behavior. Those who are trying to mislead the masses will turn their attention towards any persons showing the

---

[1] Matthew 10:16 "Behold, I send you out as sheep in the midst of wolves; so be shrewd as serpents and innocent as doves."

Jefferson Daniel Seal

power and willingness to expose their deceit. That's the reason Jesus doesn't stop with telling us just to be shrewd. He immediately goes on to advise us to remain as innocent as doves. The evil forces of this world are hostile to believers. Not incidentally hostile, but rather *purposefully* hostile. Just as wolves are intentional about the harm they inflict upon sheep, so it is with those under Satan's control. They will try and destroy anyone found standing in their way. Thus, the Democrats give away their strategy in the **DPP**:

> *"We will appoint judges who defend the constitutional principles of liberty and equality for all,"* [**DPP** pg. 24]

Again, the Democrats make use of flowery words to supplant their real message by covering it over with some actual truth. But, isn't that what Judges are already supposed to be doing? The Democrat Party wants to appoint judges who will adhere to <u>their</u> plan of promoting Satan's agenda at the expense of God's tried and true way of living honorable lives. The picture of genuine legality is depicted by a blindfolded woman meting out justice in a fair and impartial manner. But Jesus is warning His followers they can forget about such treatment from the world. Satan's adherents will drag Christians into court on the most minor of offenses. Fortunately, the Bible gives away their demonic strategy. [2] Jesus is teaching us to be

---

[2] Matthew 10:17 "But beware of men, for they will hand you over to the courts."

Christlike in a godless world, combining wisdom of the serpent, with the innocence of the dove. Christians will be persecuted, using the very laws the heathen choose not to follow. Here's yet another example:

> *"We will protect a woman's right to safe and legal abortion, curb billionaires' influence over elections because they understand that Citizens United has fundamentally damaged our democracy,"* [**DPP** pg. 24]

Satan has embarked on a campaign in which he is attempting to legitimize social affairs which go opposite to Biblical teaching. Abortion, gay marriage and contempt for Scripture are the main three issues he's currently using. It's all part of his master plan. Even today, we have a significant number of churches which preach in strong favor of these hot button social issues. Pastors are no longer united in their message; "Abortion is murder." Many congregations now routinely embrace gay and lesbian clergy within their pulpits. And many more parishioners readily deny the inerrant nature of the Bible. Openly disagreeing with such policy inside the halls of the sanctuary will lead to increasing trouble for the true believer.[3] It's all part of Satan's plan. He's driving the strategies and plans of the Democrat Party in his

---

[3] Matthew 10:17 "But beware of men, for they will hand you over to the courts and scourge you in the synagogues;"

Jefferson Daniel Seal

diabolical efforts to achieve legitimizing evil and sinful living.

Have you ever wondered why Satan and his crowd are pro-abortion, pro-gay marriage and anti-Bible? It would seem not to really make any difference to normal life, would it? But I assure you—there is very good reason for these actions. Just like any con or swindle, the success of it is determined almost exclusively by the setup. Mankind is currently being desensitized to certain demonic behaviors which will become rampant during the final seven-year period of his time on Earth. The Bible tells us the time before the Second Coming of Jesus Christ will be similar to the days before the flood. [4] As outlined in the book; **The End is Near**, the three main behaviors rampant before the flood were: extreme violence, gross sexual impurity and widespread idolatry. Those behaviors led God to destroy civilization, after safely removing His people.

Satan is once again setting the same stage for the End Times. Abortion on demand numbs people to extreme forms of violence against the most innocent of persons. When the Antichrist takes over the world commerce system, no one will be able to buy or sell without having his mark upon them. Any attempt to bypass the system will be met with swift reprisal; in

---

[4] Matthew 24:37 "For the coming of the Son of Man will be just like the days of Noah."

Satan Would Be A Democrat

the form of execution by beheading. [5] Thus, the followers of the Antichrist will be the ones "eating and drinking;" as they will be able to buy food. [6] The Antichrist will deny anyone unwilling to accept his mark the ability to buy or sell legally. Such persons will be starving and will be forced to try and obtain food and supplies. They will have to resort to bypassing the system of the Antichrist; and when caught, will be charged with breaking his law. They will be publicly executed in the street for their "crimes." Just as with the murder of the unborn due to a woman's right to choose, so will it be with these innocent citizens who likewise will be murdered for the Beast's right to choose.

In the days prior to the Flood, man was engaged in widespread homosexuality. It was the logical result of *"the daughters of men choosing the fallen angels (the Nephilim) as their husbands."* [7] The offspring of the Nephilim were all male—an ironclad result of genetic crossbreeding. The Antichrist will outlaw traditional marriage, making gay marriage the only legal institution. [8] This policy will lead to the destruction of the family. I predict the Antichrist himself will be openly gay. And these conditions will persist until

---

[5] The End is Near! "In the Days of Noah, pages 268 thru 270."
[6] Matthew 24:38 "For in those days before the flood they were eating and drinking,"
[7] The End is Near! "In the Days of Noah, pages 268 thru 270."
[8] Matthew 24:38 "For in those days before the flood they were eating and drinking, marrying and giving in marriage,"

arrival of the Judgment, which will be when Jesus returns at the end of the age. [9] Remember, it was God who closed the door on the ark, so Noah and his family were at least aware when the time was near. [10]

The campaign to deny Scripture as the word of God is perhaps obvious: it allows truth to be re-defined as what Satan would have it to be. By using the issues of abortion and gay marriage, demonic forces will successfully make people choose Satan over God. Those are two hot-button issues people think they can use their intellect to decide which is right. This error in judgement will lead people to label persons adhering to Scripture as "narrow-minded Bible thumpers," putting even more distance between the Antichrist and God's truth. This contempt for Scripture will open the door leading directly to idolatry. When there is no truth, people flounder and eventually perish. The "truth" is people will have nowhere to go when the Antichrist starts demanding the citizens of the world begin worshiping him as God. [11] Satan will have won the day when this eventually happens.

---

[9] Matthew 24:38 "For in those days before the flood they were eating and drinking, marrying and giving in marriage, until the day that Noah entered the ark,"

[10] Genesis 7:16 Those that entered, male and female of all flesh, entered as God had commanded him; and the LORD closed it behind him.

[11] Revelation 13:12 He exercises all the authority of the first beast in his presence. And he makes the earth and those who dwell in it to worship the first beast.

Satan Would Be A Democrat

Everything begins with the slow and steady attack to degrade both the United States democracy, as well as isolate her citizens from Biblical teaching. The Democrat Party plan to dilute the vote also extends over to both houses of Congress:

> *"Restoring our democracy also means finally passing statehood for the District of Columbia, so that the American citizens who reside in the nation's capital have full and equal congressional rights."* [**DPP** pg. 24]

The choice for the Democrats is simple: the residents of Washington D.C. number just over 606,000 people; of whom 68 percent are Democrat, with just under 8 percent Republican. This would guarantee two to three seats to the Democrats in the House of Representatives and the addition of two more Democrat voting Senators. It would be an automatic win for them. So, what about Puerto Rico? The population of the island is 3.7 million—or about six times that of Washington, DC. Why not call for statehood for them? This reason is also simple. The percentage of Democrats in Puerto Rico is less than 50%. So, there would be <u>no</u> gain for the Democrat Party here. Therefore, it's not contained within their platform. It doesn't help them in their quest of stealing the vote.

Would it surprise you to discover the very things the Democrat Party is accusing the government of doing is part of their hidden strategy for taking control? As of September of 2019, the Democrat controlled House of Representatives is undertaking proceedings whose stated purpose is to attempt to impeach both President Donald Trump and Supreme Court Justice Brett Kavanaugh. Despite having the outcome of the Mueller investigation clearly go against their agenda, the Democrats are refusing to let go of their quest to end President Trump's presidency by any means possible. As shown by their continued attacks against the newest member of the Supreme Court, they are still fully engaged in the quest of silencing voices opposed to theirs, securing a Democrat leaning Court, all the while trying to pass laws which eliminate American's most basic rights.

All this is being done by design, with the Democrat Party leading the way. They are promising the world to under-educated voters, by issuing assurances which are impossible to keep.

> *"We believe that by making those at the top and the largest corporations pay their fair share we can pay for ambitious progressive investments that create good-paying jobs and offer security to working families without adding to the debt."* [**DPP** pg. 24]

First off, <u>none</u> of the current social programs cannot be sustained without either adding to the debt or increasing taxes. Very soon, assuming no changes are made, Social Security and Medicare obligations alone will consume 100% of the revenue taken in by the U.S. government. To believe taxing the rich and large corporations will bring in sufficient revenue to make up the difference to pay for "ambitious progressive investments" is a lie directly from the lips of Satan. This is where some basic economic knowledge will show him to be the father of all lies that he is.

The truth is the top 400 billionaires in America in 2018 earned 210 million dollars in gross income. That means income before any taxes are paid. Assuming we taxed them at 100%, this amount would still be only able to pay for one-fiftieth of the 2018 budget deficit. The top twenty corporations had a total profit of just over 300 billion dollars in 2018. Assuming they were taxed at 100%, they would pay for just over 30% of the budget deficit. Now, assume the entire wealth of the 585 billionaires living in the U.S. was confiscated, that would still only pay about 55% of the total budget of 2018 United States budget.

The Democrat Party, by hindrance of who is leading them, operates at a deficit against those choosing to follow Godly principles. Their only way to win is to dupe, swindle and scam honest citizens into believing their lies. They first get our attention by creating a moral crisis of some ilk; and then use fraud and deceit to sway public opinion away from the truth. This is their only tactic which can work. Thus, they will continue to try and steal the vote; and then our wealth in their evil quest for control. And they will

Jefferson Daniel Seal

make full use of all manner of outright lying hypocrisy in their efforts at achieving total victory.

VI. GLOBAL WARMING HOAX

Ice Age Evidence

The current buzz words in use by the Democrat Party reflecting their concern over global warming is: "Climate Change." As you'll read in this chapter, they have attempted this type of ploy on the American people, as well as the rest of the world, many, many times before. They are declaring climate change is the imperative menace and a major ordeal of this era.

"Climate change is an urgent threat and a defining challenge of our time." [**DPP** pg. 25]

This tactic is nothing new. As a matter of record, the Democrats have attempted similar gambits at least twenty times since 1967. So, please do not become alarmed at this latest attempt. Let's review some scientific facts before we get too deeply into parsing the Democrat Party rhetoric.

To begin with, the Earth has experienced at least <u>five</u> major ice ages within its 4.54-billion-year history:

Ice Age	Timing of Start
Huronian	2.1 billion years ago
Sturtian/Marinoan	710 million years ago
Andean-Saharan	460 million years ago
Karoo Ice Age	350 million years ago
Pleistocene Ice Age	2.58 million years ago

The Pleistocene glaciation, also known as the Quaternary glaciation, is an alternating series of glacial and interglacial periods, and it still ongoing. Although geologists describe the entire time period as an ice age, the popular term "Ice Age" is usually associated with just the times when the Earth contains large ice sheets. Since the Earth still has large ice sheets present, mankind is now experiencing an interglacial period. Thus, the current Ice Age is continuing, meaning we are not out of it yet. An **Ice Age** is defined as '*a long-term drop in global temperatures from the historical norm, accompanied by an extension of continental ice sheets*.' Each of the aforementioned ice ages are cyclical on timescales of between 44,000 and 110,000 years, during which the glacial ice rhythmically extends and recedes.

The precise causes of historical Ice Ages are unknown, but likely emerged due to the position of the moving continents, the composition of the atmosphere, amount of volcanic activity and the reflectivity of the Earth itself. Variations in solar output, asteroid impacts and distance from the Sun all will influence weather on the Earth as well. But, once an ice age begins, the effect of having ice cover instead of water, desert and forest will cause dramatic increases in reflectivity of sunlight; resulting in lower temperatures and increased glaciation.

Therefore, for most of the Earth's history, it has not been in an Ice Age. During normal times when no

Ice Age is present, the average global temperature is about 71 degrees F (22 C). Ice sheets are almost completely absent, found only at high altitudes in alpine glaciers. The poles are cold, but not covered in ice; with forests extending everywhere, from pole to pole. Dinosaur fossils have been discovered on both the North and South Poles. Dinosaurs were cold blooded animals, meaning they cannot survive in freezing temperatures. Thus, only about 15% of the time has the Earth been under the effects of an Ice Age; which we still are experiencing today. Note: the current average global temperature today is 58 degrees F. And that's still 13 degrees below the normal average. Yes, it's been warming up for a while now, the most recent phase beginning approximately 12,000 years ago.

This current Ice Age is well-known because mankind has had his entire history living within it. We accept having Greenland and Antarctica covered with ice as being normal, even though it's not. Just as recently as 10,000 years ago, thick glaciers covered the land as far south as Paris and Chicago. That means humans living in North America likely didn't live much farther north than the Mexican border—at least in the wintertime. The proof lies in the location of human fossils predating the last glacial period are found only in Africa, the Middle East, China, Southeast Asia, Australia, and only small parts of Europe such as Spain and southern France. But those

Jefferson Daniel Seal

facts are missing from the Democrat Party's explanation:

> *"The best science tells us that without ambitious, immediate action across our economy to cut carbon pollution and other greenhouse gases, all of these impacts will be far worse in the future."* [**DPP** pg. 25]

I'm sorry to have to put a wet blanket on their crisis parade, but <u>no</u> amount of human action is going to appreciably change a thing. The previous Ice Ages came and went without any assistance from anyone other than Mother Nature, and the hand of Almighty God. As the permafrost begins to melt, the amount of carbon flowing into the atmosphere is 10,000 times the level of carbon mankind is contributing. It's like trying to steer the Titanic by placing your hand into the ocean. You aren't going to effectively change her course; or her fate. She's still going to run into the iceberg and sink! It's the same with the Earth's climate. Even if man stopped production of all greenhouse gases today, eliminating overnight the use of fossil fuels, and methane from cows, we wouldn't be able to change or delay the coming result by any appreciable amount. But the facts of the case certainly don't stop them from trying.

> *"We cannot leave our children a planet that has been profoundly damaged."* [**DPP** pg. 25]

Satan Would Be A Democrat

Once again, the words of warning are framed in such a way that if someone rejects them, they will be labeled as being some form of debased person. As you will read, this is just the latest in a long string of manufactured crisis the Democrat Party has foisted upon the American people and the world. And, just like all the others, this crisis shall too pass. Why do I know that? I have several reasons for stating this <u>fact</u>.

First of all, God created man and gave him full dominion over the earth. [1] God foreknew everything man would do in his history, yet he issued no warnings to Adam. When you read the full account of Genesis, there are no additional instructions apart from populating the earth and subduing it for man's use. [2] As defined back on page 140, the word **subdue** is a command to essentially "go forth and conquer." And unlike with the one tree in the Garden of Eden, there were no restrictions placed upon man. If God was worried about man making too many greenhouse gasses, He'd have told us.

The truth is God is *not* worried about greenhouse gases, carbon dioxide or any other pollution man might create. The proof lies in the glacial ice record.

---

[1] Genesis 1:26 Then God said, "Let Us make man in Our image, according to Our likeness; and let them rule over the fish of the sea and over the birds of the sky and over the cattle and over all the earth, and over every creeping thing that creeps on the earth."

[2] Genesis 1:28 God blessed them; and God said to them, "Be fruitful and multiply, and fill the earth, and subdue it; and rule over the fish of the sea and over the birds of the sky and over and over every living thing that moves on the earth."

Today, the percentage of oxygen making up our atmosphere is 20.9459 percent. It has remained statistically unchanged over the past 100,000 years. Scientists know this due to ice samples taken from glaciers all over the globe. Within each core sample, the age of the ice can be determined, as well as the composition of the atmosphere at the time the ice froze. Each particle of ice is a miniature sample of the atmosphere at the moment of its formation.

Despite all the changes in the Earth's atmosphere over that lengthy time period, including the industrial age of mankind, the level of oxygen has remained constant. Scientists call it "God's Principle." Were the oxygen level in the atmosphere to become much higher, the plentiful oxygen would allow global fires to burn uncontrolled. Were it much lower, mammal life would be curtailed and even threatened. Humans would be unable to live at altitudes much above sea level, as we do today.

The final reason is the advent of the End of the Age itself. Even if all the terrible predictions being made by Democrats concerning the effects of climate change come to pass; it simply doesn't matter. There are just a scant fourteen years to the start of the Tribulation, and only twenty-one years to the bodily return of Jesus Christ, as of November 2019.[3] So, all the scare tactics about the rise of sea levels,

---

[3] The End is Near! And God Will Prove It. Jefferson Daniel Seal, Copywrite 2012

Satan Would Be A Democrat

devastating hurricanes, flooding and whatever else they are prognosticating; simply are not going to happen. Most of the dire effects of Climate Change are predicted to start about fifty years from now. Sure, the days and months are statistically getting warmer, but the rate in actuality is very slow and will not change anything significantly within the next twenty years. God says the end of this age will see the restoration of the Earth, back to a Garden of Eden state, so all the trouble which appears to be brewing will be eliminated. [4]

It's very easy to first fool and then scare school children. The same can be said for those persons who are under educated. That's the biggest reason for Satan targeting those particular groups. People with less than stellar schooling are easy prey for such scams. They are targeted for that very reason. Listen folks, Satan and his demons are not stupid. They know what they are doing. And they are having a very high level of success. But we can stop them, at least on an individual basis, by informing those persons who are being swindled of the details of the con. Just like the elderly person being pursued by scam artists for their savings, just a little information will save the day, and their money from being stolen. The facts and evidence surrounding the *current* Ice Age should be sufficient to enlighten any person; thus, preventing the continuation of them being scammed.

---

[4] Revelation 21 & 22 Please read the chapters from your own Bible.

Crisis Fabrication 101

The people of the Earth can debate the current weather conditions endlessly without coming to any real scientific consensus. The simple truth is Climate Change is indeed a fact which impacts all of our daily lives. The Democrat Party dishonestly states President Trump has called it a hoax:

> *"While Donald Trump has called climate change a 'hoax,' 2016 is on track to break global temperature records once more."* [**DPP** pg. 24]

President Trump is on record as acknowledging Climate Change is real. His issue with the Democrat Party is the same as this book. The idea of describing their effort as a hoax being perpetrated on humankind, revolves around blaming Climate Change entirely upon the activities of man. The real issue centers on how much impact can and does man's goings-on have on the environment. The remainder of this chapter focuses on what can be proven. For those who haven't been to college, the number 101 in the section title is used to identify the first class for a course of study, e.g. "Accounting 101." It's generally the first class containing basic subject material and is used as an introduction to the subject. That's what I'm doing with this section.

Perhaps the biggest part to breaking down the problem of studying Climate Change, is accurate meteorological records only go back about 200 years. The United States created its Weather Bureau as part

Satan Would Be A Democrat

of the Agricultural Department; it was established in 1890. It began the cursory task of recording of weather observations in 1892 for the purposes of improving agriculture. This time period is far too short to create any meaningful patterns when it comes to long term trends. But this fact doesn't stop the Democrats from trying to sound the alarm:

"Cities from Miami to Baltimore are already threatened by rising seas. California and the West have suffered years of brutal drought. Alaska has been scorched by wildfire. New York has been battered by superstorms, and Texas swamped by flash floods." [**DPP** pg. 25]

They are essentially saying, there's not enough time remaining before catastrophe strikes to wait and see what's really going on. "Action must be undertaken <u>now</u> before it's too late!" Using this faulty logic is how the Democrat Party attempts to spur governmental action. The problem is the Democrat Party's warnings are sounding more like crying wolf than describing real threats. There is no credible risk to Baltimore or Miami, drought in California has ended, Alaska's not burning at any rate above normal, New York and Texas have both experienced the usual flooding associated with landfalling hurricanes. And this all was resolved in the three short years since they issued the warnings. But it fits their pattern. Let's

Jefferson Daniel Seal

take a look at their track record over the past fifty years.

"Dire Famine Forecast by '75 – 'Already Too Late' "

This Headline appeared in the Salt Lake Tribune on 17 November 1967. The article went on to state it was already too late for the world to avoid a long period of global famine. Paul Ehrlich, a Stanford University biologist, stated; "The time of famines is upon us and will be at its worst and most disastrous by 1975." He stated the population of the U.S. was already too large, and called for birth control to become involuntary. He actually recommended putting sterilizing agents into staple foods and drinking water! His reasoning was the six to seven billion expected to be living by the year 2000 could not be fed. He predicted the famines would lead to thermonuclear war and extinction of the human species.

The Democrat Party immediately called for aggressive birth control measures to avoid global mass starvation. Of course, they also called for lots of governmental money to assist underdeveloped countries with their burgeoning populations. The world's current population is 7.5 billion and very few people are starving (apart from war torn areas). The call for ridiculous measures were justified as being the only way to avert the coming crisis. Guess what? Farmers around the world became far more productive, resulting in more food being available

"Foe of Pollution Sees Lack of Time"

than ever before—and at lower prices. Food became more plentiful as a result with less resulting hunger. There is far less famine in the world today than there was in 1967. On to the next crisis four years later.

"Foe of Pollution Sees Lack of Time"

The above headline came out of the mouth of the same biologist from Stanford University in Palo Alto, California. It was printed in the New York Times on August 10th, 1969. In the article, Ehrlich blamed the lack of drastic action as being a major contributor to the overall problem. Ehrlich stated; "The trouble with almost all environmental problems is that by the time we have enough evidence to convince people, you're dead." He called for drastic action to head off a catastrophic explosion fueled by runaway population growth, a limited food supply and contamination of the planet. He said mankind "would disappear in a cloud of blue steam in 20 years."

Once again, do you see the call for immediate reaction—due to insufficient time before mass death would ensue? Of course, world air quality in most major cities is far better today than it was in 1969. Los Angeles used to be bathed regularly in a layer of thick smog, now experiences only a few days per year with visible air pollution. Gone are the extreme smog days of the 1930's and 40's. This despite having more cars than any other city in America. In fact, in most third world cities, the modern automobile puts cleaner air out of the exhaust pipe than it sucks into the engine.

But that still doesn't stop the Mass Media and their demonically controlled orators from calling for austere measures needed to solve the pollution crisis.

"Scientist predicts a new ice age by 21st century"

Our next headline appeared in the Boston Globe on April 16th, 1970. The cry was climate change would create a new ice age due to air pollution obliterating the sun. James P. Lodge Jr. warned that if the current rate of increase in electric power generation continued, the demands for cooling water would boil dry the entire flow of all rivers and streams within the continental United States. Lodge, a scientist at the national center for Atmospheric Research in Boulder, Colo, warned that by the year 2000, "the consumption of oxygen in combustion processes, world-wide, would surpass all of the processes which return oxygen to the atmosphere." He further stated the lower 48 states were "already consuming more oxygen than their own green plants replace."

The world is coming up on fifty years since his dire prediction for the planet running out of oxygen, or pollution blocking out the sun and causing a rapid return of glaciers to North America. In the time since the article appeared, the planet now generates 300% more electricity to supply a population which has more than doubled. Rivers and streams all still flow in accordance with rainfall over their watershed, and as I pointed out earlier, the oxygen content of the atmosphere has remained completely constant. We are no longer worried about an impending ice age, but now global warming. The ice age prediction was likely due to a short pattern of falling temperatures across the world in the 1960's. I hope you are able to begin to pick up on the pattern of these fearmongers among the scientific community. If you were alive and old enough to know what was being reported at that time, you already know what I mean.

"Giving aspirins to cancer victims"

That's what Dr. Paul Ehrlich thought of current proposals for pollution control, as reported in the Redlands Daily Facts, on October 6, 1970. He didn't think any real action had been taken to reduce air pollution. He predicted; "The oceans will be as dead as Lake Erie in less than a decade." He also said "America will be subject to water rationing by 1974 and food rationing by 1980." The author of "The Population Bomb" and the hero of the ecological movement was in high demand back then as a speaker on college campuses. He regularly stated "DDT in our fatty tissues has reached levels high enough to cause brain damage and cirrhosis of the liver."

To begin with, Lake Erie was not dead back then and certainly isn't now. The lake has long been plagued with algae blooms due to its generally shallow depth and warm water. But, in 1999, there was a huge swarm of mayflies around Presque Isle measuring over ten miles long. These insects are a sure sign of pristine lake health, since mayflies require clean and clear water to survive. And, the oceans aren't dead yet either. DDT is a chemical which is highly effective against insects and was used to protect crops and people against disease; in particular against mosquitoes to combat malaria. The move to ban DDT was immediate and the chemical was banned in 1972. Since then, DDT has been extensively studied and has been shown to be non-genotoxic. **Genotoxicity** describes '*the property of chemical agents to damage genetic information within a cell causing mutations which may lead to cancer.*" So, the best tool being used to protect crops and people was banned on the grounds it caused cancer—which proves now to be false.

It's not good enough for Satan to try and use a crisis to get his followers into positions of power. He also uses the manufactured crisis to get man to undertake needless actions which help create the very crisis they believe they are seeking to avoid! How many millions of people have perished due to crop failure and the scourge of malaria around the globe? It is estimated by the World Health Organization (WHO) that between 300 to 500 million people are infected with Malaria on an annual basis. Out of that number, over 1 million die. Starvation driven by disease due to insects is more difficult to nail down. First off, farmers expect a certain level of failure and try to grow more than needed to account for it. Second, we don't actually know how many people starve due to a lack of food driven solely by crop failure. But the WHO estimates 36 million persons die of starvation annually. Even if just 10% of the deaths could be prevented, that's nearly 4 million souls who die each year solely due to the DDT ban.

Look, I'm not advocating the return to spraying DDT all over the world. I'm just pointing out; the politics of the early GREEN movement didn't actually care about the victims themselves. They cared more for the environment—which is actually a form of idolatry in its most basic form. **Idolatry** is defined in the dictionary as *'extreme admiration, love, or reverence for something or someone.'* Anytime something is put above the value of human life itself, I'd call it a form of extreme reverence. The Bible describes idolatry as *'worship or honor paid to any created object over the Divine Creator.'* Mankind has a long history of revering nature. Environmentalism is in essence worshipping nature over God.

Satan is quite clever. He gets man to break God's commandments via his manufactured crisis. Rather than place our trust in God to maintain our environment, Satan gets man to forget about God and instead, puts man in the role of being the one who will take care of nature. [5] He does it by using terms such

---

[5] Romans 1:21 "For although they knew God, they neither glorified Him as God, nor gave thanks to Him."

as "mother nature" and "mother earth." We neglect to accept God as Sovereign over the world; and our protector. God built in many safeguards within the fabric of His creation; such that it would be able to recover from anything He knew man would throw at it. In a prophetic nod to the Democrat Party, God labeled how He views their thinking: "futile and foolish, as influenced by Satan." That's what the Apostle Paul means by "their hearts were darkened." He goes on to say, "Although they claim to be wise, they became fools." [6]

This is the situation today within the ranks of the Democrat Party. Just sit back and watch the constant stream of garbage coming out of the media. Everything is pro-Satan and anti-God. Do you not see it everywhere? There is a very specific reason for this loss of brainpower. It's due to people are being brainwashed by demonic forces who are programming them using a large-scale deception. God says such persons have exchanged the truth about God for a lie and wound up worshipping and serving created things rather than the Creator. [7] And they're just getting started. We've only covered the freshman class so far: Crisis Fabrication 101.

---

[6] Romans 1:21-22 "But their thinking became futile and their foolish hearts were darkened. Although they claimed to be wise, they became fools."
[7] Romans 1:25 "They exchanged the truth about God for a lie, and worshipped and served created things rather than the Creator."

Satan Would Be A Democrat

You Cain't Fix Stoopid!

The last section focused on the Democrat Party's attempts at using the specter of air pollution as the initiator of world crisis. Their rather amateurish attempts were quickly dismissed; as the predicted time frame as stated for required action to be taken was far too short. Even when they got governments to move, the bureaucracy progressed so lethargically, their dire deadlines came and went without so much as a whimper from Mother Nature. As you can see from the next quote from the **DPP**, they learned from their mistake and began pushing the predictions of doom and gloom out a lot further.

"Democrats share a deep commitment to tackling the climate challenge; creating millions of good-paying middle class jobs; reducing greenhouse gas emissions more than 80 percent below 2005 levels by 2050." [**DPP** pg. 25]

The use of climate change by the Democrats is nothing new. In fact, back in 1971, after the pollution scare fizzled, the Democrats shifted gears and switched to pollution as now being the driver of climate change; but with a different twist. They began asserting climate change would be the initiation of an Ice Age due to man's activities. The following headline was seen in the Washington Post on July 9, 1971:

"U.S. Scientist Sees New Ice Age Coming"

Jefferson Daniel Seal

That's what S. I. Rasool of NASA and Columbia University predicted. He stated: "In the next 50 years the fine dust man constantly puts into the atmosphere by fossil fuel burning could screen out so much sunlight that the average temperature could drop by six degrees." He went on to say; "If sustained over several years—five to ten—such a temperature decrease could be sufficient to trigger an ice age!" The article quotes other scientists who affirm Rasool's as "a first-rate atmospheric physicist," and agree his estimates are consistent with the majority of what others have said. They immediately began calling for "the elimination of coal, oil, natural gas and automobile gasoline." They all agreed Rasool's conclusions point to one of the most serious problems facing mankind.

Notice the same argument was presented back then as it is being forwarded today; except now it has an *opposite* result. Instead of global cooling, the left is decrying global warming. In the same vein, they are claiming world-wide acceptance of their argument by the scientific community. Hey, did anybody ever come out and say despite your coalescence of the argument over the facts—you were still *wrong*? The mass media is complicit with Satan. They never come back and report their theories and notions have been proven to be in error. Instead, they move on to the next crisis. Next, the Democrats resorted to using satellites. On to the next article.

"Space satellites show new Ice Age coming fast"

In an article in The Guardian, dated January 29, 1974, Anthony Tucker warned that a rapid worldwide trend towards a mini ice age is emerging from the first long term analyses of satellite weather pictures. He went on to suggest world temperatures reached a climax between 1935 and 1955, with the average now beginning a free fall in the 1970's. He went on to state the rate of increase of snow and ice is expected to be much faster than other trends. He was advocating Global Freezing, rather than Global Warming, due to climate change. He said the data suggested the lengthening of winter, resulting in Spring arriving later; adversely effecting crops and agriculture. Contrast such logic with the early arrival of Spring as called for in the global warming rhetoric.

The ability to create an ecological crisis is never ending with the Democrat Party. Their main problem has been to create a crisis which keeps lasting traction with the people of the United States and the world community. For all their scientific data referenced, they made one big mistake. Calling for the reduction of pollutants within the atmosphere, by ceasing to burn fossil fuels might be a credible threat. After all, burning fossil fuels does indeed create pollution of the air in one form or another. But one thing they didn't think all the way through was; if we eliminate all fossil fuels, how will man keep himself warm in the expected coming Ice Age? It's very difficult to get people much excited about implementing a solution to a problem when it involves the elimination of humankind—by freezing to death none-the-less. But it still didn't stop them from continuing to try.

TIME MAGAZINE: "Another Ice Age?"

In a piece designed to represent the most up to date science of the era, Time Magazine, put in their two cents worth in a magazine article dated, June 24, 1974. They heralded drought in Africa, flooding in the U.S., Pakistan and Japan, and a particularly chilly Spring in Canada as part of a global weather climatic upheaval. They state the aggregate temperature around the globe was growing cooler over the past three decades; with the trend showing no signs of reversing. They said; "Climatological Cassandras are becoming increasing apprehensive of a harbinger of another ice age." They continued with, "telltale signs are everywhere—from the unexpected persistence and thickness of pack ice to the southward migration of the armadillo in the Midwest." Their evidence was global temperatures dropped 2.7 degrees since the 1940's, increasing Arctic ice and snow cover by 12% in 1971.

Their only offered solution was to dramatically reduce the emissions from the resulting air pollution associated with the burning of fossil fuels. Today, those words have been replaced by terms such as greenhouse gases and carbon emission credits. They are using different words, but the tactics remain

Satan Would Be A Democrat

exactly the same: scare the undereducated public into supporting legislation which would reduce the use of petroleum-based fuels. The goals were spelled out in the Paris climate accord, signed by most countries of the world in 2016.

> *"We must meet the pledge President Obama put forward in the landmark Paris Agreement, which aims to keep global temperature increases to "well below" two degrees Celsius and to pursue efforts to limit global temperature increases to 1.5 degrees Celsius."* [**DPP** pg. 25]

Wait a minute! Just a short 45 years ago, the Democrats were warning us we'd all be dealing with another ice age. The resulting loss of crops would lead the world into mass hunger and eventual starvation. The scientists even began writing books to explain their position.

The New York Times Book Review—"The Cooling"

Stephen Schneider, a climatologist at the National Center for Atmospheric Research in Boulder, Colo., wrote a book summarizing the consensus of the climatological community. In his book, "The Genesis Strategy," he warned that food reserves were an insufficient hedge against future famine. He authored the book "to explain the entire problem as responsibly and accurately as he can, to the general public." The premise of his book is based on the

Jefferson Daniel Seal

weather observation for the years 1930-1960. They were an abnormally mild stretch of temperate weather in the northern hemisphere, allowing for bumper harvests of crops over that time. So, he postulated that when his forecast of increasingly cold weather suddenly arrived, food production would plunge to perilous levels, with worldwide famine the result. The era of stable and warm climate would end suddenly with disastrous results for mankind. His book essentially stated the golden age of farming in the northern hemisphere would soon be ended.

Let me please tell you, those persons who disagreed with such "widespread scientific belief" were regularly vilified in the press. Does this all not seem overly familiar to your eyes and ears in the current political environment? The Democrat's constant attack on the burning of all fossil fuels is ongoing; their calling for their elimination remains consistent.

> *"We believe America must be running entirely on clean energy by mid-century. We will take bold steps to slash carbon pollution and protect clean air at home, lead the fight against climate change around the world,"* [**DPP** pg. 25]

The reason for this is simple: the world economy runs and flourishes on the responsible use of fossil fuels. Eliminating them would destroy global commerce overnight. And, unlike what they would have you to believe, there are no quick or cheap alternatives to their use. If there were, the world would have switched over decades ago.

By clean energy, the Dem's are saying "anything which does not burn fossil fuels." Clean energy at the present time, is in reality a *total* myth. For example, let's examine wind energy briefly. The amount of fossil fuels required to build and maintain the large wind turbines we see cluttering up the view all over the landscape, actually exceeds the amount of fossil fuel they are supposed to replace. It's an absolute fact. Each ton of steel requires 1.5 tons of coal to produce. Each wind turbine requires 250 tons of steel on average. This doesn't include the energy required to transport and erect them.

And speaking of pollution—what of the absolutely filthy dirty mining required in places like Inner Mongolia to dig up the rare earth minerals used in the manufacture of magnets and materials for all those turbines, solar panels and batteries? Mining gallium indium phosphide and gallium arsenide is both messy and dangerous business. While technology is moving forward in each area of research, the growth of maturity is very slow. The best commercially available solar panels are only just past 20%. Wind turbines have reached levels above 50%, but only by increasing the size to the point they are so large they must be placed offshore. Lead acid batteries have around an 80% efficiency "round trip rating," but this reduces

Jefferson Daniel Seal

the efficiency of the solar panels by an additional 20%. Lithium batteries have much higher efficiency (95%) but are nearly impossible to recycle. Batteries create an ecological nightmare when trying to dispose of them. And recycling is astronomically expensive.

Thus, the idea of abundant clean energy being available any time soon is an outright lie, motivated by the demonic hordes influencing the Democrat Party faithful. Let's now look at the bottom-line numbers. The world use of energy in all forms grows by approximately two percent annually. Today, if we added up all of the wind, solar and tide energy being produced annually, it amounts to less than 8 tenths of one percent of the total (.008). So, the entire quantity of renewable sources isn't even keeping up with normal growth of demand for energy. (.020) If we did produce enough wind turbines to meet <u>just</u> the annual growth, we'd have to fill up an area the size of the British Isles with wind turbines <u>every</u> year. After 50 years, we'd have filled the entire land area of Russia! It simply isn't ever going to happen.

The Democrats were unable to sell the idea of global cooling. Their assertion that pollution resulting from the burning of fossil fuels, would thereby cause the next Ice Age—failed, because there was no reliable energy alternative available. People were unwilling to return to wood stoves to heat human residences. Since there was nothing else available, which could be produced in large quantities, they lost traction with the public. "Hey, your herd of livestock are ruining the environment. You gotta stop ranching them. They produce too much methane. If we don't, we'll all freeze to death!" "Oh, okay. What do I have to replace them with?" "Nothing's available, sorry." "Oh, so we all have to starve to death, instead. I see. Well, just never mind then." The Democrats failed to foresee the creation of a Pandora's box of their own making. They were very successful in creating a widely believed public scare. They had the world's people going for a while. But their proffered resolution was in reality no solution, and so it fell on deaf ears. I enjoy learning of Satan's failures! Like a famous comedian once remarked: "You cain't fix stoopid."

An Impotent Roaring Lion

The real problem is—regardless of the crisis the Democrats try and propose, they will always get enough people to follow them. Satan is a real force to be reckoned with. And when the crisis gets resolved or disproven, the Dems just wind up trying to create another one. I guarantee regardless of the time you are reading this book, there will be some major crisis being proposed by the Democrats. It will ever be a calamity in need of some drastic solution, which will either bankrupt the wealthy, lead the government into insolvency or ruin society as we know it outright. Despite the aforementioned predicaments being shown to be relatively small threats, the pace of the

Democrats originating new problems facing humanity hasn't slowed down in the least. They are cranking them out about as fast as they can be conjured up.

> *"The Democrat Party will ensure no Americans are left out or left behind as we accelerate the transition to a clean energy economy, and be responsible stewards of our natural resources and our public lands and waters."* [**DPP** pg. 24]

Here we go again: The words in the **DPP** about being responsible stewards over our natural resources is Biblical.[8] The Bible teaches the earth is the LORD's and all it contains, so by extension we are to be found trustworthy over our management of it.[9] But, we cannot be deemed responsible if our actions harm those others who dwell in it. As mentioned earlier, the Paris Climate Accord attempts to be too aggressive in their approach to replacing fossil fuels. There's no reasonable way to "accelerate the transition" away from them to reusable energy. In July of 2017, the French announced a plan to ban all gasoline and diesel vehicles in France by 2040, as part of the Paris agreement. That's only a short 21 years away from the publication date of this book. They also stated France would no longer use coal to produce

---

[8] 1 Corinthians 4:2 "In this case, moreover, it is required of stewards that one be found trustworthy."

[9] Psalms 24:1 "The earth is the LORD's and all it contains, the world and those who dwell in it."

electricity after 2022. That's just three years distant. France, nor any other country is even remotely in any position of being able to fulfill such promises, despite assurances of investing 4 billion Euro's in an effort to boost energy efficiency.

'Great Peril to Life'; Gas Pares Away Earth's Ozone'

Professor T. M. Donahue testified before Congress concerning the next crisis waiting to befall earth. It was the danger from a huge hole in the ozone layer created by modern technology. He blamed the aerosol sprays and freon in refrigerators and air conditioners. It was postulated that fluorocarbons, released into the environment was destroying a critical part of the atmosphere. This time it was **ozone**, chemically called super oxygen, as it *'is composed of three oxygen atoms, instead of the normal two.'* The layer of ozone filters out the sun's ultraviolet rays, shielding humanity from the threat of skin cancer. At great cost and inconvenience, mankind redesigned and changed the aerosols we put into our technology; and cancelled the building of a fleet of supersonic transports as a result of the scare. We stopped putting the chlorofluorocarbons (CFCs) into our machinery and hence the atmosphere beginning in 1980.

NASA began tracking the size of the hole in 1979. While there was a surge in the size of the hole between 1979 and 2000, it has now begun shrinking

Jefferson Daniel Seal

back down to previously normal levels. What scientists learned is—the hole in the ozone follows the rise and fall of ice cover in the Antarctic. When the sea ice cover is melting, the hole in the ozone also expands. The first problem is with the levels of CFCs in the atmosphere. This relationship shows no correlation of the size of the hole to the amount of CFCs present. Another problem is the hole in the ozone *never* extends beyond Antarctica. It stays over the top of the continent. And, it only appears in the southern hemisphere during their winter—when coincidentally there isn't any sunlight. Antarctica sees nearly four months of darkness. It's impossible to get skin cancer from the sun without sunlight. And, when the sun returns in the summer, the hole in the ozone completely disappears. This is another example of a scare which precipitated action at tremendous cost but couldn't be proven that the repair actually worked.

Acid Rain Kills Life in Lakes

The next scare, called **acid rain**, appeared in April of 1980. Once again, coal fired electric power plants were the blame. '*The industrial burning of coal and other fossil fuels creates waste gases which contain sulfur and nitrogen oxides. When they combine with water in the atmosphere, they form acidic compounds, which when they fall back to earth, it's in the form of acid rain.*' This acid rain was supposed to cause great environmental harm, typically to forests

Satan Would Be A Democrat

and lakes. "We're simply not prepared to contemplate leaving the generations of the next century with hundreds of thousands of sterile lakes," said Raymond Robinson of the Canadian environmental agency. The problem was deemed to be insurmountable with lasting and irreversible damage having already occurred.

After ten years of a Congress directed study, costing the American taxpayer 537 million dollars, the problem was pronounced "not an environmental crisis." The report by the National Acid Precipitation Assessment Program (NAPA) was issued in 1990, repudiated the steep cuts in sulfur dioxide emissions as called for by ecological scientists. They said the cost of 5 billion dollars per year to control such pollution was a decided overreaction to the acid rain problem. Just as with the earlier problem of poor air quality in Los Angeles, changes in technology would lower the emissions on a more cost effective and affordable scale, with all lakes and bodies of water recovering quickly, having a full recovery inevitable without spending the huge sums of money being called for by critics. NAPA rejected the more extreme views calling the problem a crisis or potential calamity.

The Democrats always reject the answers which go against their point of view. The leaders of the party will attack any persons offering views which either disagree with or contradict their assertions of an emergency being just around the corner. This, despite they themselves, are frequently the "abusers of the environment" at a rate far in excess of middle-class Americans. Al Gore, Senator from Tennessee and Vice President, is a notable example. Despite calling for massive cuts to greenhouse gases, it was he who flew all over the globe in an older, very inefficient business sized jet, whose engines produced many more times the pollution than a newer one. He could have saved many thousands of tons of carbon simply by riding on a commercial airliner; just like everybody else. How is such behavior being in any way a good steward of the environment? It is the term 'hypocrite' which comes to mind.

The Democrat Party wants to have it both ways. First, the rich leaders and supporters of the party want to keep their wealth and opulent lifestyle. They never offer to bear any of the burden. Second, they believe the extreme cuts in greenhouse gases and carbon credits being called for will not hurt the American worker.

> *"Democrats reject the notion that we have to choose between protecting our planet and creating good-paying jobs. We can and we will do both."* [**DPP** pg. 24]

I have news for them; things just don't work that way in the real world. I don't care how many times a person demands it; cutting off their nose to spite their face, is never a workable solution. Satan doesn't seem to care. He continues to drive his demonic message in

Satan Would Be A Democrat

hopes of catching God Almighty in some mistake. By studying man's history, it sure looks to me that Satan only wants to be able to prove God wrong just one time. Allow me the privilege of one example.

Adolph Hitler was driven by an extreme sense of nationalism to return Germany to the state she was prior to the start of WWI. He began covertly arming Germany and preparing her for war in secret. His actions directly led to the Second World War. At some point he became demonically possessed and started killing Jews. I'm sure many members of the Nazi party were likewise affected. Before Germany was defeated, it managed to kill fully one-half of the Jews in the world. It took until 2016—over 70 years!— before the Jewish population worldwide returned to pre-1940 levels. Satan was attempting to exterminate the Jews. Had Hitler been slightly more successful, there would not have been a population large enough to return to Jerusalem in 1948 and create the state of Israel. As it was, they held on through four regional wars by their fingernails.

The example the Bible gives for followers of Christ is the same Moses gave to the Hebrews during their Exodus from Egypt. When the ten plagues had been leveled against the Egyptians at terrible cost, Pharaoh finally and reluctantly agreed to allow the Hebrews to depart their life of slavery. Notice, despite going on a long journey to Mount Sinai, and then on to the Promised Land, God didn't have them take any extra

Jefferson Daniel Seal

supplies. He said He would meet their needs. A few days after leaving, Pharaoh had a change of heart and assembled his army and came after the Hebrews in force. It was not to return them to Egypt, but rather to bury them in the desert. Thus, Moses and his people found themselves trapped between a reed sea and Pharaoh's army. [10]

As would be natural, the Hebrew people wanted to panic and run. But there was nowhere to go. They were trapped. The words of Moses ring loudly across the ages. He told them: "Shut UP!" and to "Stand Still!" This got their attention. The point is there's nothing which could be done anyway. Then Moses said, "Observe your Salvation!" The lesson today is crystal clear. God is telling His followers the same message. "Ignore the loudly proclaimed warnings of coming catastrophes." Our faith is in the hands of God; and not the hands of men. Despite repeated calls for action, take none. Live your normal life. And finally, be calm, while waiting and watching for your salvation. The promised attacks are merely a threat. Satan is just an impotent roaring lion, toothless against believers.

---

[10] The Time is Near – Volume I Read the full story of why the original Hebrew of Old Testament of Bible translates into "reed sea" instead of "Red Sea."

Satan Would Be A Democrat

VII. HEALTH AND SAFETY RUSE

Death, Domination & Dejection

The Democrat Party is making a stab at increasing health care coverage to a point whereby they want it to become universal for all Americans. Their claim is health care is a *right* and not a privilege. They further seek to clarify that people should be put before profits. Once again, their flowery words seem to beckon to the reasonable side of our brain.

"Democrats believe that health care is a right, not a privilege, and our health care system should put people before profits." [**DPP** pg. 32]

To begin with, a **right** is defined as '*a moral or legal entitlement to have or obtain something.*' So, the Democrats are saying health care should be a *legal entitlement* for any person. There's a lot of discussion surrounding the word "entitlements" lately; particularly within budgetary circles. The entitlements portion of the government budget is completely out of control, and on the verge of bankrupting this great nation. Do we continue to expand and push entitlements to the point there's no benefits remaining for anyone? That describes Satan's wish perfectly and precisely what he is pursuing.

So, what are entitlements really? An **entitlement** means '*the belief that a person is inherently deserving of certain privileges.*' **Inherently** is another word for

Jefferson Daniel Seal

'*essential*.' **Deserving** translates to '*worthy*.' Are we to assume then Health Care is an essential right for all Americans? Read for yourself the words of the American Declaration of Independence:

> "*We hold these truths to be self-evident, that all men are created equal, that they are endowed by their Creator with certain unalienable Rights, that among these are Life, Liberty and the pursuit of Happiness.*"

Just to be clear: there is <u>no</u> mention of "Health Care" anywhere within the full text of the document. The Democrats would have you believe "Health Care" is part and parcel of a person's life, as defined by the Declaration itself. Well, let's once again take a detailed look at their words to see if it's fact or fiction.

The framers of the American Declaration of Independence, especially Thomas Jefferson, were disciples of a man named John Locke. He was an English philosopher and physician, widely regarded as the most influential of Enlightenment thinkers. In 1689, Locke wrote a book entitled; "Two Treatises of Government," where he argued that government existed for the *sole* purpose of protecting the **property** of its citizens. This forms the basic premise of the entire Declaration of Independence. Locke went on to define such property as '*a person's life, liberty and estate*.' This was all no accident. Locke's concept of man started with his personal belief in the account of creation, as detailed in the Bible. He equated natural law with Biblical revelation, as both were created by God. Locke derived the fundamental concepts of his political theory directly from Scriptural texts. Keep this in mind as we discuss the basic theory of the American government.

We start with the idea of what is encompassed within a person's life, as intended by the Declaration of Independence. A **person's life** is defined as '*the period beginning at some point after their conception but prior to their birth; and ending with the physical death of their body.*' While you might disagree with my stated definition, the Biblical account proves many times; God names and also inhabits people, while they are still in the womb. [1] The right to life therefore begins within the womb; and ends upon the natural, accidental or predetermined physical death of the body. That right is not to be infringed upon otherwise. One of the basic tenets of Locke is all humans were created equally free, and therefore governments needed the consent of the governed. A baby could *never* give consent to its own death.

The second element of property reflects our **liberty**. It's defined simply as '*the power or scope to act or behave as one pleases.*' It's the right to choose what you do and where you do it. So long as your behavior doesn't tread on or infringe upon those

---

[1] Luke 1:15 "For he will be great in the sight of the LORD; and he will drink no wine or liquor, and he will be filled with the Holy Spirit from the time within his mother's womb."

around you, liberty is freedom to do what you so desire. It's frequently described as "being free within society from oppressive restrictions imposed by authority on one's way of life, behavior or political views." By the way, **property** is defined as '*the right to the possession, use, or disposal of things which you own.*' A person essentially owns the *time* between their birth and death. Society doesn't begin legally holding a person responsible for their actions until around their 18th birthday, but that still doesn't mean they don't own their juvenile years. They just aren't held legally accountable for them.

The third and final element of **property** is '*the money and property a person owns.*' This reflects our assets, capital, holdings and wealth. A person's behavior largely determines the level of success they attain with their life. Once more, we're back to God's law of sowing and reaping. If you work hard, all the while obeying God's rules for good and honorable behavior, you will be successful and reap good from what you have sown. If you don't, then you won't. So, what responsibility does government then have in this equation?

The short answer is; only our protection. The preamble of the Constitution grants the federal government authority to raise and maintain a military to provide for the common defense of Americans "property." Note: this authority for protection is <u>not</u> a guarantee of success or failure; only a guarantee of

Satan Would Be A Democrat

a person's right to determine their own outcome. If you make poor choices, your protection only extends to your right to do so. The government was never put there to serve in the role of bailing out citizens who make poor choices. It's there to assure people the freedom to pursue happiness, but not certify they attain it. In the same way, the government is not here to guarantee a person's health, via a health care system.

A **person's health** is defined as '*a person's mental or physical condition.*' Would you not agree the *average* person during their lives has significant control over their own health? We all choose whether to go to the gym, or instead smoke a pack of cigarettes per day. Some choose to do illegal drugs while others try and eat healthy. Some folks will brush their teeth three times per day, floss and see their dentist twice per year. Others will do none of those things. Our "Life" becomes the sum of all of our choices. A lot can be said about our overall health as well. "A person can't control getting cancer or many diseases which are genetic. What about them?" In the same way, we will not all become wealthy millionaires; people must make the most of what they have been given—just as in Jesus's parable about the Talents. We are all created equal, but do not enjoy equal circumstances.

So, the question remains: Is Health Care a right and or a privilege? A **privilege** is defined as '*a special* *advantage granted or available only to a particular person or group.'* When you grant a privilege to everyone, doesn't it cease being a privilege, by the very definition of the word? Not according to the Democrats. They tout their success to this point in time by ignoring the truth.

> *"Democrats have been fighting to secure universal health care for the American people for generations, and we are proud to be the party that passed Medicare, Medicaid, and the Affordable Care Act."* [**DPP** pg. 31]

But, has these programs really been a successful avenue for the American people? Let's examine the baseline numbers.

The total of the U.S. Government annual budget for 2015 equaled 3.8 **trillion** dollars. A trillion is *'the number one followed by twelve zeros.'* It is a thousand billion. Using $100 bills, a million dollars would fit easily inside a couple of large grocery bags. Using the same $100 bill, a billion dollars would completely fill the average sized grocery store, sacked up from floor to ceiling. It's a very big number! There are three parts of spending to the U.S. government budget: **Entitlements** ($2.45 trillion), **Discretionary Spending** ($1.1 trillion) and **Interest** on the Debt ($229 billion). Translated, it means 64.8% of the budget goes towards **Entitlements**, 29.1% to **Discretionary Spending** and 6.1% to **Interest** on the debt.

Satan Would Be A Democrat

To put these numbers in relatable terms, we are going to assume the annual budget of the United States equals exactly one hundred dollars annually. Medicare, Medicaid and Social Security add up to $56.80 of the **Entitlement's** total allotment of $64.80. The military receives $15.88 of the **Discretionary Spending's** $28.90 total. And $6.10 goes to pay **Interest** on the debt. That means just $21.22 cents is left to pay for <u>every</u> other program of the federal budget. So, in real terms, 64% of every tax dollar is already going into Democrat Party initiated programs.

The Federal deficit for 2015 was 425 billion dollars, amounting to 3.2% of the total budget; or $3.20 using our example. So, as we discuss the additional cost for all the programs being proposed by the Democrat Party, I want you to keep these figures in mind. Because the primary focus should not be on the merit of the programs themselves, but rather on the feasibility of paying for them. It does no good to add in all the free and beneficial packages when the result will be the bankruptcy of the United States. Remember, the primary responsibility of government is to provide security for the citizen's property.

While the use of the dictionary and the calculator might seem laborious to you, the reason I use them is because words and numbers have both meaning and consequence. I want you to see precisely what the Democrat Party is seeking. Only then can you appreciate and understand what their true goals are.

Jefferson Daniel Seal

And perhaps more importantly, learn their true aim is not focused primarily on improving the lifestyle and standard of living of the American citizen. Instead, their efforts are directed squarely at destroying the financial health and wealth of the United States. Please don't forget God's immutable law of sowing and reaping. If we run this country like an open ATM, we will reap the crops of financial ruin. It is guaranteed! We must remain responsible stewards of what God has given to us.

Again, taking their words at face value, makes them sound reasonable and even rational. But, when they are weighed against the words of the Bible, they are found in dire need of want. When we study what the Democrat Party is in reality seeking to achieve; is it not the authority whereby they can impose oppressive restrictions upon one's way of life, behavior and political views? The Democrat Party is not pursuing liberty. Instead, they are pursuing the very opposite; claiming they know what's best for the individual—which goes directly opposite of the very definition of the word! And, as I've pointed out repeatedly, it goes opposite to the Word of God.

America is still a great nation, founded and based upon a Judeo-Christian ethic, where we honor the God of Abraham, Isaac and Joseph through the way in which we live out our lives. John Locke's work had strong influence on the framers of the Declaration of Independence. They wrote of man's inalienable rights, an idea Locke codified. Remember the mention of a person's property equals their life, liberty and estate? Would it surprise you to learn this too is based on solid Biblical principles? The Democrat Party's policies, if they are allowed to be fully implemented, would lead to death, domination and dejection.

Satan's Security Number

At the behest of his party, President Franklin D. Roosevelt signed what was called the "Old-Age, Survivors and Disability Insurance" (OASDI) program into law on 14 August 1935. What most folks don't know, is the program was supposedly put into place to primarily take care of those senior adults who outlived their offspring. It was a normal practice for elderly parents to go and live with their children following their retirement from working. There were no 401K's or retirement plans per se back then. It was expected any able-bodied person (usually the men) would go to work, all the while saving for their retirement. This system seemed to function pretty well until the Great Depression hit; resulting in wiping out the savings accounts of most person's overnight.

This was the impetus the Democrats used to begin what is now the largest consumer of American tax revenue: The Social Security Administration. The program was to be funded primarily through payroll taxes, collected by the IRS and formally entrusted to

Jefferson Daniel Seal

the Federal Old-Age and Survivors Insurance Trust Fund. This was the proffered solution to having elderly adults with no place to go after their children were no longer able to care for them. The life expectancy in the United States in the 1930's was only 58 for men and 62 for women.

So, when a person lived into their 70's and 80's (actually more common than most people believe) they would live beyond the lifespan of their kids, if they had any. What usually happened is; the man would work until he died or retired. At that point, the couple would live on their accumulated savings. When those savings were exhausted, the survivors (usually just the wife) would go and live with one of her children. This was the way things were back after the turn of the 19th century.

The OASDI was written allegedly to take care of these "elderly orphans of society." It was sold to the Congress based on the concept of an insurance policy. A premium would be paid, until at such time the benefit would be needed. The premium would be collected via a payroll tax, which would be relatively small, and would be used to ease suffering on the elderly. In 1937, the payroll tax was set at 2% of earnings, on an annual maximum of $3,000 earned. This amounted to a maximum premium of $60 annually ($5 per month). In 1937 there were 53,236 beneficiaries, each receiving an average payout of $24. Sounds fairly reasonable, right? That's the way

Satan always makes his plans sound. But the devil lies in the details of his schemes!

In order to be eligible to collect the OASDI benefits, a person had to be registered. This was the beginning of the United States Social Security Number (SSN). Only workers who had been enrolled in the program and who worked at least "40 quarters" were eligible to receive benefits. A **quarter** **of** **coverage** means '*three calendar months whereby the worker earned the stated minimum amount of pay*.' For 2019 that minimum number was $1,320. However, the Social Security Administration looks at how much a person earned within the year and divides that figure by the minimum required to earn credit for a quarter. So if a person earns $5,280 in January and February of 2019 and doesn't work the rest of the year, they will receive credit for four quarters of work! ($5,280 divided by $1,320 equals 4.)

The retirement age was set at 65 by law. Initially, not very many people lived long enough to collect benefits. But this fact guaranteed the program was entirely solvent under these rules. The real problem was the camel had gotten his nose under the tent! The Democrats wasted no time expanding the program to include single mothers, their children, early retirement age, high cost of living adjustments, disability and Medicare health benefits. Along the way they added alcoholics, drug addicts and prisoners to the benefit roles. By 2019, the payroll tax was up

Jefferson Daniel Seal

to 15.3% on maximum earnings of $128,400. This amounts to an annual tax of $19,645.20 per worker (or $1,637.10 per month). As of 2008, the number of beneficiaries of Social Security reached a staggering 51 million persons, receiving an average benefit of $12,089.04. The program will become insolvent by 2034 unless even more changes are made. What do you think is going to happen?

I predict more increases are going to be made to the payroll tax. Additionally, they will push out the age whereby normal persons will become eligible to receive benefits. The beginning age of 65 has now been moved out to 67. Full benefits can now only be received for persons reaching their 70th birthday. And one day soon, they will begin **means testing** benefits. What this means is '*the Democrats will set an income threshold in order to receive benefits.*'

So, for example, anyone earning more than $80K after retirement (total of investments and pensions) per year will begin to see their government benefit shrink. By the time a person earns say $250K, their benefit will be reduced to zero. A form of this is already happening. For persons earning more than 250K in retirement income, they are being charged over $900 per month for Medicare medical benefits EACH. Just watch and observe, my friends. The Democrats will never cease to fight their war against the wealthy, hardworking citizens regardless of the circumstances.

Satan Would Be A Democrat

The Democrat party states the claim in the 2016 **DPP**. They will not quit trying to make health care a fundamental right for all.

"Democrats will never falter in our generations-long fight to guarantee health care as a fundamental right for every American." [**DPP** pg. 32]

Once more, the words sound rosy, do they not? The problem with the Democrats making anything a fundamental right, lies in the details of how to pay for it. Money doesn't grow on trees and someone must be taxed in order to satisfy the bill. For example, what if the worker or person was wealthy enough to not need universal health care coverage? They still cannot opt out of the program. The fundamental right comes with mandatory participation. It's the same way with Social Security. There is no way to opt out. A person will have 16% of their pay taken by the government, whether the person wants the insurance or not. Recall the discussion about liberty? There is no real liberty surrounding Social Security programs.

Now, the Democrats want every person to have access to Medicare, whether they ever worked 40 quarters, or not:

"As part of that guarantee, Americans should be able to access public coverage through a

public option, and those over 55 should be able to opt into Medicare." [**DPP** pg. 32]

They will not rest until every benefit becomes universal, to include hosts of persons who did not earn it. The problem with such policy is two part. First, someone who sowed bad seed with their lives, shouldn't be entitled to receive the same benefits as persons who did sow proper seed. This is a clear violation of God's Law. Second, by taking such action, the Democrats are attempting to override the natural consequences of reaping. Again, this is sinful behavior and goes against Biblical teaching. Recall the discussion about sowing and reaping, back on page 89: "Don't be fooled! For God *cannot* be ridiculed. You WILL reap from what you have sown."

As you can see, Satan's manner of governing can be summed up in the phrase: "My way or the highway!" Make no mistake; Social Security in these United States has reached the level of being a form of socialism. **Socialism** is defined as *'a political and economic theory of social organization which advocates the means of production, distribution and exchange should be owned or regulated by the government as a whole.'* While the government doesn't yet control the means of production, they do control and regulate distribution of Social Security benefits. Socialism was viewed as a steppingstone to communism. **Communism** is defined as *'a political theory advocating class warfare leading to a society* *in which all property is publicly owned, with each person paid according to their needs.'* Read the definition again, paying very close attention to the words on the page.

Now, compare those words with what the Democrat Party Platform of 2016 is advocating. Examine the proceedings of the Democrat Party and realistically evaluate them in light of the concrete actions being taken; and <u>not</u> their stated objectives. Now, can you truthfully say the Democrat Party is not leading the United States down a path to utter destruction? Just as the Roman Empire was taken down, Satan would like nothing more than to destroy the greatest nation this world has seen; since the creation of Adam and Eve. A nation founded upon Biblically based principles, which embrace the idea of one God Almighty and His law.

Soon, everything the Democrat Party is attempting to achieve, will be successfully implemented by the man soon to come, called "the Antichrist" in the Bible. He will force everyone to accept his mark before they will be allowed to participate in any form of commerce or social services. He will take the meaning of "mandatory" to a whole new level. In fact, those refusing to accept his mark will be publicly and gruesomely executed via beheading. The Bible teaches us the number associated with him will be 666. For all the facts, go to DWJDMinistries.com and order a copy of the book: The Antichrist Revealed.

Jefferson Daniel Seal

Friends, information is power. Get the information now while you can. Before the Demoncrats make it impossible to obtain. Do it before the implementation of Satan's Security Number!

Clinging Tightly to Faith

This book fiercely advocates the idea whereby human beings can come totally under the influence of satanic forces. This influence can be as benign as listening to propaganda on television and the mass media, all the way to the point of experiencing outright demonic possession. I will use the Holy Bible to prove this fact, as well as explain how Satan can compel unsuspecting persons to believe a lie. Those targeted persons are ordinary people who have been duped, swindled and conned—or are being pursued for such. There's no other way to say it: the raging struggle for the hearts and minds of humanity is still under way.

For those persons who fail to accept this premise, the Bible is very clear about the subject matter. We are in essence discussing a person's mental health. I'm defining a person who has a bill of **clean mental health** as being *'free from demonic influence.'* Any infestation of the mind by satanic beings would then be my characterization of being *'mentally unhealthy.'* The Democrat Party is on record as taking mental health issues just as solemn as they do physical care.

"We must treat mental health issues with the same care and seriousness that we treat issues of physical health." [**DPP** pg. 34]

Certainly, *most* medical conditions and afflictions are not demonically influenced in any way. But I'm not talking about those cases. The Bible tells us Jesus healed persons from all sorts of various ailments and conditions. [2] Notice, one of the afflictions is called "demoniacs." The Greek word used in the footnoted verse is **daimonzomai** [*dahee-mon-ID-zom-ahee*] and means *'under the power of a demon.'* Clearly, demonic possession was, and remains a real condition. This is the type of mental health issue of which I speak.

There are many levels of demonic possession, as explained throughout Scripture. A person can be severely affected; or just suffer varying degrees of mental persuasion. For example, Jesus drove a demon from a man, who was rendered speechless when possessed. [3] Another time Jesus cast out a demon from a young boy, which had caused him to become both deaf and mute. [4] We discover

---

[2] Matthew 4:24 The News about Him spread throughout all Syria; and they brought to Him all who were ill, those suffering with various diseases and pains, demoniacs, epileptics, paralytics; and He healed them.

[3] Luke 11:14 Jesus was driving out a demon that was mute. When the demon left, the man who had been mute spoke, and the crowd was amazed.

[4] Mark 9:25 When Jesus saw that a crowd was rapidly gathering, He rebuked the unclean spirit, saying to it, "You deaf and mute spirit, I command you, come out of him and do not enter him again."

Jefferson Daniel Seal

throughout the New Testament that demon possession can cause some people to become extremely violent, [5] be blind and mute, [6] have super-human strength, [7] have greater than normal insight, [8] run around naked, [9] and become mentally unstable. [10] Apparently, demons can have only limited power over persons; as they are able to cause certain conditions and illnesses. And while the medical community at large doesn't accept the idea demonic of possession as being a genuine health condition, such an opinion certainly doesn't prove demonic possession is a fairytale. God excluded demons from the physical realm after the Great Flood; but He didn't exclude them from the Spiritual domain. [11]

Perhaps the first question in your mind is: "What does the footnoted verse mean by the words 'this darkness'?" [12] The answer is provided within the text in black and white. Quite simply: Satan, the devil, his demonic forces. The devil is waging a war against humanity using weapons the Bible describes as "schemes." The Greek word used is **methodeia**

---

[5] Matthew 8:28-34 Please read the passage from your Bible.
[6] Matthew 12:22 Please read the passage from your Bible.
[7] Mark 5:2-7 Please read the passage from your Bible.
[8] Mark 5:2-7 Please read the passage from your Bible.
[9] Luke 8:27 Please read the passage from your Bible.
[10] Matthew 17:15-18 Please read the passage from your Bible.
[11] Ephesians 6:12 For our struggle is not against flesh and blood, but against the rulers, against the powers, against the world forces of this darkness, against the spiritual forces of wickedness in the heavenly places.
[12] Ephesians 6:11 Put on the full armor of God, so that you will be able to stand firm against the schemes of the devil.

Satan Would Be A Democrat

[*meth-oh-DAY-eh-ah*] and means '*cunning arts, deceit, craft, trickery.*' These are the very same tactics which frauds, schemers, and con artists employ against their hunted quarry. Just like with swindlers, there is a solid defense to be had. You might be wondering; "How can we defend ourselves against demons we cannot hear or see?" Believe it or not, but you've already started on building up your protection to defend yourself; it began when you picked up and began reading this book! The Apostle Paul advises us to put on the *full* armor of God so that when the evil ones arrive, and begin their task of trying to fool you, you'll be able to stand firm. [13] Paul then gives us a complete list of what composes spiritual armor. [14]

God's armor is not an option! You either put it on; or risk being totally defeated. Make no mistake; you and everyone you know are all engaged in a full-blown war! Ignoring the fact only increases your chances of becoming a casualty. Unlike the con artists and frauds who are after a portion of your hard-earned money, the forces of this darkness are after your soul! While they can't literally steal your soul, they can and will embezzle any chance you have of spending eternity with God in Heaven. That's the purpose of their con. Just like with Adam and Eve, they want you to lose what the first humans had put

---

[13] Ephesians 6:13 Therefore, take up the full armor of God, so that you will be able to resist in the evil day, and having done everything, to stand firm.
[14] Ephesians 6:15 thru 18 Please study this passage from your Bible.

Jefferson Daniel Seal

at risk: their ability to live in Heaven, within the presence of Almighty God. Only those who put on the armor and wear it properly—will be the ones who stand a chance of avoiding the eternal torment which will be the Lake of Fire. Losing the war should not be an option for you! Why would you allow the devil and his fallen demons to sway you over to their side?

Okay, assume for the moment the Bible is just a made-up book. Suppose all of it is just a myth, brought forward by people who have been described as; "the basket of deplorables; the racist, sexist, homophobic, xenophobic, Islamophobic—you name it;" [15] those bitter souls who "cling to their God and their guns, and are anti-immigrant." [16] Even if every word of Scripture is completely false and the direct result of superstition and hyperbole—why does EVERY belief supported by the Democrat Party fly opposite of what Scripture says? Recall the analogy about being in a war? As a former military leader, war planner and policy formulation expert, I can tell you; it's a waste of time putting *any* focus on those forces who are of no threat to you. There's a reason the

---

[15] Hillary Rodham Clinton, September 9th, 2016: "You know, just to be grossly generalistic, you could put half of Trump's supporters into what I call the basket of deplorables. Right? [Laughter/applause]. The racist, sexist, homophobic, xenophobic, Islamophobic—you name it."

[16] Barrack Hussein Obama, April 6th, 2008: Referring to working class voters in old industrial towns decimated by job losses, the future president said; "They get bitter, they cling to guns or religion or antipathy to people who aren't like them or anti-immigrant sentiment or anti-trade sentiment as a way to explain their frustrations."

Satan Would Be A Democrat

Democrat Party comes after such persons: It's because they are the PRIME threat to the survival of their schemes.

This war is not being fought with bullets, missiles and bombs. No, it's being fought with lies, deception and demonically driven laws and policies. Look at the footnoted comments from two recent prominent Democrat Party leaders and compare them to what is going on today. Everything they are accusing the Christian side of doing in the war is precisely the tactics the Democrats are employing against them! Remember, the "rust belt" was created by Democrat policies. In the same way those same policies are creating the current homelessness and drug epidemics. Why are the twenty worst cities for crime being run by Democrats? The answer is simple: Satan desires them to be managed that way. He wants crime to become so bad, the police have to cease enforcing lesser rules. He wants to destroy people's hope and peace.

I've worked in programs designed to feed the hungry, assist the needy and care for the elderly. In the overwhelming cases we worked and observed, alcoholism, drug addiction and mental incapacitation were the three forces driving 95% of the people we saw into difficult circumstances. So, what is the Democrat solution?

"The Democrat Party supports a robust mental health workforce, and promotion of

> *better integration of the behavioral and general health care systems."* [**DPP** pg. 34]

They are calling for more bureaucratically driven policies. They see the root problem as being what is an obvious lie; people lack adequate access to health care, as defined as the availability of both mental and physical treatment. Anyone can enter an urgent care facility or emergency room in the U.S.—including illegal aliens—and they will not be denied care. Instead, while recognizing the existence of the epidemic, they ignore the true cause and therefore also the solution.

> *"We must also expand community-based treatment for substance abuse disorders and mental health conditions and fully enforce our parity law."* [**DPP** pg. 34]

The true cause of the mental breakdown within society is the Spiritual war. The people suffering from the work of the demons are the casualties being caused by the fighting. There may or may not be help for such persons. But there is still help for those not yet injured by the fighting. The Bible gives us the tools for our defense. First off, protect yourself by searching for, then listening to, and finally heeding the TRUTH. [17] The strongest weapon Satan can employ against humanity are endless lies. The truth is out there. It's any and every morsal which agrees with

---

[17] Ephesians 6:14 "HAVING GIRDED YOUR LOINS WITH THE TRUTH."

Satan Would Be A Democrat

the words in the Bible. Second, ensure your behavior reflects what the Bible says is right or righteous, and not what mankind says is good. [18] This is the fundamental practice God has ordained: you will then reap good crops from your sowing of good seed.

Our behavior matters and will absolutely impact our mental health. Paul then says, "Put on the shoes which will allow the bringing of the Gospel of Peace." [19] The word **Gospel** means '*good news*.' Rather than repeat all the garbage of doom and gloom being preached by the Democrats, instead share the Good News of Jesus Christ with people. That will do more for them than any physical item you might bring. The fourth item Paul advises us to do is to take up the shield of faith. [20] Placing our trust in God will allow us to ignore the lies of the devil and his demonic cohorts. The barbs will then be unable to gain zero traction with Christ's followers and is equivalent to extinguishing the flaming arrows of Satan.

The fifth element of our armor is accepting the gift of salvation from Jesus. [21] Salvation cannot be earned nor merited; just accepted. The helmet symbolically protects our mind and ultimately our soul from all the

---

[18] Ephesians 6:14 "HAVING PUT ON THE BREASTPLATE OF RIGHTEOUSNESS."

[19] Ephesians 6:15 "SHOD YOUR FEET WITH THE PREPARATION OF THE GOSPEL OF PEACE."

[20] Ephesians 6:16 "in addition to those things, take up the shield of faith, with which you will be able to extinguish all the flaming arrows of the evil one."

[21] Ephesians 6:17 "And take THE HELMET OF SALVATION,"

Jefferson Daniel Seal

satanic garbage. It is the free gift of Jesus offered to any who will agree to worship and follow after Him. Hand in glove with our acceptance of Jesus comes the sixth element of our armor: God's Holy Spirit. He is our true defender and is described as our only offensive weapon: a sword. [22] I know your Bible says "Word of God"—which is completely correct, so long as you envision His living voice—the Holy Spirit. The word used in the text is **rhema** [*HRAY-mah*] which means literally '*a word spoken by a living voice*.' The Greek language uses an entirely different word when talking about God's Word—**lagos**. This word means '*God's written text—the Bible*'. The Holy Spirit certainly uses the text of the Bible when He speaks to us. It's important to know the Holy Spirit is our only weapon used for our defense; but it is not wielded by us. The Holy Spirit is a fully-fledged member of the Trinity. We have no control over Him.

The 7th and final part of our armor is prayer. [23] The word used is **deeseos** [*DEE-she-oohs*]. It means '*heart felt petition, arising out of deep and personal urgent need*.' That is the perfect description of true and real prayer. On your bended knees, before God Almighty in total submission; calling on Him to defeat the forces of evil to bring about the protection you and

---

[22] Ephesians 6:17 "And the sword of the Spirit, which is the living voice of God."

[23] Ephesians 6:18 "With all prayer and petition pray at all times in the Spirit, and with this view, be on the alert with all perseverance and petition for all the saints."

the other saints (followers of Jesus) are seeking. If people want to have any chance of defeating Satan, these items of armor are the *only* things which will guarantee success. Anything else you may try will result in failure and possibly your eternal damnation. You can be made completely secure within the hand of God Himself. It does require a level of effort to put on the armor of God. But once you do, you'll be so glad you did! Only then will you truly be considered part of "a basket of deplorables," by the demonic forces of Satan. The Bible says all who call upon the LORD will be saved. [24] It's ultimately your choice. No one can force you to pick one side or the other. Just remember; there's no higher honor in God's eyes than clinging tightly to your faith.

Demons of the Airwaves

Please make no mistake; despite being thwarted by God at nearly every turn, Satan still does rule and run this world system. He was awarded reign over the Earth when Adam and Eve ceded it to him, following their sinning in the Garden of Eden. [25] That's the reason Satan went after them in the first place. Satan desires to rule and to be worshipped. It's the whole reason he was removed from his position as chief of the angels. He sought to be above God Himself. God

---

[24] Romans 10:13 for "WHOEVER WILL CALL ON THE NAME OF THE LORD WILL BE SAVED."

[25] John 12:31 "Now judgment is upon this world; now the ruler of this world will be cast out."

Jefferson Daniel Seal

still retains full authority over the Earth, but Satan has gained control over the world system. That's why as followers of Christ, we must still put on the armor of God—for our protection. Otherwise, just like Adam and Eve, we too will be duped by the king of swindlers and frauds. The "father of all lies" holds the advantage over those without God's armor wrapped tightly around them.

We have proof of this fact in Scripture. When we read of the start of Jesus' ministry, the first thing to happen to Him was Satan showed up. Satan attempted to tempt Jesus, in the same way he tempted Eve. Recall, Jesus went out into a deserted place immediately after being baptized in the Jordan River by John. When He came up out of the water, the Holy Spirit descended upon Him like a dove. [26] After forty days of fasting, Satan offered to give Jesus all the kingdoms on the Earth, were He to bow His knee and worship him. [27] With the Holy Spirit, Jesus was able to refuse Satan's offer, despite being in a very weakened condition. The armor of God is *sufficient* for us. But, one day soon, Satan will make the same offer to the man who will become the Antichrist. And unlike Jesus,

---

[26] Matthew 3:16 After being baptized, Jesus came up immediately from the water; and behold, the heavens were opened, and he saw the Spirit of God descending as a dove and lighting on Him.

[27] Matthew 4:8-9 Again, the devil took Him to a very high mountain and showed Him all the kingdoms of the world and their glory; and he said to Him, "All these things I will give You, if you kneel down and worship me."

Satan Would Be A Democrat

the Antichrist will gladly accept the devil's evil offer. It's important to remember; it's still Satan's to give.

Satan is successful due to his ability to blind the minds of men to the truth of what's really going on in the world. The Bible says very plainly: "the god of this world is capable of blinding the minds of the *unbelieving.*" [28] The footnoted verse is talking about Satan; as he is the god of this world. Notice the verse defines whose minds he is able to blind: "the minds of the unbelieving." Jesus is the Truth, and so we read those under Satan's hand cannot see the light of the gospel of the glory of Jesus Christ. [29] That's why I have been saying all along; "If you are truly accepting of the things the Democrat Party stands for, you are being duped, conned and swindled by the father of all lies— Satan!" Listen my friends, you can see the truth laid out logically before you; and it costs absolutely nothing to view it. Also, it won't hurt you and you don't have to commit to anything beforehand. But it does require you to open up your eyes in order to see it. That's the sole purpose of my work: getting people to see God's Truth.

The Bible describes these *unbelievers* as ordinary persons, walking their way through life, behaving just like everybody else; and doing what is currently

---

[28] 2 Corinthians 4:4 In whose case the god of this world has blinded the minds of the unbelieving.

[29] 2 Corinthians 4:4 So that they might not see the light of the gospel of the glory of Christ, who is in the image of God.

customary. [30] Following the crowd is what most people do. That's why it's a crowd; everybody is clustered together. Just like a herd of cattle, there is security in numbers. People are loathed to admit it, but we all tend to follow the crowd. Human beings, for all their talk of independence, are closer in reality to behaving like a bunch of lemmings. That's the basis of the demonic mantra: "Do what everybody else is doing; don't stand out. Conform to the norm!" The bad news is those unbelievers are being led according to the wishes of the ruler of this world. In a most amazing discovery—the Bible even tells us how Satan does it.

You see, Satan is a finite being. That means he can only be in one place at any given time. God Almighty is infinite and omnipresent. [31] **Infinite** means '*to be without limits or to not be finite.*' To say God is infinite is to acknowledge He is not limited by the constrictions of the created universe. God created the universe and made all the rules as well. Therefore, He is not bound or restricted by those rules. God is and can be everywhere at the same time. He's not limited by time or space, as we and the angels are. But it really doesn't matter. God <u>is</u>; period. That's the name He gave to Moses when asked what He should be

---

[30] Ephesians 2:2 "in which you formerly walked according to the current customs of this world,"
[31] Psalms 139:7 "Where can I go from Your Spirit? Or where can I flee from Your presence?"

called. [32] This is not true of Satan. He still is limited by whatever constraints God put on angels. They can do more than mortal man, but they are yet limited in the spiritual realm. So, how does Satan exercise control over what so many people think and believe?

Satan can clearly go into and possess people; as the book of Revelation reveals on many occasions. And so can demons; as we observed in the previous section. But again, each entity can only be inside one person at a time. Multiple demons can even inhabit one person. But they cannot indwell more than one. Which brings me to my next point. Satan has a horde of demons who follow and obey him. We know from Scripture they amount to one-third of the angels God created to serve Him. [33] While we don't know the actual total number of angels, we know the quantity of them is large enough to be called "a myriad." [34] Since angels were created to be protectors [35] and ministering agents, [36] it's logical there are a limited number, as compared to the world's total population. So, while Satan controls a large army, he's limited by

---

[32] Exodus 3:14 God said to Moses, "I AM WHO I AM;" and He said, "Thus you shall say to the sons of Israel, I AM has sent me to you."
[33] Revelation 12:3-4 "a great red dragon having seven heads and ten horns, and on his heads were seven diadems. And his tail swept away a third of the stars of heaven and threw them down to earth."
[34] Hebrews 12:22 But you have come to Mount Zion and to the city of the living God, the heavenly Jerusalem, and to myriads of angels.
[35] Psalms 34:7 "The angel of the LORD encamps around those who fear Him, and He delivers them."
[36] Hebrews 1:14 "Are not all angels ministering agents sent to serve those who will inherit salvation?"

Jefferson Daniel Seal

an actual number which is insufficient to have his agents everywhere. He needs a force multiplier; and I know he's found one.

As I have done many times, I go back to the original languages of the Bible to study what God actually said to the ones who wrote it down. Man's intellect and viewpoint changes over time. The advancement of technology *slowly* catches up with what God already foreknew; which He had the scribes of the Bible write on the pages of Scripture. Look now at Ephesians 2:2:

> *"in which you formerly walked according to the* **course** *of this world, according to the* **prince** *of the* **power** *of the* **air**, *of the* **spirit** *that is now working in the sons of disobedience."*

This is how the verse appears in the New American Standard version of the Bible. Within the context of the verse, Paul is describing how we have been made alive in Christ, after being dead in our sin and trespasses. That is what he means when he says; "in which you formerly walked according to the **course** of this world. The Greek word used here is **aion** [*ahee-OHN*] and means '*a period of time, age.*' Another way to phrase it would be to say, '*current customs of the day.*' Now, look closely at the next phrase where it reads; "according to the prince of the power of the air," what does that mean?

You can search across all the reference Bibles you can find, searching for an explanation; but nothing I found comes even close to describing what that sentence actually means. Here's what I came up with using the original language:

> *"in which you formerly walked according to the current customs of this world, according to the ruler of the influencers of the airwaves, the voices now working in the sons of disobedience."*

The above verse reflects a literal translation directly from the original Greek. Look up **Ephesians 2:2** in your Bible; it doesn't matter which translation you have. Where you see the word air in your Bible, the original Greek uses the word **aeros**. It's the plural version of the Greek word **aer** [*ah-ayr*] which means simply 'air.' So, the word in your Bible should be translated 'airs' in order to be more correct. Instead of putting the word "airs" in the verse, I chose the word "airwaves." You'll see why shortly, but it's the only word I could think of which would fit logically into the scenario Scripture is giving us. This is yet another reason to go back to the original languages.

There's nothing really *wrong* with the current translation, but I believe it falls short of what God is telling us. The word "airs" or perhaps "atmospheres" doesn't make sense within the <u>context</u> of the verse. I don't think it means demons operate within the

Jefferson Daniel Seal

atmosphere alone. We already know they can work within the spiritual realm, which I believe means they operate *anywhere*. If God indeed meant 'airwaves,' how would the *original* people recording Scripture write the word down if they had no idea what it meant? It's the same way with the Apostle John in Revelation, describing some kind of attack helicopter. He had no way of knowing what it was. I think the scribes had to write "airs" in the text and let God and the Holy Spirit define the term. Now, how would translators write the word? They wrote "air" just as they did. The time for the true meaning hadn't yet arrived.

Since mankind is now getting closer to the end times, God, just as He promised, is slowly unsealing the words of prophecy. So therefore, in light of that knowledge, what would the translators write today? "Airwaves." We now know what airwaves are and the efficiency with which they operate. And we also know how they can be used to quickly propagate propaganda all over the world. Satan is a master manipulator of people, so it makes sense he would take control of the airwaves. We see his hand all over the persons who are working in the field of broadcasting media. Just turn on any news show and watch for more than ten minutes and you'll quickly see what I'm saying. This explains why the term "fake news" is now so prevalent.

Satan Would Be A Democrat

The word for authority used in the verse is **exousias** [*ex-oo-SEE-ahs*] which is also in plural form. The word must therefore mean *'authorities, influencers, or powers.'* So, the ruler mentioned in the verse is over all of those "authorities, influencers or powers," who are the actual persons *controlling* the airwaves. When examined within the context of the verse, I believe the word "influencers" becomes the clear choice. The word used for spirit is **pneuma** [*PNYOO-ma*] and can mean *'breath, wind or spirit.'* The actual word used is once again in plural form; **pneumatos**, [*PNYOO-ma-toes*], and so must mean *'breaths, winds or spirits.* Demons aren't spirits, so we can rule that one out. Using the word "winds" in the verse wouldn't make any sense either. That leaves just "breaths." When we speak, we use our **breaths**; which allows our **voices** to be heard. This led me to conclude the verse means *'people speaking, alluding to their voices.'*

So, what **Ephesians 2:2** is in reality telling us: "Persons who are <u>not</u> aligned with Jesus Christ, are still living their lives according to the current customs of the world, a system ruled and controlled by Satan, the devil. They are conducting their existence according to the world forces of this current darkness, who are controlling the voices on the airwaves. Satan's demons are working among the sons of disobedience—who are persons willingly working under the influence of demonic forces. Those influencers would become the voice of Satan himself! Therefore, just as the Bible prophesied long ago, the modern mass media would be controlled by demons of the airwaves.

Sons of Disobedience

It's a Biblical fact: man is <u>not</u> permitted to interpret Scripture. [37] I know your Bible says; "No prophecy of Scripture... ;" but the translators added in the words: "prophecy of" which are not present within the original text. The Greek word used for **Scripture** is **graphe** [*graf-FAY*] and means '*a writing, a written thing, the Holy Scriptures*.' The word for **Prophecy** used in the second half of the verse is **propheteia** [*prof-fay-TEA-ah*] and means '*any discourse emanating from Divine inspiration and declaring the purposes of God, whether by reproving and admonishing the wicked, <u>or</u> comforting the afflicted, <u>or</u> revealing things hidden; especially via the foretelling of future events*.' So, essentially the whole of Scripture is **propheteia**, and not just the parts we today refer to as prophecy. Every word of the Bible is Divinely inspired, written down by men moved by the Holy Spirit.

As such, there are written rules contained within the verses of the Bible telling us exactly how to figure out what texts mean. Anytime we try to determine or

---

[37] 2 Peter 1:20-21 But know this first of all, that no Scripture is a matter of one's own interpretation, for no prophecy was ever made by an act of human will, but by men moved by the Holy Spirit spoken from God.

confirm the true meaning of Scripture, God has left certain clues to assist us. In my book, How to Study the Bible (available through DWJDMinistries.com) I thoroughly go over and cover in detail each method used to break down Scripture. The bottom line is: Men are not permitted to interpret the verses in the Bible. Not one bit! We must access the Holy Spirit, along with the instructions contained within God's Word to understand what He is saying. God informed us there is a way to properly study and hear His word. And, the Holy Spirit will bring us all to the same point as to the actual meaning of the words in the Bible. If someone is deviating from the Truth, flee from the sound of their voice. [38] Allow me the luxury of giving you one example.

Did you notice the phrase, "the sons of disobedience" at the end of **Ephesians 2:2**, in the last section? We need to figure out what God is telling us. So, we apply our knowledge for how to properly interpret Scripture. We begin with the word for **disobedience**. It is **apeitheia** [*ah-PAY-thee-ah*] and it appears a total of six times in Scripture. It has an interesting definition. It means '*obstinacy towards God, obstinate opposition toward the Divine Will.*' **Obstinate** is defined as '*stubborn refusal to change one's opinion or chosen course of action, despite*

---

[38] Romans 16:17 "I appeal to you, brothers, to watch out for those who cause divisions and create obstacles contrary to doctrine that you have been taught; avoid them."

attempts to persuade one to do so.' You can see this obstinance displayed within the mass media on a daily basis. They fight and rail against anything of or from God.

The phrase "**sons of disobedience**" appears just twice in the Bible. The word for **sons** is **huios** [*hwee-OS*] and here is used to describe '*one who is a follower of another, a pupil or disciple.*' I've reproduced **Ephesians 2:2** here for full context of the phrase.

> *"in which you formerly walked according to the current customs of this world, according to the ruler of the influencers of the airwaves, the voices now working in the sons of disobedience."*

The **sons of disobedience** mentioned in Ephesians are clearly disciples of Satan. By definition, they are '*persons following the lead of someone who is working against the will of God.*' Satan is that being. And Satan is also the ruler of the "influencers of the airwaves," now working **in** the sons of disobedience. The word for **in** is **en** [*en*] and is a preposition meaning '*properly, in (inside, within); figuratively "in the realm (sphere) of.*' So, we have been given a clear picture of satanic forces working within persons who are being influenced by evil.

As you will soon see, God is ever consistent in His word. It's what makes the Bible a truly miraculous document. When two verses containing the same

Satan Would Be A Democrat

phrase are studied together, they can then be used to help explain each other. When we read the second verse in Ephesians containing the exact same phrase, we get immediate affirmation for our work with explaining the meaning of Ephesians 2:2. Look now at **Ephesians 5:6**:

> *"Let no one deceive you with empty words, for because of these things the wrath of God comes upon the sons of disobedience."*

The verse begins with a warning: "Let no one deceive you with empty words." The word for **empty** is **kenos** [*ken-OS*] and means *'morally empty, foolish, worthless, pretentious.'* This is the *only* time where this word appears in the Bible. Let's define each word of its definition separately:

Morally: *'with reference to the principles of right or wrong.'*

Empty: *'(of words or a gesture) lacking meaning or sincerity.'*

Foolish: *'(of a person or action) lacking good sense or judgment; unwise.'*

Worthless: *'(of a person) having no good qualities; deserving contempt.'*

Pretentious: *'attempting to impress by affecting greater importance, talent, culture, etc., that what is actually possessed.'*

Take a moment and study each definition carefully in light of the leaders of the Democrat Party and the content of their platform. Now tell me; aren't those words a perfect description of the Democrat Party's leadership behavior? Let's use the **DPP** statement on a woman's right to reproductive care to evaluate their voices in light of God's Word. Try and use an *open* mind to this approach so you can truly see what *God* says about their words and actions. Ignore any voices, in your head or otherwise, which might attempt to influence your thought process. This is what they wrote concerning woman's reproductive health:

> *"We believe unequivocally, like the majority of Americans, that every woman should have access to quality reproductive health care services, including safe and legal abortion—regardless of where she lives, how much money she makes, or how she is insured."* [**DPP** pg. 33]

So, now I will take each phrase of their statement and break it down via the words used to define the word "empty" in **Ephesians 5:6**:

Morally: *"...including safe and legal abortion—..."* We've discussed this topic already. Abortion is never safe for the unborn baby. And God doesn't care about man's definition of legality. Man's law can *never* override God's Laws. The Bible clearly states in the sixth commandment, using a direct word-for-word

Satan Would Be A Democrat

translation from the Hebrew: "You shall not commit murder." [39] Abortion is the needless killing of an innocent person. This crime of abortion perfectly meets the definition of murder.

Empty: "*...like the majority of Americans...*" God doesn't respect the majority consensus of any public opinion poll. As I discussed before, God is not swayed by what people think. This phrase means nothing before God; and is therefore, devoid of meaning. God says His thoughts are *not* our thoughts. [40] He is God Almighty; the Creator. We are the created.

Foolish: "*Every woman should have access to quality reproductive health care service...*" There isn't any logical and sane person in America who would disagree with this statement. But the truth is; every citizen who wants it already has access to quality reproductive care. There are a lot of FREE programs available for women to obtain OBGYN services. But this does not reflect the reality of what the Democrats are actually saying. Their cloaked affirmation for women's reproductive health care is really a demand for unrestricted access to abortion. And that's what makes it a foolish statement. God is against it. Most American's don't want abortion on demand to be

---

[39] Exodus 20:13 "You shall not commit murder."
[40] Isaiah 55:8 "For My thoughts are not your thoughts, nor are your ways My ways," declares the LORD.

Jefferson Daniel Seal

legal. They have made it abundantly clear at the polls.

Worthless: "...*regardless of where she lives, how much she makes, or how she is insured.*' Looking behind the curtain reveals the Democrats are once again discussing abortion and not simply OBGYN care. The locale where a woman lives has little bearing on the availability of health care. But it can determine whether abortion is legally available to her or not. The retail cost for abortion in the United States ranges from a low of $295 to a high of $3,000. Most insurance companies do not cover abortions. They are viewed as *elective* procedures. But, none of this should ever matter. On demand abortion should *never* be legal, so discussing the where, the how much, and the coverage of it is merely rearranging the deck chairs on the Titanic. Regardless of what avenue the Democrats pursue, it's deemed to be a worthless endeavor before God. The ship still sinks in the end.

Pretentious: "*We believe unequivocally...*" The word **unequivocally** means '*in a way that leaves no doubt.*' The Democrats are attempting to convince American women that they are the Party who is on their side: unequivocally! Just like the majority of Americans! Guess what? Women are <u>the</u> majority of Americans! This statement is attempting to impress their faithful flock in a way which is deceiving; as well as ostentatious. Another inconvenient fact is that most women themselves are <u>not</u> in favor of abortion on

Satan Would Be A Democrat

demand. The manner in which the Democrat Party tries to sell its wares is exaggerated, deceitful and pompous. Who does this sound like to you?

The Bible is clear in its instruction: "Let no one deceive you with empty words, for because of these carefully crafted lies, the wrath of God will fall upon the sons of disobedience." Just like with the law of sowing and reaping, God is promising His rage and anger will be brought down on those who are following the voices of Satan and his demons. Can you begin to see the subterfuge and duplicity of the Democrat Party? Are they not being led by the Father of all Lies? If you can, try and understand you are being duped, swindled and deceived by the best conman there ever was—the devil himself. Should you remain within the crowd of those heeding the lying words of the sons of disobedience, you too will suffer the total wrath of God Almighty in the coming days which lie soon ahead.

Jefferson Daniel Seal

VIII. BRAINWASHING 101

Testing All Voices

Now that we've learned Satan and his demons are the demonic forces behind the majority of the voices on the modern-day airwaves, we must be as wise as serpents to avoid being brainwashed by their messages. [1] This brings up an excellent question: "Surely there are voices on the airwaves devoid of Satan's influence. How do we know which messages are pure, untainted by evil, and come from God?" That's the best question anyone can ask! Since we can observe the Democrats are operating within the realm of Satan, along with a lot of Republicans, Libertarians, Independents, as well as others; every message must be tested to determine its true source. Otherwise, like Adam and Eve, and millions of others, we can be fooled by satanic forces. They are clever and shrewd with their dealings.

The very first thing we can do to avoid being "brainwashed" is not to believe everything we hear on television or read on the Internet. Sounding official is usually a good way to get unsuspecting persons to do your bidding. Satan knows this tactic and uses it often. So do the scam artists, who call up pretending to be detectives, police officers or some other form of law enforcement. The Bible tells us to <u>not</u> believe

---

[1] Matthew 10:16 "Behold, I send you out as sheep in the midst of wolves; so be shrewd as serpents and innocent as doves."

Jefferson Daniel Seal

every voice we hear. [2] The word used in the verse is **pneumati** [*PNYOO-mah-tea*] and means '*wind, breath, spirit.*' As before, I translated it "voice." But, there's a double meaning here. Every voice has a brain behind it. And that brain is potentially controlled by either God or a demonic being. Hence the Bible warning to "test all the voices to determine whether they are from God, or not." [3]

The reason for this warning is God is well aware Satan and his horde are placing men under psychological attack. The definition of the word **brainwashing** is '*the process of pressuring someone into adopting radically different beliefs by using systematic and often forcible means.*' The description of the process of brainwashing by referring to it as "**systematic**" is right on course. This word is defined to mean '*done or acting according to a fixed plan or system; methodical.*' This is precisely what Satan is utilizing; a methodical approach to implementing his plan. He hasn't really changed tactics over the thousands of years he's been assailing mankind. We see the very same systematic approach being utilized within the Democrat Party. The term we would use today is "Progressive." This book has been describing their process since the first page.

So, why would God be worried about people being brainwashed? It's because He loves mankind and

---

[2] 1 John 4:1 "Beloved, do not believe every voice."
[3] 1 John 4:1 "but test the voices to see whether they are from God."

Satan Would Be A Democrat

doesn't want to lose a single person to the Lake of Fire.[4] The word for perish is **apolesthai** [*ap-POL-less-stigh*] and means '*utterly destroyed, cut off entirely (from God).*' God is well aware Satan can radically influence persons toward his evil side of the balance sheet. It all began with Adam and Eve. So, our Heavenly Father warns us "that many false prophets have gone out into the world."[5] The Bible uses one word for false prophets, it is **pseudoprophetai** [*psyoo-coe-prof-FEY-tie*] and means '*pseudo prophets.*' The word **pseudo** means '*not genuine; spurious or sham.*' Isn't this word definition a perfect description of the persons we've been discussing? It can also mean '*a pretentious or insincere person.*' Again, isn't this an apt description of those leading the Democrat Party? Unless you're still among those drinking Satan's Kool aide, you know the answer.

The second half of the word is "prophets." A **prophet** is '*anyone who makes predictions, laying claim to their absolute veracity.*' A prophet or their message does not have to be somehow related to God and the Bible. All they need be is someone pretending to speak words of truth, but in fact are phonies and imposters. Modern day leaders of the Democrat Party are indeed such charlatans. They specialize in the art of misimpression that they are

---

[4] 2 Peter 3:9 The LORD is not slow to fulfill His promise as some understand slowness, but is patient with you, not wanting anyone to perish but for everyone to come to repentance.
[5] 1 John 4:1 "because many false prophets have gone out into the world."

Jefferson Daniel Seal

somehow working for the benefit of the world with their message. When in fact, they are actually operating for self-benefit or for the promotion of their benefactor. In chapter six, I outlined many of the modern-day predictions of those associated with the Democrat Party agenda. Every person was issuing dire warnings of calamities to come, strongly asserting the accuracy of their message. In the end, they've all been proven false by both science and reality.

The good news is the Bible informs us how to determine if a voice comes from God or not. Every voice which confesses that Jesus Christ has come in the flesh is from God. [6] Essentially, any person who willingly will state: Jesus Christ is God's one and only Son, was born of a virgin, and came down to Earth in human form, is from God. It's the message of the Gospel. If they are willing to publicly admit it, they are from God. If they refuse to do so, or skate around the issue as being irrelevant or immaterial; they are not from God. [7] The Bible says such is the voice of the antichrist, who we've been warned is soon coming, and the voice of whom is already present within this world. There is only one power capable of seeing the future—and it's God Almighty. Any other prophet by definition is a false or pseudo prophet.

---

[6] 1 John 4:2 "By this you know the Voice of God: every voice that confesses that Jesus Christ has come in the flesh is from God."
[7] 1 John 4:3 "and every voice that does not confess Jesus is from God; this is the voice of the antichrist, of which you have already heard that it is coming, and now it is already in the world."

Satan Would Be A Democrat

That's why I have labored to examine the **DPP** in light of the Holy Word of God. As you can plainly see for yourself, every tenet of their document flies in the opposite direction of Biblical guidance. Look at the following sentences. We'll examine it against Biblical principles:

> *"Our values of inclusion and tolerance inspire hope around the world and make us safer at home."* [**DPP** pg. 40]

First off, as we've already proven, God is not about inclusion and tolerance. **Inclusion** is '*the practice or providing equal access to opportunities and resources for people who might otherwise be excluded or marginalized.* God is absolutely for inclusion; but only on <u>His</u> terms. God requires repentance, or a change of ways for a person to be *included*. The Democrats demand no such change, but rather embrace people as they are. See the BIG difference between the two viewpoints? Also, **tolerance** is defined as '*the willingness to tolerate sin, expressed in the opinions and/or behavior of one that does not necessarily agree with God's law.*'

Clearly, God's standards are not negotiable. **Sin** is by definition '*any activity violating God's Law.*' So, why would ignoring God's Law inspire hope around the world? By using the words of anti-God propaganda, the Democrats are giving false hope to those persons who have no interest in following God.

It's deliberately misleading and quite deceitful. And, I guarantee the safety and security of these United States is far from being made safer by such policies. Satan hates the United States. I suppose the Democrats believe that were the U.S. to become a total pagan nation, Satan's forces would then leave us alone. That's an entirely wrong conclusion. All we need do is look at the Roman Republic. It was destroyed by Satanic forces under the hand of Islam. Who really thinks the same fate doesn't await America; were we to abandon our faith in God?

God is telling us the time when the entire world will be brainwashed by the antichrist has not yet arrived. There is yet time to avoid being fooled by the greatest con artist of all time; the devil. Paul told us to "Let no one deceive you in any way, for it [the brainwashing] will not come until the Tribulation begins when the antichrist is revealed." [8] That day is coming. You can read my other books to discover the date. As of the publication date of this book, it's only fourteen short years away. That's less than a decade and a half. Now mind you, this is not my prophecy, but rather God's prophecy, which comes directly out of His Word. That's the only way to explain how I can identify any dates in the future. It is entirely God's

---

[8] 2 Thessalonians 2:3 "Let no one deceive you in any way, for it [The Tribulation] will not arrive until the rebellion occurs and the man of lawlessness (the son of destruction) [aka the antichrist] is revealed."

prophecy. Here's another pseudo prophecy by the Democrat Party:

"The world will be more secure, stable, and peaceful when all people are able to reach their God-given potential and live in freedom and dignity." [**DPP** pg. 40]

Under their leadership, the Democrats are predicting the world will become a more peaceful arena, whereby all people will be safe. They even invoke the name of God. That prophetic message really sounds nice, right? God Himself predicted such a message would emanate from the voices of mankind. Look now at **1st Thessalonians 5:3**:

"While they are saying, 'Peace and safety!' then destruction will come upon them suddenly like labor pains upon a woman with child, and they will not escape."

The Bible clearly tells us the End Times are anything but peaceful and secure. It says the Great Tribulation will be the worst time in the whole of human history. The Antichrist will remove all person's freedom by demanding they take his mark and worship him. Where's the dignity in being beheaded for those who refuse to comply? The only solution is to become a believer in and follower of Jesus. We must heed only the real Words of God Almighty. Begin testing all the voices you hear to find and discover the Truth!

Israel's Right to Exist

God always issues warnings to mankind of coming times of trouble. While the world (via the Democrat Party) is currently predicting peace and safety; just the opposite situation is instead rapidly coming down the pike towards humanity. The people of this world are speeding down a long, wide freeway, happily driving along, believing the well-placed lies of Satan telling them that everything is on the path towards a higher good. In truth, they are driving past all the warning signs lining the side of the road, informing them the major highway bridge just ahead over the "Gorge of Eternity" is out! Satan and his demonic hoard keep removing and concealing all the cones and barricades which God's people place along the road. Once more, please open your mind to the greatest con in history. It's being played out right before your very eyes!

God says the prophesied destruction will come upon the world suddenly; like labor pains upon a pregnant woman. The analogy of a pregnant woman describes quite graphically how things approaching the End Times are going to play out. First of all, a woman who conceives a baby will soon afterwards know she is pregnant. The baby slowly growing inside her will reach a size where he or she can no longer be missed. The "End Times" or the "End of this Age" officially started on God's stopwatch on 14 May 1948, when the Nation of Israel appeared again on the map.

Satan Would Be A Democrat

This event was predicted over 3,000 years ahead of time and came to pass on the <u>very</u> day it was prophesied. When you read of the mathematical precision God employed in His calculations, you will be astounded and in awe of His regal power. Read "<u>The End is Near—and God will Prove It</u>" for all the details. That was the first modern-day prophesied date to come to pass; with many more soon to follow!

Secondly, a pregnant woman knows the approximate time when she is due to deliver. The normal period of gestation is usually nine months. The mother has a rough idea of how long she has until the baby comes. And until her labor begins, she can carry on with her life relatively unconcerned with the baby. She can see her bump grow and even feel the baby moving inside her. This describes people of the world today. They can physically see the nation of Israel. They can feel the turmoil in the Middle East making headlines on an almost weekly basis. So, the mention of Israel is nearly continuous within all elements of the media. Most religions teach the significance of Israel's reappearance is THE major prophetic sign marking the beginning of the end.

Satan meanwhile, via his political parties all around the world, are each denying Israel's right to even exist! They lay claim to Israel being an illegitimate state and unlawfully founded. They say, "the Jews stole the land." The Arab countries surrounding Israel have attacked her repeatedly over the seventy years she's been a nation; all the while openly calling for the annihilation of the Hebrew people. A hefty significant number of Jewish Americans are members of the Democrat Party. The result is the Democrat Party is clever in the fact they don't undertake hostile action against Israel openly. Look at what they say instead in the 2016 Platform:

> *"A strong and secure Israel is vital to the United States because we share overarching strategic interests and the common values of democracy, equality, tolerance, and pluralism."* [**DPP** pg. 45]

But again, don't let their lies fool you. This is just another ploy to placate some within their ranks. This particular phrase is buried deep within a paragraph which begins by first calling for more support of Israel's enemies. The Democrats would have the United States give aid to those countries under the guise of helping refugees, seeking greater economic opportunity and freedom. Of course, the Dem's can't resist sticking two foul words on the end of what would be a good sentence: tolerance and pluralism.

I've already defined tolerance. **Pluralism** is *'a political theory calling for power sharing among a number of political parties.'* For the noninitiated, the Democrat Party is calling for Israel to share power with the Palestinians over the same territory—the land which has belonged to Israel alone over the past 4,000 years. Despite their name, the Palestinians have <u>zero</u> historical claim to Palestine. This is equivalent to the United States agreeing to share power with the horde of illegal aliens who have infiltrated the border. Palestinians have <u>zero</u> historic rights to the land of Israel as a group. But, is that what the Democratic Party calls for in their 2016 platform manifesto? Read for yourself:

> *"That is why we will always support Israel's right to defend itself, including by retaining its qualitative military edge, and oppose any effort to delegitimize Israel, including at the United Nations or through the Boycott, Divestment, and Sanctions Movement."* [**DPP** pg. 44]

How many of you reading this book are familiar with the Boycott, Divestment, and Sanctions Movement (BDS)? As you can see for yourself, the Democrat Party is clearly on record as being <u>opposed</u> to any effort to implement it. Now for the rest of the story!

BDS is a Palestinian-led campaign promoting various forms of economic boycott against Israel. Essentially, they are calling for withdrawal from disputed territories, removal of the barrier in the West Bank, and the previously described "Right of Return." [page 108] **<u>Nineteen</u>** Democrat Party members of the United States congress introduced legislation attempting to pass BDS into law, despite 37 states already having regulations on the books specifically *outlawing* BDS. Type the following link into your browser to examine this for yourself.

https://www.congress.gov/bill/116th-congress/house-resolution/496/text.

For those of you doing the math, this equates to ten percent of the Democrat representatives elected to Congress! Four of the members have identified themselves as "The Squad" due to their particularly offensive progressive agenda and antisemitic stands. The likely origin of the term "Squad" comes from a hip-hop group called Terror Squad originating from the Bronx. Since the leader of "The Squad" is from there and has self-identified herself with the term, few people believe the moniker to be either inaccurate or an imprecise description of "The Squad's" true purposes in Congress.

Shamefully, the Democrat controlled Congress stood by and did absolutely nothing. They did not censure or condemn any of the leaders or cosponsors who introduced the bill. The reason is simple: They are in reality *not* opposed to the legislation. In their view, the only problem is that it was introduced too early to be palatable to the American people. Satan knows what he wants and that's why "The Squad" was not chastised or reprimanded in any manner following their attempt at punishing Israel. Instead, we read of more lies in the **DPP**:

> *"We will continue to work toward a two-state solution of the Israeli-Palestinian*

conflict negotiated directly by the parties that guarantees Israel's future as a secure and democratic Jewish state with recognized borders and provides the Palestinians with independence, sovereignty, and dignity." [**DPP** pg. 45]

The Democrat Party is not going to stop their sneaky and sleazy attempts at delegitimizing and destabilizing the nation of Israel. Their call for a "Two-State Solution" is disingenuous; fully knowing it will <u>never</u> happen on their terms. The reason is; both sides are *vehemently* opposed to the idea. Why? It's due to both Israel and the Palestinians want *Jerusalem* as their capital city. Israel is on record saying it will *never* agree to any deal which sees Jerusalem shared or divided in any way. On the other side, the Palestinians say they will not cede their claim and access to their holy sites, <u>all</u> of which are located in East Jerusalem.

Despite all the grandstanding, the Bible says there will soon be a peace treaty between the two sides; but no one apart from God can foretell the details of it. All we know is it will be "a firm treaty." Particulars of which only the man who brokers the peace deal will know. He will be the man the Bible calls "The Antichrist." What do you bet he's a politician from out of the Democrat Party? I already know who he is; and you can too. Just pick up a copy of my book: **<u>The Antichrist Revealed</u>** off the website. The Democrats are ever hedging their bets, while attempting to sound like they support Israel. The simple truth is Satan hates Jerusalem and Israel; and will do everything in his power to destroy the state of Israel and the Jewish people. Just look at the statements and actions of nearly all the countries in the Middle East. The reason is they are fully under the control of Satan and his Islamic religion. Do you disagree? Let's look at just <u>one</u> of the facts.

The third most holy shrine in Islam is the Dome of the Rock. It's an eight-sided building (octagon) which sits squarely over Israel's most holy site—the foundation stone of Solomon's Temple. On the inside of each wall of the Islamic Temple is an inscription from the Koran. Each verse hanging on each of the eight walls, outright denies the existence of Jesus Christ, as God's only Son. This is why the Bible describes this building as: "The Abomination which causes desolation." [9] Satan will *never* willingly agree to surrender the building. That's why when the man known as the Antichrist is seen standing in the rebuilt Jewish Temple, it will have replaced the Mosque currently sitting in its place. Again, the Democrats shield their true intentions with flowery words of praise for all people of faiths.

---

[9] Matthew 24:15 "Therefore when you see the ABOMINATION OF DESOLATION which was spoken of through Daniel the prophet, standing in the holy place."

"While Jerusalem is a matter for final status negotiations, it should remain the capital of Israel, an undivided city accessible to people of all faiths. Israelis deserve security, recognition, and a normal life free from terror and incitement. Palestinians should be free to govern themselves in their own viable state, in peace and dignity." [**DPP** pg. 45]

The simple truth is the Democrat Party's words continue to belie their true intentions. But I've always advocated to judge a person's true intentions *not* by what they say; but always by what they do and how they behave. The only exception to my rule is: "If you have enough history with a person and have learned to trust their words because they match their every action—then do it."

The Democrat Party says all the right things; saying Israel has a right to defend herself, that they are a vital ally to the United States, worthy of having undisputed borders as well as an undivided capital city. But by closely examining what the Democrats and their supporting organizations are actually doing, reveals an entirely different reality. Their actions match their real agenda. Their words are lies; Satan and his hordes are working day and night to remove Israel's right to exist within this world.

Jefferson Daniel Seal

Major Labor Pains

Denying the legitimacy of a thing is another key tactic employed by the Democrat Party. **Legitimacy** is defined as *'the ability to be defended with logic or justification.'* Thus, if the legitimacy of someone or something is denied, then there's no logical reason to rise to their defense. As you watch the media, pay careful attention to the words being spoken about the people and things which the Democrats are opposed to. You will see time and again this same tactic employed: they deny the legitimacy of their enemies. As the political season for 2020 approaches, the Democrats are frantic with trying to deny the legitimacy of President Trump. They are using every lie and invented falsehood to try and impeach him. Why? It's because they already suspect he will easily win reelection; should they be unable to discover a way to remove him prior to the voting.

I don't think it was by accident Jesus compared the biggest sign marking the start of the "End of the Age" to a woman's labor pains. I know for a fact God does nothing by chance. The Democrat Party affirmation: "Abortion is a woman's right to choose," is an example of using this tactic. By stating "a woman has the right to choose," they make it sound like there's multiple choices, of which are all equal. A *pregnant* woman has essentially two choices: 1) carry the baby to full term, or 2) abort the pregnancy. They will offer many reasons as to why she might want to make the

Satan Would Be A Democrat

second choice. Perhaps, she's not ready to begin raising children; she might be unmarried and financially unable to bear the burden; or any host of other reasonable sounding justifications for not having a baby. By focusing on just the woman and *her* desires; it's easy to forget the other person in the equation: the baby. This is the first step to denying the baby's legitimacy.

The baby is still a person, who just hasn't developed enough within the womb to be able to survive on their own. The Bible is clear: God names people from conception, and not only after their birth. Both John the Baptist, and Jesus were named while early on in the womb. God told Abraham he was to name his son Isaac well before he was even conceived. [10] Those who are in favor of abortion instead refuse to acknowledge there's even a baby involved. They will refer to the unborn person as anything but. They will use terms such as "fetus," "embryo," "zygote" or "fertilized egg;" purposely avoiding the use of any term which indicates it's a baby, child or person. By denying the legitimacy of the unborn, they can then ignore the person's right to exist. Democrats never actually go on to say anything bad about babies or children. Nope, that would be the bad, sad truth—something they can't afford to do.

---

[10] Genesis 17:19 But God said, "No, but Sarah your wife will bear you a son, and you shall call his name Isaac;"

Instead, they just ignore the rights of the unborn baby by denying it's a legitimate person.

The effect of denying the legitimacy of the unborn is to place the _rights_ of the unborn child below the _wishes_ of the mother. A **right** is defined as '_that which is morally correct, just or honorable._' A **wish** or **desire** is '_a strong feeling of wanting something (or not) or for something to happen (or not)._' A desire on the part of one person falls far below the rights of another. Our judicial and legal system is based on the principles found in the Biblical Ten Commandments, which totally affirm God's Law. And, by delegitimizing the child, they remove their right to even exist. By the way, _no_ mother has the unimpeded right to determine whether her baby lives or dies. In the very rare cases where a pregnancy puts the life of the mother in mortal danger, we can all admit the mother's right to live then outweighs that of her unborn baby. Back in the Garden of Eden, Satan questioned the legitimacy of God's word, while prodding Eve to sin. [11] This is an age-old tactic still being employed daily.

Jesus in His remarks on the "End of the Age," described the coming turmoil preceding the Great Tribulation as "merely the beginning of birth pains." [12] Labor pains are what nature uses to signal to the

---

[11] Genesis 3:4 The serpent said to the woman, "You surely will not die!"
[12] Matthew 24:8 "But all these things are merely the beginning of birth pangs."

expecting mother that the birth of her baby is at hand. The closer the baby gets to their birth, the more intense the labor pains become. They also come more frequently, adding to the mother's overall pain and discomfort. The approach of the end of this age is taking shape to model a woman's delivery. The delivery of the baby is akin to the conveyance of destruction upon the sons of disobedience. The Greek word for **destruction** is **olethros** [*OL-leth-ross*] and means '*death, doom, ruination.*' The end of Satan and his followers will soon be coming. The end is now in sight. As of the publication date of this book, the bodily return of Jesus Christ is only twenty-one years away.

As you watch the signs prophesied to precede the return of Jesus, notice that since the rebirth of Israel, they have begun to both multiply and intensify.[13] The world today is in a different place than where it was back in 1948. A person can certainly ignore the prophetic signs present in the world today, but they do so at their peril. This is yet another area where Satan attempts to deny legitimacy: "End Times Prophecy." By attacking those who are preaching the soon arrival of the end of Adam's race, by heralding the message of "the end is near," the devil is seeking to silence those voices, by drowning them out in a sea of voices of his own making. We have already shown where the mass media is already nearly universally

---

[13] Matthew 24:1-14 Please read the verses using your own Bible.

controlled by Satan. He controls the Democrats, and they control the vast majority of the media. Just today, a whistleblower from within CNN, gave irrefutable video proof of the clear bias of the CEO of the network. Satan will not stop at any means to silence God's voices—whoever they are.

The only true way to determine the truth is go to the sole source proven to be an untainted repository: The Holy Bible. Anything which agrees with the Word of God is accurate and thereby truth. Anything which goes opposite or conflicts with it in any way, is therefore a falsehood or lie. It really is that simple. The Bible predicted the emergence of the Nation of Israel from out of antiquity. Not only that, but God intricately prophesied the date would fall exactly 932,400 days *after* He put them into captivity. God counts the day they went into captivity, plus all the days in between, and adds in the day they declared their freedom to arrive at His total. The Israeli declaration of Independence happened precisely 2,590 Biblical years (360 days/year) after God allowed King Nebuchadnezzar to remove their sovereignty. God foreknew the future and named the moment of their release right down to the very day. Of course, Satan doesn't want you to know that. So, he instead seeks to delegitimize the Nation of Israel itself.

Get all the facts before you decide what's correct concerning Israel. Allow me to present a few relevant particulars here on these pages. **1. The Hebrew** people are the only persons to reemerge out of the ashes of antiquity with the same genetic makeup as what they had before. Apart from the Jewish race, this has never happened before. The modern-day Jews are the direct descendants of the tribe of Israel. They have the DNA to prove it. **2. The land of Israel was given to them by God Himself, way back before any current tribe or group of people might have been living in the area.** In case you didn't know, God gave them the Promised Land forever. After the American Civil War, the famous American writer Samuel Clemens (Mark Twain), traveled to the Promised Land to write a series of articles for a San Francisco newspaper. In many of these letters, he detailed how the Promised Land was all but devoid of people. He wrote "a person could travel for days, nary seeing any person." This is consistent with all written records from than time.

There was no thriving local population which the Jews replaced when they began emigrating from other countries shortly after Clemens's letters were published. **3. The Jews began their return to Israel, largely beginning in the late 1800's, continuing right up to the present time.** As the Jews moved in, *purchasing* the lands they used for farming and ranching, laborers from surrounding areas began to come to Israel to find work. Just as with America, these poorer workers had a higher birthrate than did the wealthier landowners. The population of the

Promised Land burgeoned with the returning Jews, as well as with the laborers from adjoining lands. No land was stolen from the Palestinians or Arabs as the lies of Satan will state. The Jewish population continued to grow and flourish.

After WWI, with the defeat of the Turks, the British were given mandate over the land of Palestine. Their job was to administratively govern the geographic area and provide for security. With all the infighting between Arabs and Jews, the British found themselves expending lots of blood and treasure; all for a whole bunch of nothing. Israel didn't have any of the oil, gas and natural resources other middle east areas contained. While their mandate was set to expire in November of 1948, the Brit's made plans to depart early to avoid more bloodshed and violence. So, they secretly began preparation to leave on May 15th, 1948. **4. The Jews got wind of the British plan and instead declared her independence at 5 PM on the day before.** The fateful date was: May 14th, 1948. They unwittingly did it on the very day which God had prophetically ordained. They were unable to do it on the actual date the British departed, as it was the Sabbath and was forbidden for performing any work.

Another 40 years would pass before the world learned of the symmetry of God's planning. Despite what those following Satan might say, the timing of the Israeli independence could not have been an event planned by men—as they didn't know about

Satan Would Be A Democrat

the prophesied date prior to their declaration. Now that we can see the timing, it makes uncovering other prophetic dates very easy. This forms the basis for the prophecy you will see revealed within my other books. God alone foreknew all the events I write about. And it was His Holy Spirit which kept the timing secret until the time of the end was approaching. God's prophetic stopwatch was started on the 14th of May 1948. The long prophesied major labor pains marking the beginning of man's end, as revealed by Jesus, could now begin.

Time of Jacob's Trouble

People of this age should know we are approaching the period the Bible calls, "The time of Jacob's Trouble." God Himself is the One who makes the following guarantee: "Of all the epochs experienced by the Human Race, this soon coming time of trouble will be the worst of them all." [14] The Great Tribulation is going to be more terrible than even the Great Flood of Noah's time. Recall during the worldwide deluge of water, all of humanity was drowned except for the eight persons contained safely within the Ark. Jesus said of the coming age; "Were God to not intervene—ALL of human life would be ended during the seven years of

---

[14] Matthew 24:21 "For then there will be a great tribulation, such as has not occurred since the beginning of the world until now, nor ever will."

Jefferson Daniel Seal

Tribulation." [15] But you are unlikely to ever hear any such things mentioned on any prominent newscast. Satan will simply not allow it.

We can and should expect the world system controlled by Satan to spend every possible resource denying any information about a coming Tribulation. They will describe such reports as nonsense and fairy tales, conjured up from within the minds of delusionary religious folks. The demonic forces will attempt to cast dispersion and doubt upon any of God's prophets speaking out about what is soon to come. Despite the amazing prophecies which have already come true, the world media chooses to ignore such miracles. Instead, they divert and dilute man's attention by focusing on garbage and falsehoods. They will devote endless hours to the discussion of the predictions of frauds; such as Nostradamus and Jeane Dixon. Numerous television shows and documentaries deliberate the existence of aliens from other solar systems; while others examine the dark world of paranormal manifestations; all without one single shred of proof.

It would seem man is interested in listening to practically anyone talk about almost *anything*, so long as Godly truth isn't part of the discussion. It's even reached the point; where the more ridiculous or frivolous the theory, the more rapt attention the

---

[15] Matthew 24:22 "Unless those days had been cut short, no life would have been saved."

Satan Would Be A Democrat

media heaps upon it. This carefully managed and manipulated news, winds up creating celebrities out of persons, whose only claim to fame is some inconsequential conjecture or speculation. Watch the media for any length of time and you'll see that's a fact. Yet, despite all the shortcomings, these persons are held by the media in much higher regard than God's prophets. They will attempt—just as I discussed herein—to delegitimize any persons who try and speak the truth as found within the word of God. They will vehemently deny the end of the world is at hand; and arrogantly do it using all available resources. But, that's not what God spoke to the prophet Jeremiah. [16] Jeremiah was the one who warned of the coming time of Jacob's trouble.

The prophet Jeremiah was the son of Hilkiah, a Jewish priest from the tribe of Benjamin. [17] He lived in the 7th century BC, before the tribe of Israel was cast into captivity by Nebuchadnezzar in 606 BC. [18] Jeremiah had been called into prophetic ministry twenty years earlier, to warn the Hebrew people of God's coming Judgment. Notice from reading the footnote, God knew Jeremiah before he was even conceived. And, He consecrated Jeremiah as a

---

[16] Jeremiah 30:1 This is the word that came to Jeremiah from the LORD:
[17] Jeremiah 1:1 The words of Jeremiah the son of Hilkiah, of the priests who were in Anathoth in the land of Benjamin,
[18] Jeremiah 1:2 to whom the word of the LORD came in the days of Josiah the son of Amon, king of Judah, in the thirteenth year of his reign.

Jefferson Daniel Seal

prophet prior to his birth! [19] His task was to warn them of the coming destruction of Jerusalem, prophesied to occur nineteen years after the Hebrews went back into slavery. This was due to the nation of Israel's unfaithfulness to the laws of the covenant, and their open worship of Baal. Jeremiah condemned the Jews for their sin and iniquity before God. The LORD instructed Jeremiah to make a wooden yoke to represent the warning God was placing them into captivity. [20] When the other prophets *opposed* his message, God exchanged a breakable wooden yoke for one made of iron! [21]

Just as man cannot change the Word of God, neither can he change history; although Satan attempts to do so every day. All of the prophecies Jeremiah spoke of concerning Israel came to pass, exactly on the timetable laid out by God. King Nebuchadnezzar, of the Babylonians, invaded three times, and on each occasion removed one of the three elements of the nation's freedom. The first visit saw their sovereignty removed. The next trip saw the Hebrew security taken away. And, on their final jaunt, the Babylonians eliminated the Hebrew's ability to

---

[19] Jeremiah 1:5 "Before I formed you in the womb I knew you, And before you were born I consecrated you; I have appointed you a prophet to the nations.

[20] Jeremiah 27:2 Thus says the LORD to me; "Make for yourself bonds and yokes and put them on your neck,"

[21] Jeremiah 28:13 "Go and speak to Hananiah, saying, 'Thus says the LORD, "You have broken the yokes of wood, but you have made instead of them yokes of iron."

Satan Would Be A Democrat

worship; by destroying first Solomon's Temple and shortly thereafter the entire city of Jerusalem itself, to include the walls and gates.

God then spoke to Jeremiah of Israel's eventual scattering over all the globe. And He told of their restoration from her "Diaspora." The word "Diaspora" refers to the 25 centuries-long Jewish hiatus from the Promised Land. The word **Diaspora** is a transliteration of the Greek word **diaspeiro** [*dee-as-PIE-row*] meaning '*to sow throughout, distribute in foreign lands, scatter abroad like one would strew seed for farming.*' The scattering of the Hebrew people following the three Babylonian invasions was the fulfillment of that prophecy. The Jews remained dispersed for over 2,500 years before God brought them back together again. They returned to their homeland in 1948 with the creation of the nation of Israel. Exactly as the prophet Jeremiah was told by God to write in a book the words spoken by Him. [22]

God then foretold the people of Israel would come back from their captivity and be restored into their historical homeland. [23] This happened on 14 May 1948. By the way, secular historians have recently begun propagating the lie which alleges Israel was formed solely by a United Nations Mandate. Nothing

---

[22] Jeremiah 30:2 "This is what the LORD, the God of Israel, says: 'Write in a book all the words I have spoken to you."

[23] Jeremiah 30:3 "The days are coming," declares the LORD, "when I will bring my people Israel and Judah back from captivity and restore them to the land I gave their ancestors to possess," says the LORD.

could be further from the truth. Just as I reported, history proves the Jews declared her independence on a Friday and began waging a war of survival the very next day. The nation's freedom was secured and forged by God in a hail of Arab gunfire. The British did issue a document thirty years earlier, now called "the Balfour Declaration," back on the 2nd of November 1917. It was a public statement announcing only *support* for the establishment of a national home for the Jewish people in Palestine. This represented the first public expression of support for Zionism by a major political power; but set no timetable for action.

Following the end of WWI, the British were awarded control over the area of Palestine for the purposes of providing overall security as well as administrative control. The allies had defeated the Ottoman Empire; and Britain and France split control over the area called "Palestine." For the next three decades, the British struggled with their attempts at managing their area; they did an adequate job despite being in the midst of fighting for survival during WWII. After the end of world-wide hostilities, the United Nations in 1947, decided to forcibly implement a partition plan which no side wanted for the region. They basically attempted to split up the nation we today recognize as Israel, into arbitrary, randomly selected segments. The date for establishing the partition plan was on 1 August 1948.

The Brits quickly realized this would never be

acceptable to either side, and began making plans to leave, before more of their blood and treasure was wasted. The reasons for their decision were explained in His Majesty's Principle Secretary for Foreign Affairs in a secretly delivered speech to the House of Commons on 18 February 1947. In his remarks he said:

> "His Majesty's Government have been faced with an irreconcilable conflict of principles. There are in Palestine about 1,200,000 Arabs and 600,000 Jews. For the Jews the essential point of principle is the creation of a sovereign Jewish State. For the Arabs, the essential point of principle is to resist to the last man, establishment of Jewish sovereignty in any part of Palestine."

He went on to state the discussions between Arab and Jew clearly have no prospect of resolution by any settlement which can be negotiated. Britain was given a mandate without an expiration date. Mandates were intended to end upon the independence of the mandated territory. The British government had taken the position there was nothing in law to prevent termination due to frustration of purpose.

The British knew there would be widespread violence and even war, were the partition plan to be implemented and applied, just as it had been preconceived. The Jews had a long history of living in squalor; the only thing keeping them going was the dream of returning to their blessed Promised Land. No U.N. commission could take that away from them. So, the Brits quickly agreed to the withdrawal date of 1 August 1948. But they stated a piecemeal departure of their people would be highly risky to their interests at best. Once the withdrawal of military forces was underway, law and order could no longer be provided, and security of British citizens could not be guaranteed. So, the British selected a date well in advance of 1 August 1948 in which to depart. They had in mind the 15th of May 1948. To preclude violence, they kept the date secret, subject to further negotiations with the United Nations.

However, the Hebrew Intelligence agency, Haganah, quickly learned of the planned early departure and informed senior Jewish leaders; who then made plans of their own. They decided to declare their independence one day prior to the British withdrawal; ignoring the UN Partition Plan. They knew the Promised Land belonged to them alone. No one could take it from them. God had made an unbreakable promise to Abraham. Little did they know, but these Hebrew patriots were unwittingly fulfilling a major prophecy straight out of God's word. They were going to reestablish the nation of Israel after being absent from the world stage for nearly 2,600 years. It was time to start the stopwatch counting down to the time of Jacob's trouble.

IX. BREAKING FREE FROM SATAN

Jesus Alone is LORD

As you've hopefully endeavored to carefully read and study the preceding information, it is my fervent prayer you've reached a fair-minded and proper conclusion: "The modern Democrat Party is being led by none other than Satan himself." Any person of sound mind using rational thought, prudently examining the evidence provided herein, would be hard pressed to arrive at a different finding. And, if indeed it truly is Satan leading the adherents of the Democrat Party down the proverbial primrose path, the next question which must be asked is: "Just exactly *where* is he leading them?" Well, there's only one place Satan and his horde will guide mankind, and that's in <u>any</u> direction steering away from the word of God. He will do anything to stop people from hearing the Good News of Jesus Christ.

The Bible teaches there is *only* one way to get to Heaven; and it is through God's Son, Jesus. [1] There is no other way: not by Islam, not via Buddhism, nor thru Hinduism. The <u>only</u> road leading to God the Father, runs directly through Jesus. Jesus is the <u>only</u> path. Every other route or direction is a waste of your time and energy. As such, Satan is going to fight tooth and nail to stop any word of Jesus from being spread

---

[1] John 14:6 Jesus answered, "I am the way and the truth and the life. No one comes to the Father except through me."

anywhere around the globe. Jesus was very specific; He said if we knew Him, we would know God the Father as well. [2] Thus, it makes sense Satan and his demonic horde will allow other religions to talk all about God; so long as they don't mention Jesus in the light of being God's only Son. He can be a prophet, He can be a good teacher, He can be a famous Rabbi; it doesn't matter. They just will never equate Jesus with being God. The reason for doing this? It's because apart from acknowledging Jesus as equal with God Himself, the channel to God the Father is blocked. Jesus _is_ the pathway to the Father.

Paul, in his writings to the Philippians, made it clear: "Christ Jesus, who being in the form of God, did not consider it _robbery_ for Himself to be equal with God." [3] The word for **robbery** used in the text is the Greek word **harpagmon** [_har-pag-MON_]. This is the only time it's used in Scripture. It means '_the act of seizing for one's own use, robbery_.' Today we'd use the term "_stolen honor_" to discuss such an act. But Jesus was not stealing any of God's honor or glory by laying claim to being equal with God. Instead, He made it known, He intentionally emptied Himself, willingly taking on the position of a slave, to be made

---

[2] John 14:7 "If you really know me, you will know my Father as well."
[3] Philippians 2:5-6 "Let this attitude be in yourselves, which was also in Christ Jesus, who although existing in the form of God, did not consider it to be robbery to be equal with God."

Satan Would Be A Democrat

in the likeness of humans. [4] Thus, it cannot be denied; while Jesus willingly accepted such an infinitesimally lower position in God's cosmos, He did not relinquish His role as being fully God, equal to God the Father. Jesus, as God, took on the flesh of a man, humbling Himself to the point of death; execution on a cruel cross by crucifixion, for the sole purpose of saving mankind. [5] Friends, I ask you to seriously consider; "Is there any greater *humility* than that?"

Due to the completely selfless act of Jesus, our salvation hinges on Him alone. No one else could have done what He did. That's why there's no other name whereby men might be saved. The Bible says God "highly exalted Jesus," bestowing upon Him a name which is above every other name. [6] God awarded Jesus the highest possible honor; the result of His willing sacrifice for mankind. But with God's affirmation also comes a prophetic warning. "So, at the name of Jesus, EVERY KNEE WILL BOW, of those who are in heaven and on earth and under the earth." [7] In case you were unsure, that list includes you, me and anyone else you might know, or anyone who ever

---

[4] Philippians 2:7 "but emptied Himself, taking the position of a bond-servant, and being made in the likeness of men."

[5] Philippians 2:8 "Being found in the appearance as a man, He humbled Himself by becoming obedient to the point of death, even death on a cross."

[6] Philippians 2:9 "For this reason also God highly exalted Him and bestowed on Him the name which is above every name,"

[7] Philippians 2:10 "So that at the name of Jesus EVERY KNEE WILL BOW, of those who are in heaven and on the earth and under the earth,"

Jefferson Daniel Seal

lived. It includes everybody. Paul goes on to explain "every tongue will confess that Jesus Christ is LORD, to the glory of God the Father." [8] There will be no exceptions: everyone will do it.

So, any religion which does not embrace Jesus as LORD GOD, <u>cannot</u> be referring to Almighty God, the Father of Jesus. Any mention they make, must by definition, be discussing a different god. The proof is simple: if they don't know Jesus, then they cannot know God the Father. It's really that simple. There's just no other way to God. That's why any organization, like the Democrat Party, while linked to Satan, will not equate Jesus to being God's Son. The truth is, demons are actually prevented from denying Jesus is the Christ. They already know who He is. [9] And I believe God stops them short from denying Jesus is the Christ. So, with that limitation in mind, their task becomes an effort at deception. We must never be permitted to know who Jesus really is. So, Satan will stop at nothing to ensure the name of Jesus Christ is kept from ever even being spoken of; or mentioned in any positive light. That explains why Satan uses deception to con and swindle men.

He will even attempt to craftily attack the minds of Christians, to steer them away from the message of

---

[8] Philippians 2:11 "and that every tongue will confess that Jesus Christ is LORD, to the glory of God the Father."
[9] Matthew 8:29 And they cried out, saying, "What business do we have with each other, Son of God? Have you come here to torment us before the time?"

God's salvation. [10] As we read in 2 Corinthians, the 11th chapter, we see even Paul was concerned about Satan's craftiness. He was worried that Satan would lead Christians astray from the simplicity and innate purity which comes from devotion to Christ. The truth is most Christian oriented churches add in additional rules and guidelines which have the effect of polluting the Gospel. They do it in ways which might seem like good ideas at the time. For example, some will decry and criticize the impact on the members of the congregation the effects of alcohol, dancing, electrical musical instruments, etc., all in the name of Christian purity. The effect of such preaching is never good.

In the case of drinking alcohol, Paul in his letter to the Ephesians, said' "Do not get drunk on wine, which leads to dissipation. Instead, be filled with the Holy Spirit." [11] The Greek word used is **methyskesthe** [*meth-EES-kes-they*] and means '*to become drunk*.' Once again, this word is only used the one time in Scripture. Wasn't this the perfect place to say, "Don't drink wine?" I think so. But that's not what Paul said. The proof lies in the context of his words. Paul said getting drunk can lead to "dissipation." The Greek word used here is **asotia** [*as-oh-TEE-ah*] which means

---

[10] 2 Corinthians 11:3 But I am afraid that, as the serpent deceived Eve by his craftiness, your minds will be led astray from the simplicity and purity of devotion to Christ.

[11] Ephesians 5:18 Do not get drunk on wine, which leads to debauchery. Instead, be filled with the Spirit,

'*spiritual wastefulness*.' He was clearly warning us against engaging in the dulling of our minds via the excessive consumption of wine. Such 'spiritual wastefulness' could result in excessive behavior, after which might follow dire consequences. That's why his advice: "Be filled instead with the Holy Spirit."

We already know Satan is cunning and sneaky. He's scammed and conned the vast majority of the members of the largest political party in the United States; and he's done it without them even knowing. Satan's got them following policies which are clearly anti-God, and which lead men deeper into sin. All the while, deceiving them into believing that what they're doing is in the best interest of humanity; when in fact, it's actually furthering his own evil purposes. You've got to admit, Satan's got one sly and shrewd underhanded operation going. And it's going quite strongly.

If you've been part of his operation—even unwittingly, your ability to escape the clutches of his reach is limited. In fact, there's only one way to achieve it. You need to become a believer in and follower of Jesus Christ. Apart from the strong influence of the Holy Spirit, your chances of breaking free from the grip of Satanic forces is quite slim. Even now, as you watch the Democrat candidates for president of the United States on television, it's impossible to fail to see who they are actually representing. Any in-depth study of their stated

Satan Would Be A Democrat

policies shows the true nature of their intentions. Remember, it's not what one says which matters; it's what they do which convict them in the soon-coming court of God's judgment. The path man is on is headed towards a time of sheer terror—and not peace and safety as the Democrat Party would have you believe. [12] Think you're strong enough to endure the time of Tribulation? Well, think again.

God says, "Every strong man will have his hands on his stomach like a woman in labor, every face turned deathly pale." [13] Unless you've experienced an event in your life where everyone around you was scared to death, you have no idea what God is talking about in this verse. But, as you begin to look around at all the happenings in this world just now, it's actually getting easier to envision such a time soon coming. The prophet Jeremiah said, "How awful that day will be! No other will be like it." [14] Unless you want to be part of such a day, God's advice is simple: "Come as you are to the feet of My Son." Only then will you be able to break free from the grip of Satan and his demons. Recognize Jesus alone is LORD and Savior.

---

[12] Jeremiah 30:4-5 These are the words the LORD spoke concerning Israel and Judah: "This is what the LORD says: " 'Cries of fear are heard—terror, not peace.' "

[13] Jeremiah 30:6 Ask and see: Can a man bear children? Then why do I see every strong man with his hands on his stomach like a woman in labor, every face turned deathly pale?

[14] Jeremiah 30:7 How awful that day will be! No other will be like it.

Jefferson Daniel Seal

Hell On Earth!

In order to break Satan's grip over one's mind, a person must find some way to view the truth. They need to get past all the noise within the world media. The "talking heads" and "voices of reason" from among the airwaves must be ignored. Recall from the first section, Satan is working very hard at deceiving all of us. He deftly cloaks each lie within a carefully chosen dialog of limited truth. Then, making crafty use of language, he twists the truth into half-truths, deceiving men into taking steps into sin. It was this same tactic which allowed Satan to defraud Eve. After the deed was done, Eve *knew* she'd been deceived into eating the forbidden fruit. And she also knew who it was that deceived her. [15] Satan is still in the business of telling sugar-coated lies. "The Democrat Party is the only party who will stand up for the rights of all people!" [16] His lies haven't stopped being told.

Upon first glance, it does appear Satan's words are accurate. The Democrat Party *seems* to be the organization who supports people being oppressed and opposed within society at large: Women want control over their own bodies, the LGBTQ community wants marriage just like everyone else, wealthy persons have plenty of money to share with the less fortunate, major corporations should be forced to

---

[15] Genesis 3:13 Then the LORD God said to the woman, "What is this you have done?" The woman said, "The serpent deceived me, and I ate."
[16] Genesis 3:4 "You will certainly not die," the serpent said to the woman."

Satan Would Be A Democrat

share profits with workers, anyone who wants to come to the U.S. should be allowed in regardless of their status, and racism by white people is rampant in America. Satan knows if a lie is repeated often enough, people will begin assuming it must therefore be factual. This was exactly how the Devil first got Eve, and then Adam to fall. He's still diligently working his con against us! He will not cease doing so until God Himself locks him up in the bottomless abyss. [17]

In the meanwhile, Satan is telling mankind, "It will only happen when the Democrat party gets into power, that all the ills of society can then be banished! Those racist Republicans are just a continuing threat to the safety and security of the United States!" [18] So, drinking the sweet tasting Democrat Party Kool-Aid is pretty simple, and quite easy to swallow. After all, who doesn't want to help and support those who are being unfairly oppressed? So, persons open up their wallets and support the Democrat Party with both their money and their vote. [19] And, they also encourage and coerce those around them into doing the same thing. [20] The real problem

---

[17] Revelation 20:2 And he laid hold of the dragon, the serpent of old, who is the devil and Satan, and bound him for a thousand years.

[18] Genesis 3:5 "For God knows that when you eat from it your eyes will be opened, and you will be like God, knowing good and evil."

[19] Genesis 3:6 When the woman saw that the fruit of the tree was good for food and pleasing to the eye, and also desirable for gaining wisdom, she took some and ate it.

[20] Genesis 3:6 She also gave some to her husband, who was with her, and he ate it.

for those following Satan, is his planted seeds of lies only become exposed when the crops begin to sprout above the ground. It's only then when the real result of what's been done can no longer be hidden. [21]

Look at the moral and ethical condition of America today. Homelessness and poverty *abound*. Drug use is *skyrocketing*. Homosexuality is becoming radically normalized throughout society. All of this, despite the government spending vast amounts of money on welfare programs designed to eradicate poverty and raise the standard of living for poorer Americans. Like my grandad used to say: "All them seeds of sinful livin' is comin' home to roost!" The more America and the world follow Satan's agenda, the worse our problems become. Indeed, God <u>will</u> <u>not</u> be ridiculed; this world is beginning to reap in earnest the sins of Satan we've chosen via deceit to sow. And, it's only going to be getting worse. If you think today is bad; you ain't seen nothing yet!

Have you taken notice of the dramatic increase in civil violence all over the globe? Unless you've been lying somewhere in a coma, I'm sure you have. Of course, Satan will tell you, "It's all part and parcel of global warming!" Again, that's just another ridiculous lie. Well, once more, we must look to the words of Jesus to discover the truth of the situation. Look at His words in Matthew 24:7:

---

[21] Genesis 3:7 Then the eyes of both of them were opened, and they realized they were naked;

"For nation will rise up against nation, and kingdom against kingdom, and various places there will be famines and earthquakes."

This is how the verse appears in most modern translations of the Bible today. Let me ask you: "Is there <u>any</u> event contained within this sentence which tells you something *specific* which can be used to pinpoint a particular time in human history?" I would say absolutely not. As translated, this is just about the most generic sentence possible. After all, for the whole of man's history, nation has risen up against nation, kingdom against kingdom, and famines and earthquakes have occurred with strict regularity all over the world. This is where digging into the Scriptures pays huge dividends.

We begin with the word used for **nations**. It is the word ethos [*ETH-os*] and means '*ethnicity, tribe or clan.*' So, Jesus is telling us, "ethnic groups would rise up against other ethnic groups." Violence will be committed in the name of race and/or ethnicity of one's people. It can be tribal warfare based on cultural differences, or any conflict based on societal disparities between peoples of another race. Since the end of WWII, this type of conflict has been the main source of skirmishes and combat around the globe. The next word we examine is **kingdoms**. The word used is basileian [*bah-sil-LAY-ee-an*]. It translates to mean '*authority, sovereignty, dominion.*'

Jefferson Daniel Seal

The definition states the word basileian *'does not pertain to an actual kingdom itself, but rather the authority to rule said kingdom.'* The word authority means *'the power or right to give orders, make decisions, and enforce obedience.'*

So Jesus saying, "kingdom would be fighting against kingdom" is nothing more than a struggle over power. In the United States, we see it happening on the news every day. The Democrats are fighting with Republicans over the right to hold sway over policy. As we've seen, Satan is running the Democrat Party in an attempt to seize control of power. So, another way to state the words of Jesus would be: "political parties will fight against other political parties." The struggle between Republicans and Democrats is over the right to rule, to be able to exercise authority and dominion over the people. Going back to the original languages of the Bible is quite revealing when viewed within the context of our time.

The next word we examine in the verse is **famines**. The Greek word used is limoi [*lee-MOY*]. This word means *'famine, scarcity, destitution.'* Destitution is *'poverty so extreme one lacks the means to provide for themselves.'* Think mass starvation due to a lack of the means to obtain food. Eventually, the Antichrist will force this issue when he forbids all those refusing to take his mark from buying or selling. The next word we examine is seizmoi [*sice-MOY*]. While today we use the word **earthquake**, when discussing seismic

Satan Would Be A Democrat

activity; that's not the original meaning. The historical meaning of the word was *'commotion, turmoil, upheaval on a grand scale.'* Imagine large scale riots involving most of the population and you get the right idea. And finally, the word for **various places** is topous [*TOP-os*]. It literally means *'marked off spaces for settling and dwelling.'* Today we'd say, *'inhabited spaces.'* One gets the idea of the plots and zoning areas used to define the layout of cities and towns, delineating the use of space.

So, in order to understand what Jesus is warning us about in Matthew 24:7, we need to put in the words we defined using the *original* Greek language, along with the resulting context, to yield the following sentence:

> *"For ethnic group will rise up against ethnic group, and political party against political party, and in cities and towns there will be great scarcity and destitution, due to severe turmoil and upheaval among the people."*

Do you not see Jesus is warning us; "Mankind is going to be engaged in the ideological fight of their lives!" We already see whispers of what is soon coming, within society of our world today. Those who were witness to the Judge Kavanaugh hearings for his appointment to the Supreme Court, can clearly see what's coming. There's no middle ground upon which any compromise can be built. The Party with the power is going to rule regardless of the wishes of the other side. The fighting is going to become so severe; people will eventually starve to death as a result of the calamity. The same situation is what has caused all the violence in the Middle East all these many years. Both sides are diametrically opposed with no real chance for compromise.

I want you to imagine for a moment a United States where Hillary Clinton won the election for President. We'd now have a Supreme Court with a 5 vs 4, or perhaps even a 6 vs 3 liberal crooked bend to it. Most of the elements of Satan's agenda would be in the process of being implemented. Abortion would become unrestricted, freedom of Christian speech would be greatly impaired, the rules for gun ownership would become severely restricted, borders would be opened, social programs would quickly grow out of control. The country would very quickly fall into civil strife and struggle as peoples of differing ideology resisted the forced changes being imposed upon them.

The dissension and discord between the different political parties would continue to grow daily until it exploded in violence upon the streets. Once people were forced to accept a new reality driven by the left, they would immediately begin fighting and brawling over differing ideological issues. I honestly believe this country would have eventually found itself in a second Civil War were Hillary Clinton (or any other

Satan Would Be A Democrat

Democrat for that matter) to have won the 2016 election. But Trump winning the election has seen politics remain far from peaceful. The Democrats are all suffering from the effects of "Trump Derangement Syndrome." But the reality is; all he's done thus far is to slow the steady slide of the U.S. society towards one mirroring Sodom and Gomorrah. When God begins to move this nation towards reformation, that's the time you'll begin to see Hell on Earth!

Seeing All These Things

Jesus and His disciples entered Jerusalem on Palm Sunday; precisely as prophesied. That time He came as a lowly servant, ready to fulfill His role in the redemption of mankind. Jesus entered the city via the Golden Gate, riding on a donkey, accompanied by His little band of twelve, exactly as the Bible said He would. They then went into the Temple to have a look around. His disciples were quite impressed by the magnificence of Herod's temple buildings; and they told Him so. [22] Remember, these disciples were not what we'd describe as sophisticated, educated and polished persons at that time in their lives. They were what the Democrats of today would describe as "bitter men, clinging to their God, and their guns."

Jesus was having none of such admiration for an evil man's achievement. He replied by saying, "Oh,

---

[22] Matthew 24:1 Jesus came out from the temple and was going away when His disciples come up to point out the temple buildings to Him.

Jefferson Daniel Seal

you mean all of this 'grandiose architecture'?" Jesus then gestured towards the magnificent buildings of Herod's Temple. "Well, let me just tell you, there'll not be a single stone left standing on top of another; all of this will be leveled!" [23] And so, a bit over 36 years later, the Temple was destroyed by the forces of the Roman Empire, on the 23rd of July, 70 AD. The disciples were caught completely unawares by the words of the LORD. They associated the worship of God with the Temple. They were still missing the fact that the very man they were following was the new bridge to God.

Later on, while Jesus was sitting on the Mount of Olives, they came to Him privately asking three separate questions: [24]

1) Tell us, when will these things happen?
2) What will be the sign of Your coming?
3) What will be the sign for the end of the age?

Jesus spends essentially the rest of the chapter answering their questions. Please note, when you read through the verses, remember Jesus is responding to their questions by explaining His answers in the order in which they were asked. His answers seem confusing until you consider He is

---

[23] Matthew 24:2 And He said to them, "Do you not see all these things? Truly I say to you, not one stone here will be left upon another, which will not be torn down."

[24] Matthew 24:3 As He was sitting on the Mount of Olives, the disciples came to Him privately, saying, "Tell us, when will these things happen, and what will be the sign of Your coming, and of the end of the age?"

talking to several groups of persons. First, He was talking to His disciples, which are in the same category as all the people who lived prior to the rebirth of Israel. For these folks, it was all just interesting information concerning the future.

The next group Jesus is addressing, are those persons who are alive to witness the rebirth of the nation of Israel. He gives a parable of a budding fig tree to describe the timing. "When its branch has already become tender and puts forth its leaves, you know summer is near." [25] The fig tree represents the nation of Israel. When it reemerges from its long period of dormancy (winter) and begins to put forth leaves (grows as a nation and begins to flourish), those witnessing this event can know summer is near. Summer represents a time of redemption. So, those who are able to cognitively recognize the miraculous rebirth of the nation of Israel can then KNOW they are living in the "End Times."

The next group of persons Jesus is addressing; are those people alive to witness most, if not all of His prophetic statements come to pass. These folks will have no excuse from which to escape judgment. They will have seen the fulfillment of prophecy in their lifetimes. [26] This group of people can be further

---

[25] Matthew 24:32 "Now learn the parable from the fig tree: when its branch has already become tender and puts forth its leaves, you know that summer is near;"

[26] Matthew 24:33 "So, you too, when you see all these things, recognize that He is near, right at the door."

Jefferson Daniel Seal

divided into several parts. The first part is made up of those persons who become true followers of Jesus Christ at some point *prior* to the Rapture. These people will be well aware of prophetic Scripture and will be ready when the Rapture happens. They will be secretly and suddenly removed prior to the start of "The Great Tribulation." These are those people who have truly been "born again."

The other folks who see the signs, but ignore them for too long, will be left behind. This graphically points to the purpose for DWJD Ministries: get people to both see the signs and become followers of Jesus Christ. God is willing that no people should perish, and by association, so are we! It is my belief a large portion of these folks will refuse to accept the "mark of the beast" as offered by the Antichrist and will suffer the consequences. They will either starve to death or be beheaded as the penalty for attempting to buy or sell outside of the system. They will be resurrected on the other side of the Tribulation, following God recreating the world into a garden of Eden state.

That leaves two groups of people remaining. They are the ones who ignore the End Times signs at their peril. They have no Biblical knowledge and thus have no real awareness of what is happening or coming next. Most of these persons will agree to follow the Antichrist and will embrace him as God. If you think you can wait until the end to accept Christ as LORD and Savior, allow me to warn you. God says He will allow Satan to deceive all remaining people with the coming of the Antichrist. [27] The arrival of the Antichrist will be in accordance with the work of Satan. He will use all sorts of displays of power using signs and wonders of his own to support his lies. [28] God is not being unkind. He's just allowing those who pursue wickedness to be deceived because they are on the road to hell by choice. They are the ones who refuse the message of the Gospel, snubbing God's offer of salvation. [29]

This will lead to their eternal death in the Lake of Fire. These people will not be resurrected back to the Earth. They will be sent to Hell. [30] Their next moment of awareness will be at God's Great White Throne of Judgment. The other group is the Jews who flee to Petra to be protected and nourished by God for the last 3 ½ years. They will survive the Tribulation and be the prodigy of Abraham God prophesied would endure forever. And so, they shall ever be.

---

[27] 2 Thessalonians 2:11 "For this reason God sends them a powerful delusion so that they will believe the lie."

[28] 2 Thessalonians 2:9 "The coming of the lawless one will be in accordance with how Satan works. He will use all sorts of displays of power through signs and wonders that serve the lie,"

[29] 2 Thessalonians 2:10 "and all the ways that wickedness deceives those who are perishing. They perish because they refused to love the truth and so be saved."

[30] 2 Thessalonians 2:12 "and so all will be condemned who have not believed the truth but have delighted in wickedness."

Jefferson Daniel Seal

So, who are you going to trust? The Word of the Almighty, as recorded within the pages of the Bible? Or, the words of people who are speaking and working under the direct influence of Satanic beings? The Bible says if you are not a follower of God, then it initially will seem undesirable to you. But Joshua then asks the following question: "Are you going to stick with the current crowd you've been hanging with?" As you've just read, they don't actually have much of an idea of what's really going on. And, they are clearly being guided by lying, cheating and deceiving spirits, who can't be trusted; as the truth cannot be found within them. Joshua then declares, based on the evidence... "As for me and my house, we will worship the LORD!" [31] You would do well to make the same decision.

God has decreed: "The persons seeing these signs will endure until all of the prophecy is fulfilled." So, if you are seeing these signs; even if you only recognize one or two, you are going to live long enough to see them all come to pass. [32] And anyone who loves their father or mother, or wife or kids more than the LORD

---

[31] Joshua 24:15 "But if serving the LORD seems undesirable to you, then choose for yourselves this day whom you will serve, whether the gods your ancestors served beyond the Euphrates, or the gods of the Amorites, in the land you are living. But as for me and my household, we will serve the LORD."

[32] Matthew 24:34 "Truly I say to you, this generation will not pass away until all these things take place."

Satan Would Be A Democrat

is not worthy of Him. [33] Whoever fails to take up their cross (whatever burden you believe it to be to follow the LORD) is not worthy of Him. [34] The only cause worth pursuing is the cause of Christ. What more proof do you need? You can clearly see Satan and his horde have taken control of the Democrat Party. And they are well on their way to controlling the content reaching the airwaves.

So, what are you waiting for? You've got proof God is real, Jesus is His Son, and the appearance of Israel after 2500 years marks the start of God's stopwatch for events delineating the end of this age. Satan is bent on conning you, to swindle you out of your eternal life as offered by Jesus. He has lied to you, twisted the truth with half-baked fabrications, all in the name of deceiving you from hearing the Good News as spoken of in the Bible. The storm of God's wrath will swirl down on the heads of all who reject Jesus. [35] And His fierce anger will not cease until all of His purposes are completely and totally fulfilled. God promises, in the coming days, all persons will come to understand on a personal, albeit very painful manner, as they physically experience the unabated

---

[33] Matthew 10:37 "Anyone who loves their father or mother more than Me is not worthy of Me; anyone who loves their son or daughter more than Me is not worthy of Me."

[34] Matthew 10:38 "Whoever does not take up their cross and follow Me is not worthy of Me."

[35] Jeremiah 30:23 "See, the storm of the LORD will burst out in wrath, a driving wind swirling down on the heads of the wicked."

consequences of their actions. [36] So, since you still have a little time, what are you going to do now that you are "seeing all these things?"

Footsteps to the Truth

As you have grappled with the information presented within the pages of this volume, there is obviously much more to be learned. The truth which lies herein serves as a crowbar, to the opening up of your mind to the truth of God's word. I say crowbar due to the certainty of demonic forces fighting the illumination of this candor with every fiber of their being. If you have lived a life as a long-term Democrat, then reading this much after 2020, doubtlessly, will find you witness to much of what is discussed within these pages. By now, you must KNOW absolutely, positively there is a God. In the same way, you should know Satan too is real and working against humanity. It's entirely your choice whether to accept or reject the truth. If you wish to fully accept it and throw off the yoke of deception; here's a way to go about it. I describe the process as taking 12 steps down a Roman road:

Step One: To move towards God we must first admit to ourselves we in actuality believe in Him. I can state with *certainty* that you, and everyone else on the

---

[36] Jeremiah 30:24 "The fierce anger of the LORD will not turn back until He fully accomplishes the purposes of His heart. In the days to come you will understand this."

Satan Would Be A Democrat

planet, *already* believes in God. But a person must go further and actually acknowledge His existence. No more saying things like: "God is dead!" or "Religion is for the weak minded." The Bible teaches all men have some knowledge of God. God says He made it quite plain to us. [37] But this simple belief we all have, only lets us know He exists. We must ourselves do more. We must cognitively recognize and concede that God is real and is full of love for humanity.

You now might be wondering, "What about atheists?" The dictionary says an **atheist** is '*someone who does not believe in the existence of a god or any gods.*' As I have just shown, Scripture refutes that definition. Thus, there's in reality no such thing as an atheist. God said He has revealed His invisible qualities—His eternal power and divine nature—to each and every one of us. And having been seen and understood, we are all without excuse. [38] Thus, I define an atheist as '*someone who denies the existence of YAHWEH God.*' So, you are in one of two camps: You either acknowledge the existence of God, or you deny His existence. *Everyone* believes in God.

Now, merely acknowledging God is real and coming to recognize Him is important, but this is only

---

[37] Romans 1:19 Since what may be known about God is plain to them, because God has made it plain to them.

[38] Romans 1:20 For since the creation of the world God's invisible qualities—His eternal power and divine nature—have been clearly seen, being understood from what has been made, so that people are without excuse.

the first step. *Believing* in God is <u>not</u> enough. The Bible teaches us even the demons believe in God with sufficient force to cause them to tremble just with having such knowledge. [39] No, this basic level of belief is not enough. We must go one step further and acknowledge His existence. But, that's still not the same as saying you're a follower of Him. Once you realize God is real, it's time for the next step.

Step Two: You must have an actual desire to truly want to get to know God. For this to happen, a person must come to the realization something is missing within their lives. There must be a genuine longing to search for and to find God. This desire is driven by a deep-seated need we each feel for Him. God put what amounts to a hole inside our soul which only He can fill. Everyone has it. If you lack this desire to find Him, then you can't go any further. It's a way of God saying you likely haven't fulfilled step one yet. But I would still urge anyone to pray for God's wisdom in helping them recognize His existence. Then, I would call upon Him and pray for His divine assistance. God is faithful and <u>will</u> answer your prayer.

Step Three: We each must realize we cannot come to God in our current human state. God is a perfect, righteous and holy Being; who cannot have sin within His realm. We are not good enough on our own to go

---

[39] James 2:19 You believe that there is one God. Good! Even the demons believe and tremble.

Satan Would Be A Democrat

before Him. We are sinful, unrighteous and unholy. The reason for this is we *all* are sinners. We each have sinned. Even a single sin makes us unworthy to go before God on our own merit. We can sense the sin which exists within our everyday lives. We instinctively know that we each live in a fallen state.

The truth is most of us ignore or avoid even the idea of God, thereby leading ourselves into a deeper pit of depravity. **[40]** We don't like to admit we are sinners. Interestingly enough, we just observed that very sentiment with how leaders of the Democrat Party will behave in the near future. We can come to God, but only on His terms. But, such a journey, begins with the realization we fall short of His requirements. This only proves there had to be another way for us to come to Him. And that path cannot be designed or even influenced by us. Once more, this realization of our sin must be acknowledged by each of us in that we are each a sinner. However, there is terrific news: The God of heaven loves YOU!

Step Four : Believe and accept God loves you! And not only that, but He loves you not as you should be; but as you are right now. He knows you are yet living in sin as a fully-fledged sinner! He loves you despite the fact you're still a sinner! Even in your sinful state,

---

[40] Romans 1:21 For although they knew God, they neither glorified Him as God nor gave thanks to Him, but their thinking became futile and their foolish hearts were darkened.

Jefferson Daniel Seal

God is committed to you. The Bible tells us God loves every single person in the world; and since you are part of this world, it includes you! [41] You have to admit God's love is strong and deep enough to care for you. No matter what you've done, or how you've lived, God still loves you with the deepest of affection.

Step Five: Realize God loved you so much, He took action to save you. God Almighty sent His only Son, Jesus Christ, down to earth, for the sole purpose of dying on a cruel wooden cross of pain. The action God took, was to send His Son down to earth. God had His Holy Spirit impregnate Mary, and she in-turn gave birth to Jesus. Jesus came as the **Messiah**. That's a word which means '*savior*.' Accepting God made a way through Jesus His Son, is a necessary step to realizing God had the power to redeem us. And not only that, but God had the *will* to do it. This action was done for the sole reason that Jesus would pay your sin debt. Jesus took your place on that cruel wooden cross. It's now time for more admission and some acknowledgment.

Step Six: Acknowledge your sin created a debt. You've heard it's not what you say—but what you do? Well, God loves us so much, He sent His only Son Jesus to earth, to die for humanity, demonstrating His love towards us, while we were yet unrepentant sinners.

---

[41] John 3:16 "For God so loved the whole of humanity, that HE surrendered His only Son, that who-so-ever puts their trust in Him, will never perish, but instead be given eternal life."

Satan Would Be A Democrat

God took the first step to reconciling our sin debt. [42] For all have sinned. That includes every human being who ever lived—except for Jesus Christ. The Bible teaches us sin is passed down from the father. Jesus has God as His Father. Therefore, He had no sin at birth. Remember, it's our sin that makes us incompatible with a righteous and holy God. [43] That means, without some help, we cannot be with God. The Bible teaches the consequences of our sin is eternal death. [44] The important point here is we must acknowledge we owe a debt. That's what I mean when I say, "We cannot be with God on our own." Someone had to pay off our sin debt. We are unable to do so on our own. Well, that's the bad news. It's now time for some good news as well.

Step Seven: Believe God created an avenue for us to be with Him in Heaven. He is offering us eternal life. Suppose you invented a liquid remedy which could extend a person's life for say one full year. No matter what was wrong with them; if they drank your potion, they'd live another 365 days. Well, were that true, you'd be the richest person who ever lived by far! God Almighty is offering us *eternal* life! By definition, that's something which simply cannot have a value placed upon it. It is priceless! The good news is God's

---

[42] Romans 5:8 But God demonstrates His own love toward us, in that while we were yet sinners, Christ died for us.
[43] Romans 3:23 "For all have sinned and fall short of the glory of God,"
[44] Romans 6:23 "For the wages of sin is death,"

Jefferson Daniel Seal

offer of eternal life is completely free! You will literally live _forever_! And it doesn't cost a dime. "Ah, what's the catch?" you ask. The catch is: we must believe our eternal life comes through God's Son, Jesus Christ, alone. [45] There's no other way to get to God. None. It is the only way.

Step Eight: Realize payment is required for our sin. That compulsory payment is eternal death. Since eternal life is priceless, eternal death carries an inestimable cost as well. God even said were it possible for someone to accumulate _all_ the money in the entire world—it would still be insufficient to pay down a single person's sin debt. So, the only alternative is we get sent to the eternal prison God created for the fallen angels. The Bible calls it: "The Lake of Fire." The jurisdictive sentence for our sin carries with it a length of time equal to eternity. That's the prescribed penalty for our debt. But God made a way for us to bypass that horrible fate. God sent His Son, Jesus. Jesus came directly from heaven and He knew no sin. That means He lived a perfect life. He was thus able to take our place. His death paid our sin debt and paved the way for us to be made righteous before God. [46]

Step Nine: We must reach a point where we can

---

[45] Romans 6:23 "but the free gift of God is eternal life in Christ Jesus, our LORD,"
[46] 2 Corinthians 5:21 "He who knew no sin became sin for us, that we may be made righteous before God through His death."

Satan Would Be A Democrat

trust that God is good at His word and will save us. I cannot even begin to explain to you how such a thing could happen. I can only tell you that the Bible—God's word—says it can. This is where faith comes into the picture. We must accept everything happened just the way the Bible tells us it did. Look, right now you are living in a most blessed time. You have the privilege of seeing prophecy being fulfilled all over the world. Everything is happening in the exact time, place and manner God said it would. Why would you want to not trust Him at His word? Is there anything else in this world which can begin to approach what God has displayed before us?

Step Ten : Be willing to confess Jesus Christ is LORD and that you are now a willing follower of Him. Your verbal and sincere confession reflects what's really inside your heart. The rest is easy: God says if we are willing to confess with our speech that Jesus is Lord, it's the best indication we truly trust that God raised Him from the dead. That means you accept Jesus died in your place. The Bible says, "For with the heart a person believes, resulting in our righteousness before God." That means you're not ashamed of God and Jesus. The net result is you will be awarded eternal life. [47] That's what the Bible says. "Whoever calls upon

---

[47] Romans 10:9-10 [9]"That if you confess with your mouth Jesus as LORD, and believe in your heart God raised Him from the dead, you will be saved. [10]For with the heart a person believes, resulting in righteousness, and with the mouth he confesses, resulting in salvation."

the name of the LORD will be saved."

Step Eleven: Requires us to stop right where we are in life, and actually begin calling upon the name of the LORD. That means any person who calls upon God, in the name of Jesus, to be their LORD and Savior, will be heard. The phrase "will be saved," literally means "to be rescued." You will be *rescued* from your sentence of being sent to the Lake of Fire. To call upon the LORD, simply means to talk to God in prayer. That means beginning a conversation with Him which will last the rest of your natural life. No other requirement is stated. I have included a sample prayer to get you started. It doesn't matter what words you say—or not say. God already knows the intent of your heart. He will hear your prayers regardless of what is said or not said. Pray to Him now:

> *My Heavenly Father, I confess that I am a sinner. For that I am truly sorry. I know I require a way to get to heaven, as I admit I could never do it on my own. I truly believe Jesus is your Son, who died on the cross of Calvary in my place, shedding His blood for my sin. He died for me. And, He arose from the grave on the third day, in victory over sin. I claim that victory by faith because I am trusting you to save me. Thank you for forgiving my sin, and please come into my*

---

[48] Romans 10:13 "Whoever calls upon the name of the LORD will be saved."

Satan Would Be A Democrat

heart. I am asking this for the sake of Jesus. I am putting you God, my heavenly Father, as LORD of my life. I am trusting in Jesus as my rescuer, and want to receive You into my heart to be with me forever. Thank you, God for saving me! Amen.

Step Twelve : Now, go out and begin telling others about your faith. If you just prayed that prayer, then you are now a follower of Jesus Christ. You are now on the road of that of a Christian. Saved by the blood of the lamb! The angels in Heaven are celebrating. Go and find a church of like believers in Jesus Christ. Search for a church which preaches the Bible as the error-free word of God. Look for a congregation teaching Jesus is the <u>only</u> way to God the Father. A true follower is <u>not</u> ashamed of their faith. They are proud of God and what He has done for them. Get some knowledge and begin sharing the Good News with others.

Then send us an email telling us of your new-found faith. We have many books and materials with which to get you started. If you are unable to afford these materials, we will get them to you regardless. Just email us at:

<u>info@dwjdministries.com</u>

We want to hear from you. Send us a summary in your own words about your experience of finding Jesus. This is the same thing as confessing Jesus with

Jefferson Daniel Seal

your mouth. Don't be ashamed of Him. Be proud of Him! And He will be proud of you. Be not only willing; but be excited about sharing your new faith with others. You will be greatly blessed when you do. And, more importantly, you will be allowing others to hear the good news of Jesus Christ.

What Comes Next:

You've just finished reading: **Satan Would Be a Democrat.** As you can see, proof supplied by God to man is voluminous, making it quite compelling. But you've just begun the journey. There are more volumes for you to read, study and digest. Each DWJD book has all the relevant prophecies spelled out in detail, along with the supporting verses, definitions and the words from the original languages. Friends, time is indeed short. But not so short that you cannot make the required changes to your life. The Bible is completely true and reliable. This means God is real, relevant and responsive.

He's issuing mankind 3 "Wake-Up! Calls" as the end approaches. Jesus urged His disciples 3 times while praying in the Garden of Gethsemane [Luke 22:46]: "Why are you sleeping? Get up and 'pray that you may not enter into temptation.' " The word for **temptation** is `peirasmon` [*pe-ras-eh-MON*] and means '*to be tested by calamity and affliction.*' Jesus is urging us to come to Him to avoid "a most terrible trial by fire." My experience is the modern church is fast asleep, slumbering while the ashes of the fires of Tribulation are falling down around them. It's time to wake-up! and take a strong stand for Jesus Christ!

Jefferson Daniel Seal

Note to Pastors: I am eager and willing to come and address your congregation. If you're interested, just use the email and/or phone number listed on the website to contact us to request a speaking engagement. A member of my staff will promptly return your inquiry to set up a date. There's never a fee for me to come to your church. However, my schedule is beginning to rapidly fill up, so contact us soon:

info@DWJDMinistries.com